REGULATING AUTONOMY

The chapters in this volume explore, with reference to specific examples, the nature and limits of individual autonomy in law, policy and the work of regulatory agencies. Authors ask searching questions about the nature and scope of the regulation of 'private' lives, from intimacies, personal relationships and domestic lives to reproduction. They question the extent to which the law does, or should, protect individual autonomy in those areas. In recent decades, rapid advances in the development of new technologies—particularly those concerned with human genetics and assisted reproduction—have generated new questions (practical, social, legal and ethical) about how far the state should intervene in individual decision-making in these areas. Is there an inevitable tension between individual liberty and the common good? How might a workable balance between the public and the private be struck? How, indeed, should we think about 'autonomy'?

This book is concerned with the main areas of personal life where the boundaries and limits to individual autonomy are drawn: in our intimate and domestic relationships, our sexualities, and reproduction. These essays explore the different kinds of arguments used to create and maintain those boundaries—including, for example, the protection of the vulnerable, public goods of various kinds, and the maintenance of tradition and respect for cultural practices. Individual authors address, in relation to their own chosen field, issues of where and how the boundaries around private life should be drawn, and how those boundaries are maintained and interventions justified. How are the contemporary ethical debates about autonomy constructed, and what principles do they embody? What happens when those principles become manifest in law? The chapters in this book each address aspects of these broad questions, in the context of specific contemporary debates around sexualities, reproduction and family relationships. These debates are driven by conflicts over ethical principles and changing cultural practices, as well as new dilemmas posed by technological advances.

Regulating Autonomy

Sex, Reproduction and Family

Edited by

SHELLEY DAY SCLATER
FATEMEH EBTEHAJ
EMILY JACKSON
AND
MARTIN RICHARDS

For the Cambridge Socio-Legal Group

·HART·
PUBLISHING

OXFORD AND PORTLAND, OREGON
2009

Published in North America (US and Canada) by
Hart Publishing
c/o International Specialized Book Services
920 NE 58th Avenue, Suite 300
Portland, OR 97213-3786
USA
Tel: +1 503 287 3093 or toll-free: (1) 800 944 6190
Fax: +1 503 280 8832
E-mail: orders@isbs.com
Website: http://www.isbs.com

Hart Publishing Ltd, 16C Worcester Place, Oxford, OX1 2JW
Telephone: +44 (0)1865 517530 Fax: +44 (0)1865 510710
E-mail: mail@hartpub.co.uk
Website: http://www.hartpub.co.uk

British Library Cataloguing in Publication Data
Data Available

ISBN: 978-1-84113-946-3

Typeset by Compuscript Ltd, Shannon
Printed and bound in Great Britain by
TJ International Ltd, Padstow, Cornwall

Acknowledgements

This book is the seventh in a series by the Cambridge Socio-Legal Group and is the product of a three-day workshop held in Cambridge in September 2007.

We are grateful to the *Modern Law Review* for a grant to support the workshop, and to the Cambridge Socio-Legal group for their financial support. We thank the Centre for Family Research, and Social and Political Sciences at the University of Cambridge for hosting the event, and special thanks are owed to Susan Golombok.

Our deep gratitude to the contributors for their participation in this stimulating project, and to the discussants—Belinda Brooks-Gordon, Zeynep Gürtin-Broadbent, Frances Murton and Matthew Weait—for their insightful comments and helpful suggestions. Frances Murton, as always, carefully copy-edited the manuscript.

The Editors
Cambridge
September 2008

Contents

Notes on Contributors

Belinda Brooks-Gordon is a Reader in Psychology and Social Policy at Birkbeck College, University of London. Her research addresses psychological and social policy questions on sexuality, gender and the law. A chartered psychologist with a PhD from the Law Faculty in Cambridge, her publications include: *The Price of Sex: Prostitution, Policy and Society* (Willan Publishing, 2006); *Law and Psychology: Issues for Today* (Oxford University Press, 2006) (coedited with M Freeman); *Sexuality Repositioned: Diversity and the Law* (Hart, 2004) (coedited with A Bainham, L Gelsthorpe, MH Johnson and M Richards); and *Death Rites and Rights* (Hart, 2007) (coedited with F Ebtehaj, J Herring, MH Johnson, and M Richards).

Jennie Bristow is a writer and researcher based in Kent. She was formerly commissioning editor of the online publication *spiked*, and is author of *Maybe I do: Marriage and Commitment in Singleton Society* (Academy of Ideas, 2002). Jennie is also currently working with Ellie Lee at the University of Kent on the Parenting Culture Studies project (www.parentingculturestudies.org).

Julia Davidson is Principal Lecturer in Criminology and is Manager of the Criminology Research Cluster at the University of Westminster. She has conducted research in the criminal justice area and has a PhD in Social Policy from the London School of Economics and Political Science. Dr Davidson has extensive experience of applied policy and practice research and has directed work with young victims, serious violent and sexual offenders, criminal justice practitioners and sentencers. She is author of *Child Sexual Abuse: Media Representations and Government Reactions* (Routledge, London, 2008). Dr Davidson provides regular expert advice on criminal justice issues to the media and has worked extensively with the BBC and ITN News.

Shelley Day Sclater has been a lawyer and an academic social scientist and now works as a freelance writer and researcher, most recently producing Family Studies course materials for the Open University. She was Professor of Psychosocial Studies at Univeristy of East London and has published widely on families and close relationships. Her most recent book is a co-edited one: *Emotion: A Psychosocial Approach* (Palgrave, forthcoming in 2009). Shelley was a founder member of the Cambridge Socio-Legal Group and has contributed to and co-edited a number of their books.

Fatemeh Ebtehaj is an associate member of the Centre for Family Research, University of Cambridge. Her research focuses on Iranian migrants and exiles, with a particular interest in issues related to gender, self and identity, narrative and discourse analysis. Her current research highlights the impact of migration on ageing and on the care of the elderly. She has been a contributor to, and co-editor of, the Cambridge Socio-Legal Group's *Kinship Matters* (Hart Publishing, 2006) and *Death Rites and Rights* (Hart Publishing, 2007).

John Eekelaar has published extensively in the field of family law. He held a Rhodes Scholarship from 1963 to 1965, and was awarded the Vinerian Scholarship in 1965. He was called to the Bar in 1968 at the Inner Temple. He was a Tutorial Fellow at Pembroke College from 1965 to 2005; he held a Lecturership from 1966 to 1991, and was Reader in Law until 2005. He was elected to a Fellowship of the British Academy in July 2001. He retired from teaching in 2005, and is currently Academic Director at Pembroke College. He continues research as Co-Director of the Oxford Centre for Family Law and Policy (OXFLAP).

Ann Furedi has been Chief Executive of the reproductive healthcare provider BPAS (the British Pregnancy Advisory Service) since 2003. BPAS provides more than a quarter of all abortions in England and Wales, with 87% of the charity's services provided on behalf of the NHS. Ann previously worked as Director of Policy and Communications at the Human Fertilisation and Embryology Authority and as Director of the charity Birth Control Trust. Ann has written extensively on issues relating to reproductive health and rights.

Theresa Glennon is Professor of Law at Temple University, Beasley School of Law in Philadelphia, Pennsylvania. In 2005, she was a visiting fellow at the Centre for Family Research at the University of Cambridge. Her teaching and scholarship focuses on the legal rights of children and families, with particular focus on family law, education, and disability. Her family law publications embrace a range of topics, including assisted reproductive technologies, custody relocation disputes, the effort to harmonise family law in Europe, paternity disputes, second parent adoptions, and the rights of mothers with mental illnesses in the child welfare system. Professor Glennon's most recent publication is 'Still Partners? Examining the Consequences of Post-dissolution Parenting' (2007) 41 *Family Law Quarterly* 105.

Susan Golombok is Professor of Family Research and Director of the Centre for Family Research in the Faculty of Social and Political Sciences at the University of Cambridge, and a Professorial Fellow of Newnham College, Cambridge. Her research focuses on the impact on children's social, emotional and identity development, and on parent–child relationships, of being reared in new family forms, including lesbian mother families, solo mother families, and families created by assisted reproduction procedures such as in vitro fertilisation (IVF), donor insemination, egg donation and surrogacy. She has written many academic papers on these subjects and several books including *Parenting: What Really Counts?* (Routledge, 2000) and *Growing up in a Lesbian Family* (with Fiona Tasker), (Guilford Press, 1998).

Zeynep Gürtin-Broadbent is a PhD student at the Centre for Family Research, University of Cambridge. Her research interests encompass gender and reproduction; bodies; new reproductive technologies; and the patient–clinician interface in medicine. Her PhD work looks at the experiences of Turkish women undergoing IVF in Turkey and in the UK.

Jonathan Herring is a Fellow in Law at Exeter College, University of Oxford. He is author of several books including *Criminal Law: Text, Cases and Materials* (OUP, 2008); *Criminal Law* (Palgrave, 2006); *Medical Law and Ethics* (OUP, 2008) and *Family Law* (Pearson, 2007). He has also written widely on issues relating to criminal law, family law and medical law.

Emily Jackson is Professor of Law at the London School of Economics and Political Science. She is a Member of the Human Fertilisation and Embryology Authority, the BMA Medical Ethics Committee and the Ethics Committees of the Royal College of Physicians and the Royal College of Pathologists. Her publications include *Regulating Reproduction* (Hart Publishing, 2001) and *Medical Law* (Oxford University Press, 2006).

Suzanne Jenkins (BA, LLM) is a law research student (PhD candidate) at Keele University. She is also research assistant for Keele Gender Sexuality and Law Research Group.

Martin H Johnson is Professor of Reproductive Sciences in the Anatomy School at the University of Cambridge, UK, and Vice Master of Christ's College. He was a Distinguished Visiting Scholar at the Law School at La Trobe University, Melbourne (2005–06), a member of the Human Fertilisation and Embryology Authority (1993–1999), and annual Ver Heyden de Lancey Lecturer in Medical Law at the Law School, Cambridge (2007). In 2004 he was elected a scientific Fellow of the Royal Society of Obstetricians and Gynaecologists. He is author of *Essential Reproduction* (6th edition) (Blackwell Science, 2007), co-editor of the Cambridge Socio-Legal Group's *Sexuality Repositioned* (Hart Publishing, 2004) and *Death Rites and Rights* (Hart Publishing, Oxford, 2007). Martin has authored over 230 papers on reproductive science, ethics, law and medical education. He is treasurer of the Cambridge Socio-Legal Group.

Ellie Lee is Senior Lecturer in Social Policy at the University of Kent, and the co-ordinator of Parenting Culture Studies (www.parentingculturestudies. org). She researches in the areas of the sociology of reproduction, family and health. Her publications include *Abortion, Motherhood and Mental Health, Medicalizing reproduction in the United States and Great Britain* (Aldine Transaction, 2003); *Real Bodies, A Sociological Introduction* (edited with Mary Evans) (Palgrave, 2002); and *Abortion Law and Politics Today* (Macmillan, 1998). Her recent research projects have been about second-trimester abortion, and infant-feeding, and these studies are reported in journals including *Health, Risk and Society, Sociology of Health and Illness,* and *Reproductive Health Matters*.

Mavis Maclean CBE is Joint Director of the Oxford Centre for Family Law and Policy (OXFLAP) in the Department of Social Policy, University of Oxford, and Academic Adviser to the Ministry of Justice. She is former President of the Research Committee on the Sociology of Law and a Fellow of the International Institute for the Sociology of Law in Oñati, Spain. She has written extensively on family law issues, particularly the position of women and children after divorce and separation. She was a panel member of the Bristol Royal Infirmary Inquiry.

Elena Martellozzo is a Lecturer in Criminology and Research Methods at the University of Westminster. Elena is currently conducting PhD fieldwork at New Scotland Yard analysing case studies of online grooming and distribution of indecent images of children and studying police practice. Elena's primary research interests lie at the intersection between cybercrime, child abuse and policing. She recently co-authored, with her supervisor Dr Julia Davidson, a book chapter 'Protecting children online: towards a safer internet' in G Letherby *et al* (Eds), *Sex as Crime* (Willan, forthcoming) and a journal article 'Protecting Vulnerable Children in Cyberspace from Sexual Abuse in the United Kingdom' *(in Police Investigations Police Practice & Research: An International Journal (PPR)*, forthcoming), where she presents some of her primary doctoral research findings.

Frances Murton is an associate member of the Centre for Family Research, University of Cambridge and has worked on a number of studies on the psychosocial aspects of new genetic and reproductive technologies. She was formerly a social worker specialising in work with children and families, and a family mediator. She has assisted the editors of earlier publications from the Cambridge Socio-Legal Group.

Kerry Petersen is an Associate Professor at the Law School, La Trobe University, Melbourne. Her main research interests are in law and medicine and human reproduction law. In 2005, she visited the UK as an Australian

Bicentennial Fellow and conducted research into the regulation of assisted reproductive technology (ART) within a comparative framework. She has published extensively in these areas and co-edited *Disputes and Dilemmas in Health Law* (The Federation Press, 2006) with Ian Freckelton. She is currently working on an Australian Research Council-funded research project which examines the impact of legal and professional regulation on ART clinical practice throughout Australia and New Zealand.

Jan Pryor is Associate Professor and Director of the Roy McKenzie Centre for the Study of Families at Victoria University, Wellington, New Zealand. She co-authored *Children in Changing Families. Life After Parental Separation* (Blackwell, 2001), and is editor of the *International Handbook on Stepfamilies* (John Wiley, 2008). Her main foci of research are into the outcomes for children and adults of divorce and step-family formation.

Martin Richards is Emeritus Professor of Family Research at the Centre for Family Research, University of Cambridge. His research is focused on psychosocial aspects of new genetic and reproductive technologies. He is a member of the Human Fertilisation and Embryology Law and Ethics Committee and BioBank UK Ethics and Governance Council. He has been a contributor to and co-editor of earlier Socio-Legal Group volumes. Recent articles have been published in *New Genetics and Society and Studies in the History and Philosophy of Biological and Biomedical Sciences*.

Laura Riley is Press and Public Policy Manager of BPAS and previously Director of the charity Progress Educational Trust. Laura contributed to *Human Fertilisation and Embryology: Reproducing Regulation* (Cavendish, 2006).

Helen Reece is Reader in Law at Birkbeck College, University of London. Her main research interest concerns regulation of the family. She is currently researching conceptions of responsibility, particularly parental responsibility, and interpretations of domestic violence. She is the author of *Divorcing Responsibly* (Hart Publishing, 2003) and several recent articles including 'The End of Domestic Violence' (2006) 69 *Modern Law Review* 770–91.

Matthew Weait qualified as a barrister and is now Senior Lecturer in Law and Legal Studies at Birkbeck College, University of London. Matthew has taught law at the University of Oxford, the Open University and Keele University. He was one of the founding members of the Birkbeck College Law School, where he worked from 1992–99. Matthew's teaching interests are in the fields of criminal law, public law and human rights, and his research centres on the impact of law on people living with HIV and AIDS.

In addition to his university work, Matthew spent time as Parliamentary Legal Officer to Lord Lester of Herne Hill QC and has undertaken research and policy development work for a number of international organisations, including the World Health Organization and UNAIDS. His book, *Intimacy and Responsibility: the Criminalisation of HIV Transmission* was published by Glasshouse Press in 2007.

1

Introduction: Autonomy and Private Life

EMILY JACKSON AND SHELLEY DAY SCLATER

I. INTRODUCTION

THE CHAPTERS IN this edited collection address the question of how far the state should interfere with individual autonomy. Should decisions relating to our intimate lives and our domestic relationships be free from state interference? Or when, and on what basis, might interventions into our private lives be justified?

According to the *Oxford English Dictionary*, 'autonomy', from the Greek for self-rule, means 'liberty to follow one's will, personal freedom'. If *autonomy* is the right to form and pursue one's own conception of the good, free from undue scrutiny and interference, then applied to intimate lives, domestic relationships and reproductive decisions, it might require the subject to enjoy a degree of *privacy*.

Anita Allen has suggested that 'the value of privacy is, in part, that it can enable moral persons to be self-determining' (Allen, 1988, p 44). While being wholly self-determining is neither possible nor desirable, having some space in which to shape our own conception of the good, free from state interference, is undeniably important to all of us. The *Oxford English Dictionary* definition of 'privacy' is 'the state or condition of being alone, undisturbed, or free from public attention, as a matter of choice or right; seclusion; freedom from interference or intrusion'. Exercising autonomy over the most intimate aspects of our lives might then involve being able to shield some of our most private thoughts and choices from the critical gaze of others, subject only to the qualification that those thoughts and choices must not harm other people.

In recent years, communitarian and feminist critiques of these traditional conceptions of autonomy and privacy have questioned their descriptive accuracy and normative desirability. First, we are not isolated and essentially self-interested individuals, but rather we are necessarily 'socially embedded' (Mackenzie & Stoljar, 2000, p 4), and are defined by our connections with others at least as much as by our individuality. 'Erecting a wall of rights around the individual' (Nedelsky, 1990, p 167) depends upon an unrealistic conception of the self as essentially insular and self-sufficient. Rather than being isolated and alone, it is, as Bernard Williams (1973) has argued, precisely commitments, duties and relationships with others that give our lives meaning and character. Onora O'Neill (2002, p 28) puts the position starkly: 'Most contemporary accounts of autonomy see it as a form of *independence*', she says, but independence itself is a relational concept; it is always 'independence from something or other'.

Secondly, privileging 'privacy' or the 'right to be left alone' has, historically, been bad for those who lack the means or opportunities to exercise much meaningful choice over the course of their lives. Thus women's traditional confinement in the 'private' sphere has been widely recognised as socially oppressive and personally damaging (see, eg, Pateman, 1988).

Thirdly, being free from interference in our choices does not necessarily mean we will have many—or indeed any—viable options from which to choose. On the contrary, it is clear that we will sometimes have few realistic alternatives. Thus, protecting autonomy may not only involve simply an *absence* of state interference, but could require the positive provision of resources to enable someone to have a meaningful set of options. According to Joseph Raz, 'to be autonomous a person must not only be given a choice but he must also be given an adequate range of choices' (1986, p 373).

Thus, to say that autonomy requires simply the absence of restraint or intervention is insufficient. There may be times when we need help to acquire or develop the capacity, the resources or the power to shape our lives, according to our own values. In short, there may be instances when intervention is necessary in order to facilitate and support autonomy.

II. AUTONOMY IN INTIMATE LIVES AND DOMESTIC RELATIONSHIPS

The complexities of this point are introduced by Suzanne Jenkins in chapter two of this collection in her essay on prostitution. Sex work raises the question of whether the state should protect us from our own unwise choices, for example, choices that involve possible 'exploitation'. But this, in turn, begs the question of the nature of 'choice'. Some women who work in the sex industries may exercise an autonomous choice to do so (see, for example, Agustin, 2007), while others will have found themselves with few or no other options; their 'choice' to become a sex worker cannot then be understood as a realisation of autonomy, but rather as evidence that their capacity for autonomy has been compromised. For example, choice may be constrained by impoverished circumstances, or by an addiction to hard drugs. Addictions are, as McLeod and Sherwin (2000, p 271) point out, 'a form of compulsion' which 'by their very nature ... interfere with autonomy'.

The autonomy of the addict is not just limited by the physical consequences of addiction, however, but also by the way in which the addict's 'personal history has inhibited their ability to acquire the conditions necessary for autonomy' (McLeod & Sherwin, 2000, p 271). For women in this situation, we may not promote their autonomy by assuming that they are already exercising it, and 'leaving them alone'. Rather we, as a society, need to provide the resources and support (for example, treatment programmes) that will enhance the development of people's capacities to exercise autonomous control over their lives. On the other hand, it is important to recognise diversity in issues of 'choice'; pervasive stereotypes of sex workers as passive victims often paralyse thinking and bedevil attempts at intervention. As Laura Agustin (2007) shows, based on her extensive research with migrant sex workers, migrants frequently make rational choices to travel and work in the sex industry. Her work reveals the deep complexity of the contemporary sex industry and warns against making easy judgements.

Jenkins examines the vexed issue of the regulation of prostitution. There has long been controversy over what role, if any, law should play in regulating sex work. Should it, in accordance with the views of the 1957 Wolfenden Committee, be regarded as a matter of private morality? Or is the potential for harm—to the public interest generally, and to individual sex workers in particular—such that state interventions are justified? As ongoing debates around prostitution indicate, there is no easy solution, not least because 'harm' in this context is so difficult to pin down, and notions of 'harm' are further complicated by the concerns about 'exploitation' that underpin them. Is prostitution, Jenkins asks, an inherently exploitative practice?

Jenkins broadens the debate and opens up old questions to new scrutiny by moving beyond the usual suspect of female heterosexual prostitution and addressing also issues of male prostitution. In this way, she is able to challenge the dominant discourses of victimhood of female sex workers that have tended both to stultify debates and to pay insufficient attention to the agency, choices and autonomy of sex workers. Many women, Jenkins argues, make informed decisions to work in prostitution in full recognition of the potential for exploitation. Such decisions are rational, and to acknowledge this is to ask whether there is any sound basis for the legal regulation of sexual activity between consenting adults.

In chapter three, Helen Reece explores the various facets of 'violence as regulation'. She argues that some feminist campaigns against intimate violence have generated discourses that have become effective methods, not so much for controlling violence, as for regulating intimate relationships. Perhaps the most powerful critiques of the value of privacy and autonomy have come from feminists, who have pointed out that protection of the 'private sphere'—as a supposed 'haven' and as separate from the 'public sphere' and state control—has simply worked to legitimate and shield the gendered exercise of power within domestic life. As Anita Allen (1988) has argued, in the past women had too much of the wrong kinds of privacy. Enforced modesty, domestic violence and a life of drudgery are not, as Allen points out, the forms of privacy that foster moral independence. Traditionally, women's position within the so-called private sphere meant that they had minimal opportunities to shape their lives according to their own values and beliefs: Debra Morris (2000), for example, argues that privacy has been a masculinist prerogative that only enhances the vulnerability and powerlessness of women.

The mistake certain feminists have made, Reece argues in chapter three, is to blur the distinction between patriarchy as a *cause* of violence and patriarchy *as violence*. Reece critically examines the particular concept of violence that has recently taken hold within feminism—it has become a 'powerful orthodoxy' that 'coerces agreement'—and is therefore difficult to challenge. From the point of view of privacy and autonomy, concern arises, according to Reece's analysis, when these discourses are imported into regulatory processes where they then become the dominant ones.

On the positive side, the 'contextual' approach to intimate violence that feminists have struggled to foreground not only highlights the broader issue of gender relations, but also points to the profound significance of meanings. Reece's analysis shows just how much language matters; so much turns on how we *define* violence and the assumptions that are embedded in our working definitions. Definitions are important because they invoke particular discourses and set particular meanings in train. Thus, in heterosexual intimate violence, an act of, say, slapping the other, has a profoundly different meaning depending on whether it is committed by a man or by a woman. The acts are not equivalent because they have different meanings in the broader contexts of the social relations of gender; the same act has a different meaning, a different history and different consequences.

On the negative side, Reece sees the concept of violence as in danger of being stretched almost beyond definition, thus rendering underlying concepts of oppression so vague as to become almost meaningless. One upshot of these developments is that regulation of violence too easily slides into a much wider regulation of intimacy more generally, with obvious detrimental consequences for broader notions and practices of privacy and autonomy. Thus, if the category of intimate conduct that is treated as 'violence' is expanded, a very wide range of behaviours potentially becomes unacceptable and susceptible to state intervention. Feminists in the 1970s were clearly right to suggest that the concept of the 'private sphere' had too long hidden from public scrutiny the systematic abuse of women and children in domestic settings, and putting an end to the idea that domestic violence could be a 'private' matter has been of crucial importance in women's pursuit of equality and autonomy. Yet the new turn in feminist thought, as discussed by Reece, possibly has two unintended and unwanted consequences: first, it might justify radical interventions into domestic life and the imposition of an impossible new normative order from the outside and, secondly, it threatens to devalue the experiences of the survivors of serious violence by seeing their suffering in the same category as that of someone who has experienced a lesser harm.

The traditional conception of autonomy has also been regarded with suspicion by feminists on the ground that it is a concept that is fashioned according to the dictates of individualism. Thus it has been said to presuppose a rational, self-interested and essentially insular subject, who is concerned only to promote his own interests. As Lorraine Code (1991, p 77) explains:

> Autonomous man is—and should be—self-sufficient, independent, and self-reliant, a self-realizing individual who directs his efforts towards maximizing his personal gains. His independence is under constant threat from other (equally self-serving) individuals: hence he devises rules to protect himself from intrusion.

Thus, notions of autonomy have tended to over-value independence and under-value other human attributes and practices, such as caring, responsibility and our fundamental *inter-dependence* with others. Dependency is not an aberration from the norm of independence and self-sufficiency, but is rather a central feature of all human lives. We were all entirely dependent on others in our first years of life, and most of us will be dependent on others towards the ends of our lives. Many will experience periods in between when they are more or less dependent on others (Kittay, 1997, p 221). Family and intimate relationships necessarily involve both dependency upon and responsibility for others.

Nevertheless Code, along with a number of other feminists (for example, Meyers, 1989; Nedelsky, 1989), does not consider that the right response to concerns about autonomy's over-valuation of independence would be to jettison the concept of autonomy altogether. Instead, in recent years, feminists have sought to refashion the very meaning of autonomy, so that it more accurately captures the realities of human interdependence.

Thus the concept of 'relational autonomy' (Mackenzie & Stoljar, 2000) involves the recognition that we are not the isolated individuals assumed by traditional conceptions of autonomy. Instead, our development and, indeed. our entire lives *as* individuals *require* our interdependency with others (Baier, 1985). It is hard to see how any of us could become rational and reflective human beings—or, indeed, exist at all—*outside* of the social contexts in which multiple connections with others are both fundamental and non-optional. But despite our inevitable location within and reliance upon a network of relationships, our ability to make choices—albeit socially embedded ones—about the direction of our lives is nevertheless critical to our sense of self.

Drawing on the influential work of Carol Gilligan (1982), feminist theorists have argued that abstract moral reasoning in general, and an emphasis on individualistic principles such as autonomy in particular, are both distinctively 'male'. Rejecting the idea of atomised individuals, but recognising that connections with others are much more important, there has been considerable feminist interest in an 'ethic of care' (see, eg, Held, 2007). An ethic of care values relationships more highly than an individualistic notion of autonomy. It takes for granted the inevitability of dependency, and requires us to treat others with respect and compassion. An ethic of care is a useful starting point to reconceptualise autonomy as relational rather than as individual. But, as Mackenzie and Stoljar (2000, p 10) point out, care critiques can provide 'a very circumscribed reconceptualisation of autonomy. In particular, they fail to address the complex effects of oppression on agents' capacities for autonomy.' If we test the concept of relational autonomy in different areas of law, its limitations soon become apparent.

Drawing on a feminist ethic of care, in chapter four Jonathan Herring explores a concept of relational autonomy and tests the limits of its usefulness in relation to the law on rape. Central to the criminal law in the UK is the requirement that the victim did not consent to the penetrative act. Herring exposes some of the weaknesses of the concept of relational autonomy by showing its consequences for different interpretations of consent in this controversial area. A judgement about rape, within a framework of relational autonomy, would require that the sexual act be understood and interpreted in the context of the relationship between the parties and in the wider social context. Herring has opened up an important debate. The concept of relational autonomy clearly provides a richer and more nuanced understanding of human lives, decisions and choices, but its consequences need to be more fully explored in concrete contexts, and social power relations are an element that cannot be ignored. To be autonomous, in a relational sense, is to be responsive and responsible to others, and interdependent within complex networks of relationships, which will not always easily accord with the practices and expectations we have normalised in cultures that have elevated 'the individual'. Further, as Herring's analysis shows, a full understanding of the possibilities and limitations of relational autonomy demands that we develop more sophisticated thinking about the social dimensions of agency and selfhood.

Autonomy, on the relational view, is a *capacity*, the development of which requires relationships and not isolation (Nedelsky, 1989). It is also a capacity that people in general regard as important, although they may not express it using the language of autonomy. Being clear about what one wants and believes in and being able to act upon those desires and values is a form of self-governance which is generally assumed to be valuable, while recognising that our desires and beliefs, and our capacity to act upon them, are inevitably shaped, for better or worse, by the social, cultural, economic and political contexts in which we live. The personal histories of girls and women who are subjected in their domestic lives to systematic emotional, sexual or physical violence or bullying will be likely to constrain their capacities to exercise autonomy. The decision to stay with (or not to leave) a violent partner may not be an example of autonomous choice, but a reflection of the systematic chipping away at the qualities we need—such as a sense of self-worth or self-trust—in order to exercise a degree of autonomy over our lives.

Amartya Sen and Martha Nussbaum have both developed capability-based theories of justice, which have considerable resonance for a capacity-based theory of autonomy (Sen, 1999; Nussbaum, 1999). Factors that interfere with our capacity for human flourishing also, inevitably, restrict our capacity to exercise control over the direction of our lives. In the past, for example, when women lacked the tools necessary to exercise much autonomy in the private or domestic sphere, financial dependence and social norms which stigmatised single mothers and divorced women combined to make it very difficult for women to leave unsatisfactory relationships. Thus there may be many contextual factors, past and present, that mitigate the exercise of autonomy and which may be further obscured in relational models that do not take sufficient account of power relations. Where those power relations are obscured, we find instances of the tacit regulation of individuals, for example through people's participation in normative discourses and practices, such as Rose (1987) discusses in relation to 'the family'.

The focus of chapter five, by Ellie Lee and Jennie Bristow, is the tacit regulation of family life implicit in contemporary discourses and practices of feeding babies in Western cultures. Like Reece, Lee and Bristow explore an area where regulation of domestic lives occurs more covertly than overtly and where the consequences for autonomy and privacy, therefore, are that much more difficult to pinpoint. Their analysis is based on qualitative interviews with mothers about their experiences of feeding their infants; many felt that they were 'watched over' and 'monitored' by a range of health professionals but also by other mothers too. The authors show how what they call 'intensive parenting' is discursively constructed and managed, with profound consequences for parents' privacy and autonomy.

From this analysis, it is clear that the notion of choice (in this case, breast or bottle) is strongly circumscribed by morally loaded discourses that impinge not just on feeding practices but also on women's identities as mothers. These discourses are also encoded in policy and in guidelines for good practice, such that we can see, in Lee and Bristow's work, an examination of the intricate workings of regulation in this area of domestic life. They present us with a carefully worked example of the ways in which the most successful regulation is achieved, as it were, from the inside out, as people position themselves within the dominant discourses—making their choices, adjusting their aspirations and managing their anxieties (see Rose, 1987), with all that that implies for their identities, their privacy and their autonomy.

In chapter six, Mavis Maclean and John Eekelaar explore the significance of discourse and tacit regulation in the family law setting. But interestingly, in this example, we see parents resisting the power of the dominant discourses; they seem to be negotiating their way through the legal process in ways that further, rather than compromise, their autonomy.[1] Maclean and Eekelaar discuss state regulation of the family, and the consequences for parental autonomy, in the context of separation and divorce. They provide vital empirical evidence of the complex ways in which parents negotiate their autonomy, with the help of their legal advisers, against the background of private proceedings in the family courts. Parents who are unable to resolve their difficulties without recourse to the courts inevitably face the possibility of a loss of autonomy. Although 'alternative dispute resolution' (eg mediation) is often held to promote the individual autonomies of the parties, Maclean and Eekelaar's findings suggest that legal representation can be used most successfully by disputing parents to achieve durable outcomes and, crucially, to mitigate losses of autonomy.

In private family law, autonomy issues are played out in the context of considerable tensions between the discourse of welfare and the language of justice (Day Sclater & Kaganas, 2003). In recent years, the increasing dominance of the welfare discourse has tended to eclipse that of rights and justice, at the same time as individual parental autonomy has given way to the interests of children, seen as the greater good—the 'paramount' consideration. Maclean and Eekelaar's contribution reminds us that these policy imperatives are not straightforwardly implemented and that parents' desires or needs for autonomy may pose considerable barriers to state interventions when parents separate or divorce.

Several chapters in this volume problematise an important feature of traditional conceptions of autonomy, namely an emphasis upon the insular individualised self. This is underpinned by an assumption that, not only should one be able to determine one's own life course, but also one should be permitted to do so, particularly in relation to one's private life, free from external scrutiny and interference. When we designate a realm of our life as 'private' or 'personal', Allen (2003) suggests that:

> we imagine ourselves as citizens of a free society, each entitled to enjoy a number of states, feelings, thoughts, acts and relationship for which we owe others no accounting (p 1)

---

[1] For a further example of the pursuit of autonomy by parents in family law, and one that emphasises the gender dimension, see Kaganas and Day Sclater (2004).

When we are at work, for example, or driving a car, or filling in our tax return, we expect to be accountable to others for our actions, but matters of personal morality are seen as different. In order to flourish as individuals, as the Wolfenden Committee (1957) famously stated, 'there must remain a realm of private morality and immorality which is, in brief and crude terms, not the law's business'. The individual, according to John Stuart Mill (1859/1948, p 115), 'is not accountable to society for his actions, insofar as these concern the interests of no person but himself'.

But of course, very few of our 'private' actions will concern no one else. In all intimate relationships, at least two people are involved, and their accountability to each other for their conduct is, many would argue, a critical component of what it means to be close to another person. And accountability for actions in one's private life extends beyond the basic norms of decency owed to one's children, partner and other relatives. Rather we are also accountable to various state agencies for how behave in our 'private' lives.

In chapter seven, Jan Pryor's discussion of the legal regulation of step-parenthood highlights the need for a relational view of autonomy—autonomy in the step-parenting relationship is quite clearly at odds with autonomy conceived as a characteristic of an individual—but also exposes some of its limitations. First, not only does the step-parent relationship involve two people of unequal status, but it is also embedded in wider family and social contexts; thus, as we have suggested, any conception of the relational must take adequate account of social stratification and power relationships. Secondly, the debate about the regulation of step-parenting has taken place mainly on the terrain of parental and family 'rights', with remarkably little attention given to the perspectives of children; a conception of relational autonomy must be able to take account of *all* participants in the relationship but, as Day Sclater and Piper (2001) show, children have historically been marginalised or even invisible. Thirdly, the ongoing struggle to reconcile the requirements of legal regulation with the diverse and changing realities of step-family life highlights the need for any conception of relational autonomy to embrace issues of diversity and change.

So far, we have explored how autonomies are negotiated in the areas of intimacy and domestic life. In some cases, the persuasive moral power of discourse is backed up with more overtly coercive powers or institution-alised sanctions. For example, parents' duties towards their children will be enforced by a number of state bodies. If parents fail to provide adequate care, their children may be taken away, and even adopted against the parents' wishes. Payment of child support is non-optional and enforceable, and, on separation or divorce, disagreements over the division of family assets may be resolved by the courts.

Thus, accountability for 'private' decisions may take the form of straight-forward legal liability. But, as we have seen, social expectations, expressed in dominant discourses and often reinforced by professional practices or backed up by institutional power, can have equally coercive, though less visible, effects; the stigma attached to failure to comply with accepted norms can be profound. There is no legal requirement that pregnant women refrain from smoking and from drinking to excess, for example, and yet the censure that attaches to pregnant women who ignore medical advice may be just as powerful. As Lee and Bristow show, the widely promulgated assumption that 'good' mothers will breastfeed their children for at least six months exerts considerable pressure on mothers who find breastfeeding difficult or inconvenient.

Liability and accountability for conduct in one's private life is, as Allen points out 'one of the most emotionally charged forms of accountability' (2003, p 3). That men were subject to criminal sanction as a result of their sexual orientation as recently as 40 years ago now seems shockingly intolerant and cruel. On the other hand, criminal censure of rape and of the sexual abuse of children seems self-evidently justified, and any interference with the 'privacy' of rapists or paedophiles entirely warranted. The line many of us would draw here is between conduct that harms others, and conduct that does not. But even this apparently clear line that the 'harm principle' draws between situations where tolerance of difference is required, and situations where it is not, may not, as is evident from the range of views collected in this volume, be sharp or consensual enough to form the basis of public policy.

Allen argues that we are entitled to say 'none of your business!' in response to some requests for answers, but not to others (2003, p 7). But working out where this line should be drawn is by no means easy, and moreover, the line may vary between cultures and generations. Are we entitled to know about a politician's marital infidelity, or a Catholic priest's homosexuality, for example, or is it none of our business? Would it make a difference if the unfaithful politician had campaigned for the promotion of 'traditional family values', or if the priest had spoken out against the appointment of an openly gay bishop?

In addition to the web of obligations we owe to others, and the difficulty in achieving agreement over the limits of a right to say 'none of your business!', it is also worth noting the uneven distribution of privacy in society. In short, some people's domestic arrangements have always been more private than others. Single parents, for example, have often been subjected to public scrutiny and criticism (Fineman, 1991). Homeless people, or people living in institutions often find their lack of privacy humiliating and demeaning. For most people, the decision to try to 'start a family' is paradigmatically private, and their reasons for wanting children seem self-evidently 'none of the state's business'. For infertile couples, things are rather different. By having their future parenting abilities scrutinised before treatment starts, infertile couples often feel stripped of the privacy to which they would otherwise be entitled when deciding to have children (Jackson, 2002).

Some sexual activities are criminal. Until relatively recently, consenting sex between two 17-year-old males was a criminal offence. Or in *R v Brown* [1993] 2 All ER 75, the House of Lords decided that people who had engaged in consensual, sado-masochistic acts, which took place in private and which did not cause permanent injury, could nevertheless be convicted of unlawful wounding and assault. More recently still, it has been decided that knowingly or recklessly transmitting HIV to a sexual partner might amount to assault (Weait, 2005).

In chapter eight, Julia Davidson and Elena Martellozzo consider issues of autonomy and privacy in the context of the criminalisation of sex offenders, and the regulation of newer categories of offenders, including those who pursue sex with children over the internet. Proposed measures to monitor and control this group include electronic tagging, use of hormone-suppressing drugs, and the regular inspection of offenders' homes and computers, all of which represent serious inroads into privacy and autonomy, especially where such regulatory measures endure beyond the completion of formal sentences.

The 'sexual abuse' of children is an emotive issue that attracts considerable media attention, and sex offenders have become the 'folk devils' of our time. As a group, they carry considerable emotional baggage as we invest them with our deepest fears and loathings. Such is the magnitude and significance of the negative emotion we oblige them to carry for us that sex offenders represent an extreme case. Yet, they are an extreme case that, on closer examination, obliges us to look not only at the emotional work the category 'sex offender' does on our behalf, but also at the political work it achieves. For in this extreme case we see autonomy all but obliterated; in the discursive production of 'sex offenders' we see a removal of autonomy—witness the paucity of debates around proposals for 'chemical castration' in the UK, for example; it seems entirely legitimate in the face of 'risks' and potential 'harms' to children who are cast as vulnerable and in need of paternalistic protection by the state.

As Davidson and Martellozzo point out, the difficulty of weighing the individual's right to autonomy and the need to protect the vulnerable from harm in internet sex offender management is the crucial issue to which there is no simple solution. In some ways this may appear as a clear conflict of autonomies—between that of the 'offender' and that of the 'victim'. Yet, in the context of internet sex, those categories themselves are discursively constructed in ways that eclipse issues of autonomy in the first place. The danger is, argue Davidson and Martellozzo, that criminal justice measures to manage internet sex offenders represent more of an attempt to quell public anxiety rather than a genuine effort to address the complex issues of balancing individual autonomies and the public interest.

III. AUTONOMY AND REPRODUCTION

In the second part of the book, the focus of the chapters is more specifically on reproduction.

In chapter nine, Theresa Glennon opens the debate on autonomy and reproductive issues by focusing on whether markets or state regulation best promote autonomy in the area of assisted conception. Comparing the situation in the UK with that in the US, Glennon demonstrates the profound significance of context. The implication of her work is that there can be no unequivocal answer to what best assures autonomy, since autonomy itself is a concept that shifts according to context. In the US, there has long been a dominant discourse that 'big government' interferes with autonomy, whilst the vicissitudes of the market are more likely to promote it. By contrast, the regulatory regime in the UK is a fairly permissive one, lending state intervention a somewhat different meaning.

The situatedness of autonomy is a theme also taken up by Martin Johnson and Kerry Petersen in chapter ten. Discussing regulatory regimes in the UK and Australia, they unpack the notion of regulation in the context of assisted reproductive technologies (ARTs). By considering the most effective way for regulation to be achieved—the 'how' question—they oblige us to focus on the more fundamental objectives that lie behind regulation—the all-important 'why' question. It is in those objectives that we find a whole range of social concerns, elusive philosophical principles and implicit moral imperatives embedded.

Given the liberal-democratic presumption that autonomous individuals have the right to make their own informed choices, Johnson and Petersen argue, any intrusion on autonomy requires a demonstration of actual or potential harm or offence to the 'public interest'. In other words, regulation that compromises the autonomy of democratic citizens requires clear objectives not only to justify its existence but also to select appropriate regulatory instruments. But Johnson and Petersen find it difficult to unearth such clear objectives, leading them to question whether the regulatory mechanisms currently in place are suited to contemporary purposes.

In chapter eleven, Martin Richards further considers the boundaries of reproductive autonomy. Whilst agreeing with Emily Jackson (2001, p 318) that we should 'strive to carve out maximum possible respect for the reproductive autonomy of individual men and women', Richards accepts that there are some justifiable limits to reproductive autonomy. John Stuart Mill's liberal view of the state—'the only purpose for which power can rightly be exercised over any member of a civilised community, against his will, is to prevent harm to others', continues to have resonance today. Again, much then turns on what counts as 'harm'.

It is impossible to talk about reproductive choice dispassionately; not only is reproduction inevitably an emotionally loaded issue, but issues of choice are also embedded in morally loaded discourses, all the more so now that these issues are linked to advances in genetic technologies. Furthermore, contemporary debates about reproductive choice cannot help but take place in the shadow of the Eugenics movement that, not least through its associations with the atrocities committed in Nazi Germany, has tended to provoke reactions of distrust, if not downright hostility. Thus, emotive debates about the rights and wrongs of so-called 'designer babies', sex selection, human clones and the like—debates that have shed more heat than light—have dominated the media. One upshot of this has been that the social space available for debates about reproductive autonomy has tended to become Frankenstein territory, where the horrors of abjection (Kristeva, 1984) are never far away. Admirably, Richards cuts through this rhetoric and argues that social and political processes will continue to set the limits of our reproductive autonomy, as they have always done.

In chapter twelve, Susan Golombok considers a specific instance of state intrusion into reproductive autonomy: the recent—and controversial—removal, in the UK, of donor anonymity, whereby children conceived by gamete donation will, on reaching the age of 18, be entitled to identifying information about their donor/s. In Golombok's work, we can see more of the workings of those important social and political processes identified by Richards in his chapter. Crucially, whether or not donor offspring will, in practice, have access to this information depends heavily upon whether the parents choose to tell their children about the donor conception. That there is no requirement for them to do so points to the inherently ambivalent nature of the regulation; reproductive autonomy is neither supported nor destroyed, but rather remains poised and uncertain, up for negotiation.

The potential 'harm' that this regulation addresses is the risk of supposed damage to the child caused by not knowing where his/her biological roots lie. The assumption that lies behind this particular discursive construction of harm bears comment, however: 'harm' here is implicitly constructed within the long-dominant discourse of biological parenthood and thus, despite the uncertainty of the regulation, the certainty of the moral message is clear.

In chapter thirteen, Laura Riley and Anne Furedi consider some further moral messages and how they shape autonomy in the context of UK abortion law. Clearly, autonomy would best be served by a statutory recognition of autonomous decision-making and, according to recent polls, public opinion would support this. Yet, there have been repeated attempts in recent years to overhaul the law, all of which have a restrictive intent as regards the autonomy of individual women. None have yet been successful, but these attempts testify to the deep moral uncertainty that surrounds abortion and, by extension, reproductive autonomy. Abortion in the UK remains continually vulnerable to new laws restricting access, and women's reproductive autonomy is, as a result, as fragile as it is contingent. As in other areas of reproduction, abortion debates straddle the boundaries between religion and the secular, and so tend to be emotive. Those emotions are widely exploited across the media. In those debates—that never seem to reach satisfactory conclusions—abortion remains a morally ambivalent issue that is nevertheless open to pragmatic solutions at an individual level. But those solutions are already suffused with an emotivism that seeps in to fill the gap between moral uncertainty and the need to act. In the absence of consensus or any general guidelines, such solutions will rely on the moral authority given to individual feelings about what is right or wrong. What the recent polls show is that, in the end, when it comes to abortion, a woman should do what feels right to her. Nothing more, nothing less.

What the chapters in this section reveal, then, is the extent to which reproductive autonomy—and autonomy more generally—is constructed within different discourses in different contexts, and that those contexts have a significant influence on both the meanings and the practices of autonomy. Further, the discourses in which autonomy takes shape in reproductive settings are themselves sites for ongoing struggles between competing moral messages. In such a climate of moral uncertainty, it is difficult to evaluate new reproductive and genetic technologies and practices dispassionately. Where moral positions jostle for dominance, as they do in debates on reproductive autonomy, it is difficult to avoid emotivist solutions. Yet feeling does seem to be a somewhat flimsy basis for decision-making.

Finally, it is perhaps worth noting that the value attached to privacy varies between different cultures and over time. Young people are increasingly accustomed to posting very intimate information about themselves on networking websites. Some use webcams to broadcast aspects of their private lives to anyone who cares to watch. On reality TV programmes and confession-based chat shows, people often apparently expose some of their most intimate thoughts to millions of viewers. Privacy is also a relative value, in that however important we may believe it to be, it might always be trumped by other considerations. While many would argue that the current UK government has got the balance between citizens' rights to privacy and national security considerations wrong, most would accept that there is a balance to be struck.

In sum, while it is true that we value the capacity to shape our private lives according to our own beliefs and values—while we value our autonomy— it is important to recognise that we need social relationships and support in order to develop that capacity and realise it, and that our choices are both deeply socially embedded and constrained by the web of obligations that we owe to others. The model of the self-interested individual exercising 'self-government' over their life makes very little sense. As the chapters in this collection demonstrate, autonomy is a much more complex concept than simple self-determination, and its practical realisation in our domestic and intimate lives reveals us to be creatures who need social support rather than isolation in order to flourish.

The chapters in this book lay bare the all-important significance of context; autonomy appears as a fluid and contingent concept whose meanings are shaped anew with every case and situation. There cannot be any simple answer to the question of state intervention into 'private' aspects of our lives; these essays call into question the very nature of privacy, as well as the meanings, impacts and limits of autonomy, whether it is conceived of as an individual attribute or capacity, or a democratic right, or as a relational process. And, ultimately, they point to a need for us to interrogate each case or situation for whether it promotes or undermines the kind of autonomy we might be prepared to struggle for.

BIBLIOGRAPHY

Agustin, LM (2007) *Sex at the Margins: Migration, Labour Markets and the Rescue Industry,* Zed Books, London.

Allen, A (1988) *Uneasy Access: Privacy for Women in a Free Society,* Rowman and Littlefield, Lanham, MD.

Allen, AL (2003) *Why Privacy isn't Everything,* Rowman and Littlefield, Lanham, MD.

Baier, A (1985) *Postures of the Mind,* University of Minnesota Press, Minneapolis, MN.

Code, L (1991) *What can she know? Feminist Theory and the Construction of Knowledge,* Cornell University Press, Ithaca, NY.

Day Sclater, S & Kaganas, F (2003) 'Contact: Mothers, welfare and rights', in *Children and their Families: Contact, Rights and Welfare* (Eds, Bainham A, Lindley B, Richards M, Trinder L) Hart Publishing, Oxford.

Day Sclater, S and Piper, C (2001) 'Social Exclusion and the Welfare of the Child'. *Journal of Law and* Society 28(3), 409–29.

Fineman, M (1991) 'Intimacy Outside of the Natural Family: The Limits of Privacy'. *Connecticut Law Review* 23, 955.

Gilligan, C (1982) *In a Different Voice: Psychological Theory and Women's Development,* Harvard University Press, Cambridge, MA.

Held, V (2007) *The Ethics of Care: Personal, Political, Global,* Oxford University Press, Oxford.

Jackson, E (2001) *Regulating Reproduction,* Hart Publishing, Oxford.

—— (2002) 'Conception and the Irrelevance of the Welfare Principle'. *Modern Law Review* 65(2), 176–203.

Kaganas, F & Day Sclater, S (2004) 'Contact disputes: Narrative constructions of "good" parents', *Feminist Legal Studies* 12, 1–27.

Kittay, EF (1997) 'Human Dependency and Rawlsian Equality' in *Feminists Rethink the Self* (Ed, Meyers DT) Westview Press, Boulder, CO, pp 219–66.

Kristeva, J (1984) *Powers of Horror: An Essay on Abjection,* Columbia University Press, Irvington, NY.

Mackenzie, C & Stoljar, N (2000) 'Autonomy Refigured' in *Relational Autonomy: Feminist Perspectives on Autonomy, Agency and the Social Self* (Eds, Mackenzie C & Stoljar N) Oxford University Press, Oxford, pp 3–31.

McLeod, C & Sherwin, S (2000) 'Relational Autonomy, Self-Trust, and Health Care for Patients who are Oppressed' in *Relational Autonomy: Feminist Perspectives on Autonomy, Agency and the Social Self* (Eds, Mackenzie C & Stoljar N) Oxford University Press, Oxford, pp 259–79.

Meyers, DT (1989) *Self, Society and Personal Choice,* Columbia University Press, Irvington, NY.

Mill, JS (1859/1948) *On Liberty,* Oxford University Press, Oxford.

Morris, D (2000) 'Privacy, Privation, Perversity: Towards New Representation of the Personal'. *Signs* 25, 323–52.

Nedelsky, J (1989) 'Reconceiving Autonomy'. *Yale Journal of Law and Feminism* **1(1)**, 17–36.

—— (1990) 'Law, Boundaries and the Bounded Self'. *Representations* 30(1), 162–89.

Nussbaum, M (1999) *Sex and Social Justice,* Oxford University Press, Oxford.

O'Neill, O (2002) *Autonomy and Trust in Bioethics,* Cambridge University Press, Cambridge.

Pateman, C (1988) *The Sexual Contract*, Stanford University Press, Palo Alto, CA.

Raz, J (1986) *The Morality of Freedom,* Oxford University Press, Oxford.

Rose, N (1987) 'Beyond the public/private division: Law, power and the family'. *Journal of Law and Society* 14(1), 61–76.

Sen, A (1999) *Development as Freedom,* Random House, New York.

Weait, M (2005) 'The Sexual Transmission of HIV: *R v Dica*'. *Modern Law Review* 68(1), 121–34.

Williams, B (1973) *The Problem of the Self: Philosophical Papers 1956–1972,* Cambridge University Press, Cambridge.

Wolfenden Committee (1957) *The Wolfenden Committee Report on Homosexual Offences and Prostitution in England*, HMSO, London.

Part 1

Intimacies and Domestic Lives

2

Exploitation: The Role of Law in Regulating Prostitution

SUZANNE JENKINS

I. INTRODUCTION*

THERE HAS ALWAYS been considerable controversy about what role, if any, law should play in regulating prostitution, and although in Britain prostitution[1] remains legal in itself, existing legislation does make it very difficult for a prostitute to work without potentially contravening one law or another. The current laws have evolved in a piecemeal fashion. For example, under the heading of sexual offences, the system criminalises procuration, pimping and brothel-keeping, whereas loitering and soliciting for the purpose of prostitution, and kerb-crawling are public order 'street offences'. Anti-social Behaviour Orders, created by the Crime and Disorder Act (1998), have also been increasingly used against street prostitutes. These laws have been subject to ongoing review and reform in recent years, yet there remains little consensus about the best way to proceed in terms of policy. Instead, the result has been what Agustin (2006, p 34) describes as 'an endless, repetitive debate' in the literature on female prostitution, between the benefits of regulation, prohibition and legalisation or decriminalisation. Within the context of such debates, and perhaps in recognition of its significance as a feminist issue, there has been a tendency to think of a prostitute as a woman. Consequently, debates about the value and purpose of laws regulating commercial sex almost exclusively focus on the female prostitute. Indeed, until recently, in legal terminology 'a prostitute was, by definition, a woman, and a client was, by definition, a man' (Brooks-Gordon, 2003, p 28). With no male equivalent for the term 'common prostitute', the activities of male prostitution

* I am grateful to Marie Fox and John Scott, and to the participants at the 2007 Cambridge Socio-legal Group seminar for helpful comments on earlier drafts of this chapter.
[1] In this chapter, the term 'prostitute', rather than 'sex worker', is used neutrally, simply to differentiate from other types of sex work such as exotic dancing or pornography.

were regulated primarily by section 32 of the Sexual Offences Act (1956). However, in May 2004, when the Sexual Offences Act (2003) came into force, all existing legislation relating to commercial sexual offences was rephrased to employ gender-neutral terminology (section 56). Therefore, all new clauses apply equally to both men and women who sell sex. It has been suggested that by extending gender-neutrality in this way, male prostitutes may now be at risk of becoming criminalised to the same degree as female prostitutes (Bainham and Brooks-Gordon, 2004, p 282). In other words, an already controversial set of laws governing female prostitutes can now be extended to men who sell sex. According to Brooks-Gordon (2003, p 29), 'this retrograde step may make men as vulnerable as women to the law's interference in people's private lives'.

The existence of male prostitution has long been documented, and there is no doubt that male prostitution is a significant practice both nationally and internationally (Kuo, 2002, p 14). Like female prostitution it is difficult to quantify with any accuracy, however, in the UK at least, 'a generally accepted ratio of four females to one male involved in prostitution is widely held' (Barrett, 1998, p 476). The most notable difference between female prostitution and male prostitution is that the latter is largely, though not exclusively, homosexual prostitution. Of course, like their female counterparts, male prostitutes work in a number of different ways and in various venues. This includes both the more visible street-based industry as well as indoor markets such as brothels/massage parlours and increasingly as escorts operating either via agencies or independently. It is also ever-changing, and as Archard (1998, p 104) explains, not only can the economic and social status of prostitutes vary across cultures and historical periods, but they can also vary dramatically within one and the same society; that is, the prostitute can 'work the street or inhabit the penthouse'. Historically, however, regardless of the working environment, women have consistently been arrested and prosecuted more frequently for prostitution-related offences than have men (O'Neill, 1999, p 182).

In this chapter I address the gendered nature of prostitution and argue that while changes in legislative terminology do signify an important change symbolically, it is doubtful whether this move heralds any substantive transformation in gender equality. This, I contend, is the result of prevailing double standards about what constitutes appropriate male and female behaviour. In particular, this includes a tendency to neglect women's equal autonomy, in the sense of their freedom to act in accordance with their own moral values. I conclude by highlighting that, unless and until the state accepts that women can make rational, autonomous decisions to work in prostitution as men do, it is unlikely that there will be significant consequences of extending laws to male prostitutes. Despite the tinkering with the wording of legislation, women will continue to represent the target of prostitution legislation by those involved in initiating and processing criminal justice.

II. THE ROLE OF LAW

The role that law should play in regulating prostitution has long been contested. As Childs (2000, p 205) observes:

> There is disagreement not just about the scope and manner of regulation, but also as to whether law has *any* legitimate role to play in controlling this behaviour.

To address this issue, we need to consider the role of law in our society more generally, and, in particular, how decisions are made about what law should be aiming to achieve. This is not a simple task, however; as Sharpe (1998, p 151) explains, 'In a morally pluralistic society, the scope of the law is difficult to define.' For some, the role of law includes the signalling of what constitutes morally acceptable behaviour by prohibiting that which is considered to be 'wrong'. The Christian Institute, for example, remonstrates:

> The law is there to tell us what is good, helping us to define the right course of action … in the absence of all other absolutes … we look to the law to remind us what we believe (Mills, 1997, p 2).

In other words, law provides guidance in areas where doubt and uncertainty exist, including where the acceptability of certain sexual behaviours is concerned. The law does this by prohibiting particular acts, and also by governing others through formal regulation. In this way, as Anderson (2002, p 770) suggests, 'the legal and social discouragement of prostitution is seen as a way for our communities to intentionally regulate or constrain our sexual activities'.

Furthermore, because law operates 'within the context of a powerful discourse; one which is placed highly on the hierarchy of knowledges' (Smart, 1995, p 82), the guidance provided in law is deemed ultimately authoritative and thus is both highly persuasive and widely influential.

However, it can be argued that it is not the role of law to provide answers where ambiguity exists. For example, while there are fears that legalising prostitution would signify the state's validation of the use of women's bodies as commodities, those who advocate the decriminalisation of prostitution insist that decriminalisation 'does not, and would not, signify state approval of prostitution or make a judgment as to its moral status' (Sharpe, 1998, p 159). In this view, law is not about signifying or denying moral approval; individual morality is a personal judgement. It is also important to distinguish between prostitution's wrongness and the legal response that we are entitled to make to that wrongness (Satz, 1995, p 81). Therefore, although it is commonly argued that prostitution is not in the best interest of the prostitute, even if this were true, this would not necessarily warrant using the law to protect the prostitute from himself or herself. That is, even if we were to accept that exchanging sex for money is fundamentally wrong, it can still be argued that doing so does not necessarily warrant legal intervention. Barry (1979, p 236) argues, for example, that:

> It should not be the function of the law to enforce morality or values by making them legal standards under which people must live.

Similarly, Sharpe (1998, p 160) points out that there are many contentious areas of human behaviour that do not lend themselves to statutory prohibition. Indeed, this was the clear conclusion of the Wolfenden Committee, who in their report published in 1957 made radical recommendations for law reform, reflecting the argument that prostitution should be regarded as a matter of private morality. The basic attitude of the committee was that private sexual practices, whether commercialised or not, were not a matter for the interference of the criminal law, but a matter of private morality. In the view of this committee, accepting that the eradication of prostitution was unlikely, the role of law remained only to regulate the more exploitative aspects of the industry and to protect vulnerable individuals who become involved.

Historically, of course, prostitution has been viewed largely as a public health concern, an issue which has been rekindled in recent decades in recognition of fears about HIV/AIDS. Nevertheless, the principles as laid down by the Wolfenden committee remain the principles upon which much of UK prostitution legislation today is based. Therefore, although it is predominantly shaped by an understanding of prostitution as a problem of public nuisance, the role of the law still, ostensibly at least, depends on the question of whether any harm results, rather than on individual morality. Accordingly, Crown Prosecution Service guidelines state that the general objectives are fourfold: to encourage prostitutes to find routes out of prostitution and to deter those who create the demand for it; to keep prostitutes off the street to prevent annoyance to members of the public; to prevent people leading or forcing others into prostitution; and to penalise those who organise prostitutes and make a living from their earnings (CPS, 2008). Therefore, not only is the law's objective to reduce both the incidence and the public visibility of prostitution, but legal intervention is also justified by the need to protect the individual prostitute from being exploited by third parties profiting from their prostitution. This has become a particularly contentious issue. In female prostitution, for example, women are regarded as being in need of protection from exploitation, be this in the form of sexual domination or material exploitation. The extent to which this protection is warranted or desirable, however, in the view of those women who choose to work in prostitution, is controversial; not all female prostitutes relate to the notion that they are being exploited by anyone in the work that they do. In order to evaluate the role of law and its usefulness in protecting prostitutes, we need to consider the question of whether prostitutes are necessarily always victims of exploitation.

III. NOTIONS OF CHOICE

It has long been documented that feminists disagree on the question of whether a woman can validly seek recognition of her choice to engage in prostitution (Childs, 2000, p 221). Childs notes, for example, how some have compared this issue to that of abortion, arguing that feminists must defend a woman's right to choose prostitution, just as they defend a woman's right to choose abortion. Other feminists, however, argue that this type of 'choice' is as controversial as the choice to stay in an abusive relationship. Many question whether prostitution can ever be freely chosen; indeed, likening prostitution to gang rape, radical feminist, Dworkin (1992) insists, 'prostitution could not, no matter how defined, be accepted as a free choice by any woman'. Challenging dominant power relations, many feminists contend that prostitution is undoubtedly about men's power over women (Millett, 1975, p 33; Pateman, 1988; Kuo, 2002, p 143). Moreover, Pateman (1988, p 207) contends that prostitution is unlike other labour because the body cannot be separated from the individual self: 'when a prostitute contracts out use of her body she is thus selling herself in a very real sense'. However, any arguments about body ownership and one's ability to sell or hire one's body out can be interpreted as the very reason *why* women *should* be granted the right to choose to work in prostitution. As Petchesky (1995, p 395) argues:

> Feminists like Pateman, who invoke 'women's right to own their bodies' are reinforcing a language that can just as well validate their 'right' to sell their bodies' ... saying we 'own our bodies' means and can only mean that we are 'free' to sell our bodies.

The discourse of choice in relation to prostitution was brought to the fore in the late 1990s, when debate began focusing on the issue of women being trafficked for the purpose of sexual exploitation. This issue, which is now on the agenda of all major governing bodies, relies upon international human rights rhetoric, and raises the question of a dichotomy between free and forced prostitution. This discourse, which rejects issues of individual agency and consent, tends to deploy victimising terms such as 'prostituted women' and 'sexual slavery' for all migrant sex workers, rejecting the difference between 'free' and 'forced' sexual labour (see Weitzer, 2007). The belief is that no one can truly consent to prostitution and therefore any woman who is engaged in prostitution is a victim who requires rescuing from sexual slavery. However, not only has the occurrence of trafficking proved to be extremely difficult to measure, but much confusion arises from different use of terminology resulting in the conflation of both 'free' migrants who sell sex and those who have been trafficked (Agustin, 2005; 2006). It has also been argued that such sweeping generalisations 'fail to recognise the complexity and diversity of both the experiences of prostitutes and their motivations for working in prostitution' (Kuo, 2002, p 25). That a woman has chosen to travel to another country to seek work should not compromise her capacity to choose the nature of that work. As Agustin (2003, p 8) rightly asserts,

> we should be able to give credit where it is due to women and transsexuals, as well as men, who dare to make decisions to better their lives by leaving their homes to work abroad, no matter what kind of work they have to do.

Moreover, Agustin highlights how it is that, while women who work in the sex industry are consistently described in a victimising discourse, the experiences of men and transgenders who sell sex are ignored. This focus on women, insists Agustin, is because although there are many transgenders and men in the same situation, it is women that provoke the scandal (Agustin, 2007, p 11).

The negative aspects of prostitution within trafficking discourses remain widely influential both in the academic literature and the media. One particular difficulty, argues Weitzer (2007, p 451), is 'the claim that prostitution is intrinsically evil is an essentialist tenet that does not lend itself to evaluation with empirical evidence'. Furthermore, although it is often argued that people cannot give meaningful consent to the violation of their human rights (see for example, Barry, 1995), drawing upon human rights arguments can be a precarious approach to adopt. As Edwards (1997, p 57) counters:

> The prostitution issue is firmly on the human rights agenda, not only represented by a lobby arguing that it is an abrogation of fundamental human rights but represented too by the counter-claim that the right to prostitute is a fundamental human right.

This counter-claim espouses the value of free choice by individual women, and rejects interference with a woman's choice to sell sexual services, unless that choice is not made freely (Childs, 2000, p 223). It is not being suggested that the choice to work in prostitution is one that could or should be taken lightly, but that for some individuals, the option to work in prostitution may be the least unpalatable for them given their particular range of possibilities. There is of course ample evidence that women's choices can indeed be constrained, and as Chapkis (1997, p 52) submits, by being in a disadvantaged position hierarchically, very few women's lives are models of 'free choice'. However, fewer options and constrained choices do not invalidate those choices that are made. As Nussbaum (1999, p 296) maintains,

> we may grant that poor women do not have enough options ... while none-theless respecting and honouring the choices they actually make in reduced circumstances.

In other words sex in exchange for money may not be ideal, but acknowledging that cannot be taken to infer that this somehow nullifies prostitution as a valid choice. Moreover, it is worth noting that many prostitutes stress the absolute voluntariness of their entry into the profession, and indeed may assert its clear preferability to some other far less desirable forms of paid employment (Archard, 1998, p 106). Not only does it remain a valid alternative for some women, but it is neither an irreversible choice nor necessarily even a long-term decision. In fact, Kesler, herself a former prostitute, insists that

> some prostitutes state that they enjoy their work, and would choose it again; that, in effect, they do choose it every day.

That is, they choose it in full awareness of what it means to be a prostitute, and as Kesler maintains,

> just because someone cannot imagine why a woman would choose prostitu-tion, does not mean that this is not in fact exactly what has happened. (Kesler, 2002, p 223)

IV. ECONOMIC POWER

The subjects of prostitution and exploitation are often intertwined in dis-courses that point to the way in which men have taken advantage of wom-en's weaker socio-economic position. Although women are no longer tied to the home, and, ostensibly at least, enjoy equal access to education and employment, the result has not been a universal ability for women to avoid poverty or dependence upon others. It has been noted that 'the proportion of women who engage in commercial sex-work is often directly related to the economy and to levels of unemployment' (Hankins, 1996). In Britain, the 'feminisation of poverty' (Brooks-Gordon & Gelsthorpe, 2003), cou-pled with the rise in households headed by single females juggling childcare, part-time work and living on welfare benefits, means that the choice of sex work comes to makes sense for some women (Phoenix, 1999). The English Collective of Prostitutes (1997, pp 98–99), campaigning for the abolition of the laws relating to prostitution, argue that prostitution is the direct result of economic and social inequalities, and they point to statistics which illustrate the disadvantages faced by many young women.

Although there are many reasons why both men and women enter prostitution, unsurprisingly, economic factors remain the most commonly cited reasons for women (see O'Neill, 1997; Scambler and Scambler, 1997; Phoenix, 1999). However, as Ericsson (1980, p 346) rightly questions: 'How interesting is it, generally speaking, to say of a commercial phenomenon that it has economic causes?' In truth it tells us little about the decision to undertake such work. It must also be acknowledged that not all research supports the notion that economic hardship is the determining factor in turning to prostitution. For example, in her UK study investigating what social factors motivated or facilitated entry into prostitution, Sharpe (1998, p 168) found that poverty was not the sole motivating cause. Similarly Doezema (2000, p 41) explains how

> while economic motives often predominate, for many sex work is seen as a route to amassing capital or ensuring later economic independence, rather than a last resort from dire poverty.

Likewise, Kuo (2002, p 151) rejects the view that prostitution is purely the result of poverty and she points towards a number of other personal motivations, such as enjoying sex or the desire for adventure.

This notion that prostitution is not solely class- and poverty-related is borne out in the research findings of ethnographic fieldwork conducted in five US and European cities by Bernstein (2007). This research led Bernstein to question,

> if sexual labour is regarded as, at best, an unfortunate but understandable choice for women with few real alternatives, how are we to explain its apparently increasing appeal to individuals with combined racial, class, and educational advantages? (Bernstein, 2007, p 474)

Her study highlights how middle-class call girls drew on their life experiences and a 'distinctive skill set' in order to capitalise on the demands for sexual services, and the majority described themselves as 'nonmonogamous, bisexual and experimental' (Bernstein, 2007, p 477). This reinforces the idea that prostitution can be a voluntary career choice for some women. As Weitzer (2007, p 453) insists, sex workers do not necessarily see themselves as victims lacking agency. Rather, he asserts, some prostitutes, including many independent call girls and brothel workers, make conscious decisions to enter the trade and do not regard their work as degrading or oppressive.

What is being argued here is that rather than necessarily being in response to dire poverty, deciding to work as a prostitute can be in response to a range of factors that are each given weight according to the priorities of the individual. Choosing to engage in a particular occupation is not always about economic survival; it may simply represent a more attractive prospect than the more conventional employment alternatives chosen by others. It seems, however, that in the context of arguments about notions of choice, judgement about the validity of that choice tends to be based simply on the extent or level of desperation and destitution. Therefore, what is considered to be an appropriate (and therefore legitimate) response to that particular economic position rests purely on the degree to which poverty is reported. This cannot be assumed to be the only consideration. Realistically, as O'Neill (2001, p 31) points out,

> feminist thought must acknowledge that for some women, prostitution gives a good enough standard of income, relative autonomy and can be fitted in around child care.

In other words, while choosing prostitution over alternative modes of income may not constitute free choice, it is perhaps better perceived as a *rational* choice. It may be that whilst many women may make a reasoned choice to work in prostitution, a totally free choice regarding employment is something very few people truly have. But this is by no means peculiar either to prostitution or to women, and rational choice may be a more pragmatic and helpful conceptual tool in understanding how men and women make choices about how to earn their living.

Whilst we cannot ignore the social and economic contexts within which prostitution takes place, citing economic factors as they specifically relate to women is insufficient as an explanation for prostitution. Economic power will probably always play some part in justifying the decision to sell sexual services. However, men's superior economic power has never prevented male prostitution, and economic disadvantage does not explain all female prostitution. Citing economic inequalities alone is therefore simply inadequate as an explanation for all prostitution.

V. FEMALE PROSTITUTES: PATHOLOGISED AND INFANTILISED

Historically, although narratives of both male sex work and female sex work have tended to present prostitution as a product of either economic necessity or individual pathology (Scott *et al*, 2005), it has been noted that the tendency to pathologise is much stronger in relation to female sex workers (Allen, 1987, p 81; ENMP, 2003). Rather than relying on financial explanations, here there is instead a tendency to pathologise and infantilise female prostitutes by an over-emphasis on discourses of victimhood. From this perspective, economic necessity, even absolute poverty, cannot sufficiently explain why women would prostitute themselves. Instead, 'prostitution is seen to have its origins in some form of individual pathology which may be either physiologically or psychologically rooted' (Smart, 1976, p 80). In other words, rather than look to rational explanation for entry into prostitution, the tendency to pathologise manifests itself in an attitude that questions, 'What is *wrong* with these women?'. That is, logical, pragmatic justifications are dismissed in favour of more individual maladies and a tendency to challenge the soundness of mind of such otherwise 'inexplicable' women. Furthermore, women are more likely to have their motivations challenged, because:

> Whereas qualities such as strategic agency and activity are granted to both male sex-workers and their clients, they are not imagined to be qualities that are possessed by female sex-workers or their clients, all of whom are seen as suffering from some form of psychosexual deviancy. (ENMP, 2002, p 38)

In addition to this tendency to treat female prostitutes as 'ill', to reinforce their victimhood, they tend to also be infantilised in a similar manner. Marlowe elaborates thus:

> In contrast to young men, women of *any* age are treated as childlike victims; no matter what their age ... it would appear that age confers maturity and autonomy upon male, but not female, prostitutes, who are rarely represented as anything but exploited. (Marlowe, 1997, p 141)

An example of to what degree this infantilisation can affect how we present and understand prostitution is highlighted by Brooks-Gordon (2003). Referring to the Sexual Offences Bill 2003, she highlights how connections between adult prostitution and child sex offences are taken for granted:

> Clauses in the bill dealing with adult prostitution are problematic as they are placed in a section entitled 'Prostitution and Child Pornography' and inserted between child offences. This lumps the adult sex-working woman and the child together. (Brooks-Gordon, 2003, p 28)

It is within trafficking discourse that the conflation of women with children is particularly evident. For example, Agustin (2003, p 118) describes how women are infantilised in the name of protecting and 'saving' them, which denies their power and agency. Doezema (2000, p 35) argues that it is this blurring of the distinction between child and adult that helps to fix the image of the 'trafficking' victim as young and helpless. Similarly, Weitzer (2007, p 463) argues:

> Official discourse repeatedly invokes 'women and children' victims, arguably to equate women with children's vulnerability and lack of agency and to stoke popular revulsion and support for draconian measures.

In the US context, this is the result of what Weitzer calls the 'moral crusades of anti-trafficking discourse'. However, in both US and UK contexts, adult women are treated as though they need state intervention 'for their own good'. The result is, as Brooks-Gordon (2003, p 28) articulates:

> In the rush towards child protectionism, adult prostitute women may be infantilised by the law, have their right to choose removed, and be criminalised as a result.

This tendency to pathologise and infantilise female prostitutes serves not only to encourage notions of victimhood but also to further reinforce the stigmatisation and alienation of female sex workers. As discussed, the law is deemed the ultimate authority, and therefore, this tendency to infantilise women is reinforced when such conflation is given legal endorsement by denying women the right to choose legitimate employment as sex workers. The combination of being pathologised and infantilised serves to compromise women's autonomous access to the sexual, financial and social independence that is usually conferred with the status of adulthood.

VI. STIGMA AND SELF-ESTEEM

Another aspect of how women are pathologised is evident in discussions about female prostitutes' mental health and self-esteem. The way in which stigma is experienced by female sex-workers is well documented, and most female prostitutes report being affected, directly or indirectly, by society's negative views of prostitution (see, for example, Kempadoo & Doezema, 1998; O'Neill, 1999; Phoenix, 1999). It is usually considered that working as a female prostitute involves shame and that women would want to avoid disclosing their prostitute identity. The link between female prostitution and poor mental health, including low self-esteem, is similarly highlighted. However, low self-esteem is by no means universal among female prostitutes (see, for example, respondents in O'Neill, 1997, pp78–9; Nagle, 1997) and it has been argued that assuming low self-esteem to be the result of being offered payment for sexual services denies women agency and is often contested by women who choose to make their living this way (see, for example, Nagle, 1997; O'Connell Davidson, 1998). Nevertheless, discussion of female prostitution inevitably includes references to the low self-esteem resulting from involvement in prostitution. According to Bullough and Bullough (1998, pp 36–7), this argument is based on the culturally supported assumption that men enjoy, need and desire sex more than women do.

Similarly, the stigmatisation of female sex workers, argues Marlowe, is associated with a 'good girl'/'bad girl' dichotomy and the associated expectations of hegemonic femininity. Marlowe (1997, p 142) contends that boys and girls are conditioned differently in their acceptance of sexual agency and activity. He asserts that

Adolescents learn that 'good girls' abstain from sex while 'bad girls' don't, but that good boys and bad boys alike strive to have sex as often as possible as part of a normal and healthy sex drive.

Vanwesenbeeck (2001, p 268) elaborates:

> The contrast with female sex-workers may be in the possible association with biological models of masculinity, viewing sexual activity for men as normal in ways that female sex-work can never be associated with biological models of femininity and female sexuality.

Of relevance here, is the way that male prostitution can be understood and rationalised within traditional perspectives of male sexuality, yet very different pictures of male and female sexuality and sexual agency are presented. Marlowe questions the logic of making assumptions about low self-esteem, maintaining that the very opposite effect is experienced by male sex workers:

> Why would a man have low self-esteem if he's being sought out and given money for his body? Among gay men, hustlers are not stigmatised in this way—more likely, they are envied. (Marlowe, 1997, p 142)

Similarly, Parsons *et al* (2004, p 1021) report:

> Having clients request their services, they are made to feel empowered, desired, attractive, and important, and this elevates the escort's self-esteem.

In other words, unlike women who are stigmatised, men, in contrast, can be viewed by their peers as having gained in status. This is one of the most glaring differences between male and female prostitution, and this contrast appears to be the direct result of the 'double standards' present in traditional notions of femininity and masculinity.

Not only is overt sexual desire viewed as a characteristic of masculinity, but the notion that sex can be utilised as a commercial resource is similarly considered to be a specifically masculine trait. Browne and Minichiello (1996) report how it is men's ability to draw upon notions of masculinity and masculine work ethics that enables male prostitutes to adopt an occupational perspective towards their work in order to legitimise what they do. Browne and Minichiello explain how, for male prostitutes,

> being able to capitalise on personal resources in order to make money is an acceptable and legitimate way in which to prove one's masculinity and worth to society

In contrast, the same expectations cannot be applied to female prostitutes because femininity is not associated with business aptitude, and so 'the female sex-worker breaks, rather than reinforces, the rules of "proper womanhood"' (Browne and Minichiello, 1996, p 90). Therefore, men can justify and defend their decisions to use personal resources such as the sale of their sexual services. In contrast, women must be seen to conform to predominant hegemonic notions of femininity, which clearly, it seems, do not include using their sexuality instrumentally.

VII. GENDERED POLICING

The UK is not the first country to make the laws pertaining to prostitution gender-neutral. For example, Alexander (1996, p 226) notes how until the early 1990s, most, if not all, of the 50 US states' statutes explicitly defined prostitutes as female. Alexander cautions, 'despite the changes to gender-neutrality, the enforcements of such laws continue to be discriminatory'. Similarly, Allman (1999, p 14), commenting on prostitution laws in Canada, which have been gender-neutral for some time, observes how, nevertheless, 'the laws have never been applied in the same way to male sex-workers as they have been to female sex-workers'.

This may, in part, lie in police officers' discomfort in confronting gay men. Police attitudes are not influenced merely by the fact that prostitutes are commonly perceived as female, but that men engaging in male-to-male prostitution represents a particularly difficult set of challenges to confront. As West's interviewees reported, in the London Metropolitan Area, 'The Metropolitan police hated rent boys—hated the whole idea of it'. It is likely, according to West (1992, p 289), that

> such a reluctance to acknowledge and pursue men soliciting for prostitution may result, whether consciously or subliminally, in a blind eye being turned.

This tendency to avoid confronting potentially unfamiliar and possibly uncomfortable situations is similarly evident when it comes to policing off-street venues. For example, West (1992) explains how prostitutes working as masseurs or in brothels could potentially be subject to entrapment by police masquerading as clients, as women often are. However, with male prostitutes this could provoke controversy (West, 1992, p 300). Perhaps adopting the role of a potential client seeking homosexual services would be a more difficult task to perform, given stereotyped 'macho' police culture (see, for example, Reiner, 2000). Consequently, the difficulty in gathering evidence and therefore successfully securing a conviction may act as a deterrent to those initiating criminal proceedings. This may also in part explain why, as O'Neill (1999, p 180) reports, 'the police may be deploying fewer resources to policing male prostitution with the result that fewer are being detected'.

VIII. CONCLUSION

Despite having been problematised through various theoretical lenses, prostitution remains a controversial issue, and even today, 'remains a debate *between* women about ending male dominance—about ending inequality' (Jolin, 1994, p 69). This is true whether the feminist view being argued is one of sexual dominance or material inequality. However, while few would dispute the need for clear equality and neutrality in the law, in practice, in any criminal justice system, decisions have to be made about which laws will be most vigorously enforced and whom they will be enforced against. As Kuo (2002, p 66) argues, 'Understanding not just formal but actual patterns of enforcement is fundamental to understanding the nature of prostitution practice.'

In this chapter, I have argued that despite changes to the Sexual Offences Act (2003), it is unlikely that male prostitutes will now be criminalised to the extent that female prostitutes are. Patterns of enforcement are unlikely to change in the UK whilst it is primarily women who are considered to be in need of protection. In the light of a tendency to pathologise and infantilise women by an over-emphasis on discourses of victimhood, and dominant beliefs about what constitutes acceptable masculine and feminine behaviours, the female prostitute is invariably considered to be in need of rescue, moral restoration and rehabilitation. Therefore, women will remain the primary target of laws designed to regulate prostitution.

Sexual autonomy is not only about the capacity to choose what sexual practices to engage in, when and with whom, but it is also about being granted the capacity to utilise personal resources, including sexual resources, to satisfy one's particular needs and motivations. As Wilkerson (2002, p 37) argues,

> sexual agency must be understood as an important, and in some ways, key component of the liberation struggles of all disenfranchised groups, rather than a luxury to be addressed after achieving goals that might be perceived as more basic.

This would equally apply to female prostitutes, who can, and often do, make informed decisions to exercise their autonomy by choosing to work in prostitution in full recognition of the potential for exploitation. Whilst these may not be entirely 'free' decisions, they are nevertheless autonomous decisions that the state should accept. Acknowledging this may challenge traditional assumptions about the need for the law to protect prostitutes from exploitation, and so more clearly establish whether there is any sound basis for the legal regulation of commercial sexual activity between consenting adults.

BIBLIOGRAPHY

Agustin LM (2003) 'Sex, gender and migrations: Facing up to ambiguous realities'. *Soundings* 23, 1–12.

—— (2005) 'The cultural study of commercial sex'. *Sexualities* 8, 618–31.

—— (2006) 'The disappearing of a migration category: Migrants who sell sex'. *Journal of Ethnic and Migration Studies* 32, 29–47.

—— (2007) *Sex at the Margins*, Zed Books, London.

Alexander P (1996) 'Bathhouses and brothels: Symbolic sites in discourse and practice'. In *Policing Public Sex: Queer Politics and the Future of AIDS Activism* (Eds, Colter EG, Hoffman W, Pendleton E, Redick A, Serlin D) Southend Press, Boston, MA, pp 221–50.

Allen H (1987) *Justice Unbalanced: Gender, Psychiatry and Judicial Decision*, Open University Press, Milton Keynes.

Allman D (1999) *M is for Mutual A is for Acts: Male sex work and HIV/AIDS in Canada*. Co-published in Vancouver by Health Canada, AIDS Vancouver, Sex Workers Alliance of Vancouver, and the HIV Social, Behavioural and Epidemiological Studies Unit, University of Toronto.

Anderson SA (2002) 'Prostitution and sexual autonomy: Making sense of the prohibition of prostitution'. *Ethics* 112, 748–80.

Archard D (1998) *Sexual Consent*, Westview Press, Oxford.

Bainham A & Brooks-Gordon B (2004) 'Reforming the law on sexual offences' in *Sexuality Repositioned: Diversity and the Law* (Eds, Brooks-Gordon B, Gelsthorpe L, Johnson M, Bainham A) Hart Publishing, Oxford, pp 261–96.

Barrett D (1998) 'Young people and prostitution: Perpetrators in our midst'. *International Review of Law, Computers & Technology* 12, 475–86.

Barry K (1979) *Female Sexual Slavery*, Prentice-Hall Inc, Englewood Cliffs, NJ.

—— (1995) *The Prostitution of Sexuality: The Global Exploitation of Women*, New York University Press, New York.

Bernstein E (2007) 'Sex work for the middle classes'. *Sexualities* 10, 473–88.

Brooks-Gordon BM (2003) 'Gendered provisions in the Sexual Offences Bill 2003: Prostitution'. *Criminal Justice Matters* 53, 28–33.

Brooks-Gordon B & Gelsthorpe L (2003) 'Prostitutes' clients, Ken Livingstone and a new Trojan horse'. *Howard Journal of Criminal Justice* 42, 437–51.

Browne J & Minichiello V (1996) 'The social and work context of commercial sex between men'. *Australia and New Zealand Journal of Sociology* 32, 86–92.

Bullough B & Bullough VL (1998) 'Introduction—Female prostitution: Current research and changing interpretations' in *Prostitution: On Whores, Hustlers, and Johns* (Eds, Elias JE, Bullough VL, Elias V, Brewer G) Prometheus Books, New York, pp 23–44.

Chapkis W (1997) *Live Sex Acts: Women Performing Erotic Labor*, Routledge, New York.

Childs M (2000) 'Commercial sex and criminal law' in *Feminist Perspectives on Law* (Eds, Nicolson D & Bibbings L) Cavendish, London, pp 205–29.

CPS (Crown Prosecution Service) (2008) 'Offences against public morals and decency—prostitution and related offences: public interest considerations'. Available online at: http://www.cps.gov.uk/legal/p_to_r/prostitution_and_offences_against_public_morals/index.html, accessed 16 November 2008.

Doezema J (2000) 'Loose women or lost women? The re-emergence of the myth of white slavery in contemporary discourses of trafficking in women'. *Gender* 18, 23–50.

Dworkin A (1992) 'Prostitution and male supremacy'. Speech delivered at a symposium entitled 'Prostitution: from academia to activism', sponsored by *Michigan Journal of Gender and Law*. Available online at: http://gos.sbc.edu/d/dworkin3. html, accessed 23 January 2008.

Edwards S (1997) 'The legal regulation of prostitution: A human rights issue' in *Rethinking Prostitution: Purchasing Sex in the 1990s* (Eds, Scambler G & Scambler A) Routledge, London, pp 57–82.

English Collective of Prostitutes (1997) 'Campaigning for legal change' in *Rethinking Prostitution: Purchasing Sex in the 1990s* (Eds, Scambler G & Scambler A) Routledge, London, pp 83–104.

ENMP (European Network of Male Prostitutes) (2002) *Tips, Tricks and Models of Good Practice for Service Providers Considering, Planning or Implementing Services for Male Sex Workers*. Available online at: http://ec.europa.eu/health/ ph_projects/2002/com_diseases/fp_commdis_2002_exs_23_en.pdf, accessed 23 January 2008.

—— (2003) *Working Men Project: Making the Difference*. Activity Report 2003. Available online at: www.wmplondon.org.uk/documents/wmp_rw_report.pdf, accessed 23 January 2008.

Ericsson LO (1980) 'Charges against prostitution: An attempt at a philosophical assessment'. *Ethics* 90, 335–66.

Hankins K (1996) *Human Rights, Women and HIV*, Canadian HIV/AIDS Legal Network, Policy and Law Newsletter, 2(4), July 1996, www.aidslaw.ca/ maincontent/otherdocs/Newsletter/July1996/01hankine.html, last accessed September 2007, no longer available online.

Jolin A (1994) 'On the backs of working prostitutes: Feminist theory and prostitution policy'. *Crime & Delinquency* 40, 69–82.

Kempadoo K & Doezema J (Eds) (1998) *Global Sex Workers: Rights, Resistance and Redefinition*, Routledge, London.

Kesler K (2002) 'Is a feminist stance in support of prostitution possible? An exploration of current trends'. *Sexualities* 5, 219–35.

Kuo L (2002) *Prostitution Policy: Revolutionizing Practice through a Gendered Perspective*, New York University Press, New York.

Marlowe J (1997) 'It's different for boys' in *Whores and Other Feminists*, (Ed, Nagle J) Routledge, London, pp 141–4.

Millett K (1975) *The Prostitution Papers*, Paladin Books, St Albans.

Mills J (1997) 'Throwing in the towel: as concerned MPs publish a report on the issue of prostitution Chief Constables and Judges back legalisation'. *The Christian Institute*, available online at http://www.christian.org.uk/html-publications/prost .htm, accessed 23 January 2008.

Nagle J (Ed) (1997) *Whores and Other Feminists*, Routledge, London.

Nussbaum MC (1999) *Sex and Social Justice*, Oxford University Press, Oxford.

O'Connell Davidson J (1998) *Prostitution, Power and Freedom*, Polity Press, Cambridge.

O'Neill M (1997) 'Prostitute women now' in *Rethinking Prostitution: Purchasing Sex in the 1990s* (Eds, Scambler G & Scambler A) Routledge, London.

—— (1999) 'Tackling street prostitution: Towards an holistic approach'. Literature review of research on sexual exploitation, appendix *D3*-Report, commissioned by the Home Office. Available online: www.homeoffice.gov.uk/rds/pdfs04/hors279 .pdf, accessed 23 January 2008.

—— (2001) *Prostitution and Feminism: Towards a Politics of Feeling*. Polity Press, Cambridge.

Parsons JT, Koken JA, Bimbi DS (2004) 'The use of the internet by gay and bisexual male escorts: sex workers as sex educators'. *AIDS CARE* 16, 1021–35.

Pateman C (1988) *The Sexual Contract,* Polity Press, Cambridge.

Petchesky RP (1995) 'The body as property: a feminist re-vision' in *Conceiving the New World Order: The Global Politics of Reproduction.* (Eds, Ginsburg FD & Rapp R) University of California Press, Berkeley, CA.

Phoenix J (1999) *Making Sense of Prostitution*, Palgrave, Basingstoke.

Reiner R (2000) *The Politics of the Police*, 3rd Edition, Oxford University Press, Oxford.

Satz D (1995) 'Markets in women's sexual labor'. *Ethics* 106, 63–85.

Scambler G & Scambler A (Eds) (1997) *Rethinking Prostitution: Purchasing Sex in the 1990s*, Routledge, London.

Scott J, Minichiello V, Marino R, Harvey G, Jamieson M, Browne J (2005) 'Understanding the new context of the male sex work industry'. *Journal of Interpersonal Violence* 20, 320–42.

Sharpe K (1998) *Red Light, Blue Light: Prostitutes, Punters and the Police*, Ashgate Publishing, Aldershot.

Smart C (1976) *Women, Crime and Criminology: A Feminist Critique*, Routledge & Kegan Paul, London.

—— (1995) *Law, Crime and Sexuality: Essays in Feminism*, Sage Publications, London.

Vanwesenbeeck I (2001) 'Another decade of social scientific work on prostitution: A review of research 1990–2000'. *Annual Review of Sex Research* 12, 242–89.

Weitzer R (2007) 'The social construction of sex trafficking: Ideology and institutionalization of a moral crusade'. *Politics and Society,* 35, 447–75.

West DJ (1992) *Male Prostitution*, Duckworth, London.

Wilkerson A (2002) 'Disability, sex radicalism, and political agency'. *National Women's Studies Association Journal* 14, 33–57.

Legislation

Crime and Disorder Act 1998
Sexual Offences Act 1956
Sexual Offences Act 2003

3

Feminist Anti-violence Discourse as Regulation

HELEN REECE*

I. INTRODUCTION

S EVERAL WRITERS IN the United States (Hoff Sommers, 1994; Roiphe, 1994; Patai, 1998), who have become known as dissident feminists (Laframboise, 1996; see also Boyd, 2004), provide descriptions of the ways in which feminist anti-violence discourse has evolved into a highly effective means of regulating human relationships. These writers evocatively describe the environment that such discourse creates as sanitised, purifying, antiseptic, neutralised, cleansed, or sterilised. Ultimately, their warning is that rhetoric against violence leads to a distrust of informality and intimacy in human interactions. Although the dissident feminists' claims about the regulatory impact of anti-violence discourse have been heavily disputed by a diverse array of contemporary feminists (Abrams, 1994; Abrams, 1995; Minnich, 1998; Hammer, 2002; Boyd, 2004), I believe that they give an account that is both convincing and troubling about an influential strand within contemporary feminism. However, an interrogation of the regulatory impact of anti-violence discourse is not the focus of this chapter and therefore beyond its scope. What I want to refine is the analysis of feminist anti-violence discourse.

There is a popular tendency to attribute the regulatory impetus of anti-violence discourse to the wide definitions of violence predominant in this discourse (see eg Gilbert, 1994). In this chapter, I demonstrate that this is at most only part of the picture, by examining the criticisms that feminist researchers have made of non-feminist researchers who have used wide definitions of violence in the service of their own ends, specifically in the debate over gender symmetry in domestic violence. I focus in particular on the main criticism that feminist researchers have made of other research, namely that

* I am grateful to John Gillott and to the participants at the 2007 Cambridge Socio-legal Group seminar for helpful comments on earlier drafts of this chapter.

it de-contextualises violence, and I argue that feminist researchers' particular interpretation of context leads them to *define* domestic violence as what men do to women and not what women do to men.

II. WIDE DEFINITIONS OF VIOLENCE AS REGULATION

Generalisations about contemporary feminism are invariably invidious. Nevertheless, there is little doubt, and indeed it is not generally disputed, that an influential strand of contemporary feminist discourse has both pioneered and welcomed wide definitions of violence, alongside wide definitions of other related concepts such as rape, harassment and abuse (which I am including within the term 'violence' in this chapter). Examples are legion (see Elliot, 1996; Davidson & Martellozzo, this volume; Herring, this volume); to take just one:

> Violence is not one thing. It includes *force and/or violation*: force *by* the violator; violation *of* the violated. It may be physical, sexual, emotional, verbal, cognitive, visual, representational ... Violence may also comprise the creation of the conditions of violence, potential violence, threat and/or neglect. Sometimes the mere presence of someone is violating, and thus becomes violence. (Hearn, 1996c, p 43)

A body of literature has emerged from the US that argues that feminist promotion of expansive understandings of violence has evolved into a highly effective means of regulating human relationships. This outlook, which has been described as dissident feminism, highlights several ways in which such regulation occurs.

First and most apparent is regulation of the behaviour of potential perpetrators. Patai (1998) directs the most attention to this effect, in her study of the impact of what she calls 'the Sexual Harassment Industry' on US academia. She argues that regulation of perpetrators' behaviour takes the form of undermining formal rights and freedoms, principally those of due process, free association and free speech, and derivatively, in the specific context of academia, academic freedom. Going further, Roiphe (1994) suggests that, because sexual harassment may result from unconscious acts, such regulation undermines freedom of thought as well as freedom of speech, and that freedom of speech itself extends as far as 'a right to leer' (p 102).

Roiphe's predominant concern is, however, anti-violence discourse as a means of regulating the behaviour of potential victims. She highlights the way in which campaigns and laws against violence impress potential victims with a sense of fear and danger (1994; see also Fox, 1993), and she argues that current interpretations of violence portray women as passive, powerless and infantilised (see also Patai, 1998; Jenkins, this volume).

As well as examining the effect of regulating potential perpetrators' and victims' behaviour respectively, dissident feminists stress the impact that contemporary interpretations of violence have on human interaction. Dissident feminists argue that the emphasis on eliminating discomfort and offence 'demands a near total absence of unpleasantness' (Patai, 1998, p 27), requiring both hypersensitivity and hyper-vigilance. Roiphe (1994) sees barriers erected, with people keeping each other at a distance; Patai refers similarly to an obstacle course in relations between men and women. This leads to an absence of, or at least suspicion and distrust of, informal or spontaneous interactions, and to their replacement by ritually structured, formal relationships between individuals. According to Patai, behaviour becomes 'more regimented, more impersonal, more guarded ... less open, less generous, less friendly. Certainly, behaviour is transformed' (1998, p 201; see also DeKeseredy, 2000, p 737).

This form of human interaction and the consequential transformation of behaviour are *prescribed*, irrespective of the wishes of the individuals involved. Roiphe, writing specifically about anti-rape campaigns, notes:

> The movement against rape, then, not only dictates the way sex *shouldn't* be but also the way it *should be*. Sex should be gentle, it should not be aggressive; it should be absolutely equal, it should not involve domination and submission; it should be tender, not ambivalent; it should communicate respect, not consuming desire. (1994, p 60)

Dissident feminists note the elitism that is involved in this prescriptiveness when feminist anti-violence researchers place more serious interpretations on particular incidents than did the women who experienced those incidents (Hoff Sommers, 1994; see also Gartner, 1993; Gilbert, 1994). For example, dissident feminists (Hoff Sommers, 1994, pp 211–13; Roiphe, 1994, pp 51–4; see also Gilbert, 1994, p 23) highlight the fact that, while the widely quoted headline finding of the (in)famous *Ms* magazine report (1985) carried out by Koss, Gidycz and Wisniewski (1987) was that one in four women had been the victim of rape or attempted rape, only 27 per cent of the women whom Koss and others classified as rape victims defined their own experience as rape.

Regulation of relationships is reinforced by the way in which anti-violence discourse coerces agreement, through the stigmatisation of dissident voices as cold, unfeeling or heartless (Patai, 1998). Roiphe records:

> I was surprised at how many things there were not to say, at the arguments and assertions that could not be made, lines that could not be crossed, taboos that could not be broken. The feminists around me had created their own rigid orthodoxy. (1994, p 5)

There is a popular tendency to attribute the regulatory impetus of anti-violence discourse to the wide definitions of violence predominant in this discourse. But, in a sense, it is self-evident that an analysis based on wide definitions of violence could only ever be a first approximation.

Once expansive interpretations of violence had been let loose by feminist anti-violence discourse, it was inevitable that these interpretations would prove useful to other constituencies, including constituencies with aims and goals directly antithetical to the aims and goals of the inventors and instigators of such definitions of violence. In other words, while feminists often criticise non-feminists for their use of *narrow* definitions of violence (see Das Dasgupta, 2002; Hunter, 2006; Swan & Snow, 2006), they also criticise non-feminists for their use of *wide* definitions of violence to serve non-feminist ends. Clearly, wide definitions of domestic violence cannot be the full theoretical story. Accordingly, I believe that an analysis of feminist anti-violence discourse can be refined by examining how feminists respond when non-feminists make use of wide definitions of domestic violence. This is what I want to look at next.

III. THE GENDER SYMMETRY DEBATE

The context in which I wish to examine the feminist response to non-feminists' use of wide definitions of violence is the debate over whether domestic violence is symmetrical, that is, equally perpetrated by women and men. Domestic violence research is commonly divided into two relatively distinct approaches, namely a family violence (FV) approach and a violence against women (VAW) approach (Dobash & Dobash, 1992; 2004), the latter being broadly associated with a feminist perspective (Melton & Belknap, 2003). FV researchers have consistently made findings of gender symmetry in relation to domestic violence, findings that flatly contradict arguably the most basic tenet of a feminist approach to domestic violence, that domestic violence is a highly gendered phenomenon (Radford, Kelly & Hester, 1996; Melton & Belknap, 2003; Hunter, 2006; Kaganas, 2006). Accordingly, what I want to examine is the response of VAW researchers to these findings of gender symmetry.

Although the responses of VAW researchers have been multivariate, they have tended to focus on methodology. Nearly all the studies that have found gender symmetry in domestic violence have relied on some version or other of the Conflict Tactic Scales, a methodology developed by Murray Straus in the 1970s. The Conflict Tactic Scales list a series of different ways of dealing with conflict that range from verbal reasoning to verbal aggression to serious violence; respondents are then asked which of these tactics they have employed in the last year to help them to resolve conflicts that have arisen in their relationship with their partner.

While there are a number of different reasons that studies reliant on the Conflict Tactic Scales would tend to find gender symmetry in domestic violence, many centre on the breadth of the phenomenon being studied. For example, the usual scoring method adopted in these studies is that it is only necessary for a man or woman to have committed one act to be classified as violent: this means that a woman who has committed one trivial act is equated with a man who has committed several serious acts of a different nature (Dobash & Dobash, 2004, p 330).

This sets a puzzle for VAW researchers, who are hampered by their own expansive definitions of domestic violence in their criticisms of the definitions adopted by FV researchers. It is right to recognise at this juncture that there are some VAW researchers who have straightforwardly criticised the Conflict Tactic Scales for defining domestic violence too widely (Dobash & Dobash, 1979; Stark & Flitcraft, 1985; Kurz, 1989; Dobash *et al*, 2000). For example, according to Dobash and Dobash in their seminal work, *Violence Against Wives*:

> There are those who maintain that ... women ... are equally as likely to be the perpetrators of violence against their husbands as they are to be the recipients of it. Contentions of this nature make sense, and doubtful sense at that, only if one adopts a definition of physical violence that is so gross as to be trivial, including everything down to the once in a lifetime shove or push. Minor physical incidents probably occur in most marriages, and they are, of course, most regrettable, but we do not consider them to be indicative of a violent relationship nor should we speak of battered wives or battered husbands in such cases. (1980, p 11)

Dobash and Dobash are able to adopt this straightforward stance because, in their early work, they are unusual among VAW researchers in defining domestic violence particularly narrowly as 'the systematic, frequent, and brutal use of physical force' (1980, p 11). As the quotation above illustrates, in this early work Dobash and Dobash are also quite unabashed about setting up some acts of violence as uncomplicatedly worse than others (see also Dobash *et al*, 2000, p 4).

However, neither their criticism that the Conflict Tactic Scales define domestic violence too widely nor their assertion that some acts of violence are worse than others is able to flourish within contemporary VAW research, the former because it rubs against VAW researchers' own adoption of wide definitions of violence and the latter because it conflicts with the position developed by Kelly (1987) and commonly adopted by VAW researchers (see Breines & Gordon, 1983; DeKeseredy, 1994; 2000) that it is wrong to create a hierarchy of abuse. Kelly argues with particular reference to sexual violence that there is a complex range of factors that affect the meaning and impact of women's experiences of sexual violence. For example, the same event may affect women differently at various points in their life, the perceived threat may differ from the incident that materialises and the consequences of mental or emotional violence may be particularly profound. Kelly concludes that because the effects on women cannot be read off simplistically from the form of sexual violence that women experience, 'creating a hierarchy of abuse based on seriousness is inappropriate' (1987, p 49).

In their later work, Dobash and Dobash have modified their stance (2004). Their criticism is no longer the straightforward point that FV research based on the Conflict Tactic Scales employs overly broad definitions of violence but rather the related point that this body of research conflates physical and sexual acts with non-physical abusive acts. They clarify that their criticism of conflation should not be taken to imply that non-physical acts of abuse are harmless or unconsequential but only that they should be clearly differentiated from physical acts. However, this clarification does not prevent their modified stance from stagnating within contemporary VAW researchers' criticism of FV research because, as we will see and as Dobash and Dobash acknowledge, such conflation is also prevalent in VAW research.

Accordingly, the standard criticism made by VAW researchers of FV research conducted by way of the Conflict Tactics Scales is not that the latter employs overly wide definitions of violence. Rather, the standard criticism is that FV research is insensitive to context: by concentrating narrowly on discrete acts, the research de-contextualises these acts. There is undoubtedly much force in this criticism: clearly, there are distinctions that should have been drawn. One oft-quoted example in the literature is a couple who reported that they kicked each other, but a closer investigation reveals that these were playful kicks while in bed together (Margolin, 1987, p 82; see also Dempsey, 2006, p 325). Relatedly, 'throwing a lamp at a partner is very different from throwing a pillow [yet both are recorded as] throwing an object at one's partner' (Dobash & Dobash, 2004, p 329). This point can be extrapolated and the examples multiplied. In this theoretically trivial sense, there is no doubt that context is critical.

But this is not the sum total of the sense in which VAW researchers criticise FV researchers for not placing domestic violence in context. The context in which VAW researchers believe that violent acts should be studied is very different, namely the wider context of the intimate relationship (Dobash *et al*, 1992; Dobash & Dobash, 2004; see also Bible *et al*, 2002; Das Dasgupta, 2002; Herring, this volume).

It sounds almost commonsensical that domestic violence should be studied in the context of the intimate relationship, but also not particularly feminist. Studying violence in the wider context of the intimate relationship may lead to conclusions that are even more repellent to feminists than those that stem from studying violence in the absence of any context. According to Tapp and Taylor (2007), this is what happened in New Zealand in the mid 1990s.

Tapp and Taylor (2007) suggest that one of the most immediate factors that led to the New Zealand Domestic Violence Act (1995) was a report published by the Victims Task Force (Busch *et al*, 1992). In this report, *Domestic Violence and the Justice System*, the New Zealand judiciary were criticised for treating family violence as a relationship problem for which in some circumstances both parties were responsible. Although the report was influenced by feminist anti-violence discourse, in that misogyny was blamed for some of the deficiencies of the current law and one of the recommendations was that judges should receive training in domestic violence based on the power and control model,[1] the report's response to the judiciary's tendency to treat violence as a dynamic of the relationship was to recommend a focus on acts of violence without regard to the reasons for those acts. Tapp and Taylor (2007) argue that the implementation of the New Zealand Domestic Violence Act 1995 signalled the legal dominance of a feminist approach to domestic violence, and that this has since implied that little regard is given to either the origins of the violence or the dynamics within the particular family. Clearly, for VAW researchers, 'studying violence in the context of the intimate relationship' has a particular interpretation, and if this interpretation is absent, a non-feminist interpretation of context may be worse than no context at all. So what do VAW researchers mean by violence in context?

IV. VIOLENCE IN CONTEXT

VAW researchers believe that research should place domestic violence 'in an entire social context' (Breines & Gordon, 1983, p 492; Johnson, 1998, pp 40–41; see also Swan & Snow, 2006; Herring, this volume). This sounds Herculean, until a closer look reveals that the 'entire social context' actually consists of the more manageable 'context of wider power relations' (Breines & Gordon, 1983, pp 492, 511; see also Worcester, 2002; Herring, this volume), the *content* of which is *gendered power imbalances* (Brush, 1990, p 58; Dobash *et al*, 1992, p 83; Johnson & Sacco, 1995, p 291; Johnson, 1998, p 27; see also Das Dasgupta, 2002; Herring, this volume). In more detail,

> (A)lthough experienced and more easily recorded as an episode or event, violence is an extreme expression of one moment in ongoing processes through which heterosexual relationships are 'negotiated'. (Currie, 1998, p 100)

Therefore, findings from the Conflict Tactic Scales need to be situated within a framework that recognises that 'heterosexual relationships are sites of struggle between the exercise and acceptance of male power and male definitions' (Currie, 1998, p 100). Accordingly, for VAW researchers, studying

[1] See below.

violent acts in the context of an intimate relationship means studying them in the context of a relationship of domination (Brush, 1990, p 58). In other words, violence must be researched in the context of patriarchy.

We can gain a more concrete understanding of what VAW researchers mean by studying violence in the context of patriarchy when we take a closer look at the VAW approach to domestic violence. VAW research conceptualises domestic violence as a form of domination and control, with physical violence characterised as merely one tactic embedded among many, all integral to a systematic pattern of power and control (Pence & Paymar, 1993; Johnson, 1995; Hanmer, 1996; Hearn, 1996a; Johnson & Ferraro, 2000; Piispa, 2002). VAW researchers have described this cluster of control tactics variously as a 'constellation of violence' (Dobash *et al*, 2000), a 'constellation of abuse' (Dobash & Dobash, 2004, p 328), 'patriarchal terrorism' (Johnson, 1995, p 284) and the 'power and control wheel' (Pence & Paymar, 1993, p 3).

The 'constellation of violence' (or 'constellation of abuse') includes not only violent acts and injuries but also other forms of controlling and intimidating behaviour as integral and inseparable parts of the constellation (Dobash *et al*, 2000). 'Patriarchal terrorism' is similarly described as 'a form of terroristic control of wives by their husbands that involves the systematic use of not only violence, but economic subordination, threats, isolation, and other control tactics' (Johnson, 1995, p 284). The power and control wheel, arguably the most influential depiction of the dynamics of domestic violence (Dempsey, 2006), likewise places power and control in the middle, abusive behaviours on the spokes, and physical and sexual violence around the edges (Pence & Paymar, 1993).

The specific embodiment of context that VAW researchers believe is missing from FV research is the cluster of control tactics (Yllö, 1993; Johnson, 1998). For example, Yllö complains that the Conflict Tactic Scales exclude, a priori, information about economic deprivation, sexual abuse, intimidation, isolation, stalking and terrorising. More concretely, Dobash *et al* (2000, p 80) outline a detailed context for researching domestic violence in the form of a Controlling Behaviors Index that lists behaviours ranging from 'Question her about her activities' to 'Try to provoke an argument' to 'Criticise her family/friends' (see also Brush, 1990; DeKeseredy, 2000; Gordon, 2000).

There is no doubt that domestic violence can only be understood by recognising that it takes place in the context of women's inequality: women's oppression and domestic violence are intimately intertwined, both theoretically and practically. Moreover, exploring the connection between domestic violence and women's subordination leads to important insights about both phenomena. However, when contemporary VAW researchers maintain that violence must be studied in the context of patriarchy, they are not exploring the connection between the concepts of violence and patriarchy but rather are collapsing the concepts of violence and patriarchy (Liddle, 1989). The collapsing of these concepts helps to explain the significance attached to control tactics in the VAW approach to domestic violence, at the same time as the significance attached to control tactics usefully demonstrates the collapsing of the concepts.

VAW researchers regard the cluster of control tactics as at least as harmful as acts of physical or sexual violence (see Dempsey, 2006; Hunter, 2006; Stark, 2006). For VAW researchers, it is accordingly important not to become overly focused on physical or sexual acts that are seen as at most only part of an overall pattern of control (Breines & Gordon, 1983; Johnson, 1995). VAW researchers view control tactics as either a defining feature of, or at least a clear species of, domestic violence. According to Das Dasgupta (1999, p 199),

> (B)attering may or may not be established by actual acts of physical and/or sexual abuse. Coercing and terrorizing a victim are often accomplished by non-physical manipulations.

With regard to control tactics as the defining feature of domestic violence, 'battering' is defined by Hanmer (1996, p 8) as 'behaviours designed to control, dominate and express authority and power' and by Das Dasgupta (1999, p 200) similarly as 'acts that intimidate, isolate, and deny victims personal power and establish the abuser's control over them'. Hanmer (p 8) stresses that women's particular definition of violence is 'being unable to avoid becoming involved in situations and, once involved, being unable to control the process and outcome', a definition that covers visual, verbal or physical behaviour (see also Piispa, 2002).

Turning to control tactics as a species of domestic violence, an instructive example is Ramazanoglu's account of the violence of academic life. Ramazanoglu explains that while violence is most often envisaged as physical assault, restraint or the use of force, a violent academic situation is

> (N)ot so much an experience of fisticuffs and flying chairs as one of ... sarcasm, raised voices, jokes, veiled insults or the patronising put-down ... techniques of subordination ... used by academic men ... for intimidating or silencing others ... diminishing other human beings (Ramazanoglu, 1987, p 64),

demonstrating that 'violence in academic life is part of the general need for men to control women'; violence is 'widely used in academic life for purposes of social control':

> Academics are verbally highly skilled and can use verbiage to confuse and intimidate others; they are also powerful users of the voice to convey sarcasm, to interrupt, to prevent interruption and to override counter-arguments ... These verbal forms of intimidation were not generally recognised as violent until this point was made by feminists.

V. CONSEQUENCES OF VIOLENCE IN CONTEXT

The VAW approach to domestic violence represents a remarkable down-playing of the physical. This downplaying reaches its zenith when some VAW researchers choose not to count acts of physical or sexual violence as domestic violence unless they are accompanied by the appropriate cluster of control tactics. According to Das Dasgupta (1999, p 199), the

> hasty attempt to equate men and women who have used physical force against intimate partners to batterers stems from the misinterpretation of the concept of battering itself.

The non-physical is treated as profoundly more important than the physical because it both sets the context for and determines the meaning of the physical.

This means that potentially empirically verifiable statements are turned into definitions. VAW researchers have made the relatively modest converse claims that control tactics are generally associated with men's physical and sexual violence against women and are not generally associated with women's violence against men (Dobash *et al*, 1992; Das Dasgupta, 1999; Ylló, 1993; Dobash & Dobash, 2004). Both of these assertions are empirically testable, and some VAW researchers have indeed treated them as straight-forwardly empirical (Dobash *et al*, 2000; Piispa, 2002). However, while the statement that domestic violence is associated with a wider cluster of control tactics is verifiable, the statement that domestic violence is not violence unless it is associated with a wider cluster of control tactics is definitional and therefore unchallengeable by empirical evidence.

Making the presence of control tactics an essential component of domestic violence becomes both more and less significant once we realise that employing control tactics just is what men do to women, and not what women do to men. Looking first at the idea that this is what men do to women, for some VAW researchers it is not a matter of empirically investigating whether or not a man questions his female partner's activities or criticises her friends and family: instead this just is what men do:

> Although there are occasionally some fine lines between ambiguities around different forms of touch—comfort, caress, cuddle, hugging—one usually knows when they are or could be selflessly loving, taking advantage of or exerting power in touch. Such culturally specific 'knowledge' of particular men is likely, however, to neglect the full weight of power relations between men, women and young people, especially in the family. For this reason it is unlikely, and probably impossible, for men to touch in a completely non-dominant, and thus potentially non-abusing, way, unless the whole relationship is without dominance. (Hearn, 1996a, p 33; see also Ptacek, 1990, p 139)

It is impossible that 'the whole relationship is without dominance' because the 'social and psychological identity called "man" says and shows power relations. It is *"identical"'* (Hearn, 1996b, p 101).

Conversely, because women do not use control tactics against men, when women do commit acts of physical or sexual violence against men, these acts do not count as domestic violence. Women's violence to men cannot be equated to men's violence against women (Brush, 1990, p 57; Johnson & Sacco, 1995, p 291; Nazroo, 1995, p 489; Johnson, 1998, p 27; Das Dasgupta, 1999, p 212) because women's acts of violence against men just do not have the same meaning as men's acts of violence against women (Brush, 1990, p 57; Johnson & Sacco, 1995, p 291; Nazroo, 1995, p 489; Melton & Belknap, 2003, p 334). Das Dasgupta (2002, p 1378) explains in more detail that

> although both genders use violence to achieve control, women try to secure short-term command over immediate situations, whereas men tend to establish widespread authority over a much longer period.

Importantly, these gendered meanings are irrespective of intention:

> [e]ven when such results are not consciously intended, historical, political and ideological components of society *confer* these consequences on men's and women's abusive behaviors. [emphasis added]

Domestic violence is thus *defined* as what men do to women, not what women do to men (Hearn, 1996a, p 29; see also Dempsey, 2006, pp 325, 328; Dempsey, 2007, pp 917, 918).

Defining domestic violence as what men do to women and not what women do to men is the only way that VAW researchers can hold on to all of their tenets, namely the tenets of wide definitions of violence, no hierarchy of abuse and no prioritisation of the physical: VAW researchers must either adopt this definitional approach or abandon at least one of their tenets.

When Kelly (1996) confronted this difficulty in the form of wide definitions of violence used to describe women's actions as violence, she chose the latter course. She recounts her concern at hearing feminists describe themselves as having been abused by their mother as well as their father because their mother did not prevent the abuse, alongside her dismay that women researching violence in lesbian relationships were using definitions of violence that were so wide that they included manipulative behaviour, dishonesty and disrespectful treatment. It is interesting that the tenet that she chooses to recoil from is the one that she herself developed, namely the tenet that there is no hierarchy of abuse:

> When I proposed using the concept of a continuum to cover both the range of, and connections between, the violations women and girls experience at the hands

of men I never intended that be understood as suggesting that all events were the same. In that work ... we have challenged the presumption that impacts of violence can be 'read off' from the form of assault. Nonetheless, there are differences in physical and emotional damage. (Kelly, 1996, pp 41–2)

Relatedly, Dobash and Dobash (2004, p 311) suggest that part of the explanation for the findings of gender symmetry discussed above may be that women may have committed more non-physical acts such as arguing or shouting while men may have committed more physical and sexual acts of violence (see also Dobash, 2003, pp 313, 314; Swan & Snow, 2006, p 1028): with all the tenets intact and without the definitional approach outlined above, this gender discrepancy would be of no consequence. Without the premise that men do and women do not use control tactics, a wide unordered definition of domestic violence would not even enable VAW researchers to differentiate nagging wife from battering husband (see Ptacek, 1990, p 153).

VI. CONCLUSION

VAW researchers appear to disagree with FV research on the contained and justifiable methodological basis that FV researchers de-contextualise domestic violence. In reality, the VAW approach to context rules out of court the FV conclusion, because 'the only conclusion to be reached by a feminist analysis of domestic violence is that men are aggressors' (Grady, 2002, p 80). Since the context and even the conclusion of VAW research are pre-determined, the VAW approach to domestic violence ends up de-contextualising domestic violence, like the FV research. This is a shame, not least because, first, violence of course needs to be studied in context and, secondly, the feminist conclusion that women are the principal victims of domestic violence does not need ring-fencing: it would withstand open-ended empirical probing (see Reece, 2006).

BIBLIOGRAPHY

Abrams K (1994) 'Songs of innocence and experience: dominance feminism in the university'. *Yale Law Journal* 103, 1533–60.
—— (1995) 'Sex wars redux: Agency and coercion in feminist legal theory'. *Columbia Law Review* 95, 304–76.
Bible A, Das Dasgupta S, Osthoff S (2002) 'Guest editors' introduction'. *Violence Against Women* 8, 1267–70.
Boyd SB (2004) 'Backlash against feminism: Canadian custody and access reform debates of the late twentieth century'. *Canadian Journal of Women and the Law* 16, 255–90.
Breines W & Gordon L (1983) 'The new scholarship on family violence'. *Signs* 8, 490–531.

Brush LD (1990) 'Violent acts and injurious outcomes in married couples: Methodological issues in the National Survey of Families and Households'. *Gender and Society* 4, 56–67.

Busch R, Robertson N, Lapsley H (1992) *Domestic Violence and the Justice System: A Study of Breaches of Protection Orders*, Victims Task Force, New Zealand.

Currie DH (1998) 'Violent men or violent women? Whose definition counts?' in *Issues in Intimate Violence* (Ed, Bergen RK) Sage Publications, California, pp 97–111.

Das Dasgupta S (1999) 'Just like men? A critical view of violence by women' in *Coordinating Community Responses to Domestic Violence: Lessons from Duluth and Beyond* (Eds, Shepard MF & Pence EL) Sage Publications, California, pp 195–222.

—— (2002) 'A framework for understanding women's use of nonlethal violence in intimate heterosexual relationships'. *Violence Against Women* 8, 1364–89.

Date Rape: The Story of an Epidemic and Those Who Deny It. (1985, October). *Ms* magazine.

DeKeseredy WS (1994) 'Addressing the complexities of woman abuse in dating: A response to Gartner and Fox'. *Canadian Journal of Sociology* 19, 75–80.

—— (2000) 'Current controversies on defining nonlethal violence against women in intimate heterosexual relationships: Empirical implications'. *Violence Against Women* 6, 728–46.

Dempsey MM (2006) 'What counts as domestic violence? A conceptual analysis'. *William and Mary Journal of Women and the Law* 12, 301–34.

—— (2007) 'Toward a feminist state: What does "effective" prosecution of domestic violence mean?'. *Modern Law Review* 70, 908–35.

Dobash RE (2003) 'Domestic violence: arrest, prosecution, and reducing violence'. *Criminology and Public Policy* 2, 313–18.

Dobash RE & Dobash R (1980) *Violence Against Wives: A Case Against the Patriarchy*, Open Books, London.

Dobash RE & Dobash RP (1992) *Women, Violence and Social Change*, Routledge, London.

Dobash RP & Dobash RE (2004) 'Women's violence to men in intimate relationships: Working on a puzzle'. *British Journal of Criminology* 44, 324–49.

Dobash RE, Dobash RP, Cavanagh K, Lewis R (2000) *Changing Violent Men*, Sage Publications, London.

Dobash RP, Dobash RE, Wilson M, Daly M (1992) 'The myth of sexual symmetry in marital violence'. *Social Problems* 39, 71–91.

Elliot FR (1996) *Gender, Family and Society*, Macmillan, Basingstoke and London.

Fox B (1993) 'On violent men and female victims: A comment on DeKeseredy and Kelly'. *Canadian Journal of Sociology* 18, 321–4.

Gartner R (1993) 'Studying woman abuse: A comment on DeKeseredy and Kelly'. *Canadian Journal of Sociology* 18, 313–20.

Gilbert N (1994, March/April) 'Miscounting Social Ills'. *Society*, 18–26.

Gordon M (2000) 'Definitional issues in violence against women: Surveillance and research from a violence research perspective'. *Violence Against Women* 6, 747–83.

Grady A (2002) 'Female-on-male domestic abuse: Uncommon or ignored?' in *New Visions of Crime Victims* (Eds, Hoyle C & Young R) Hart Publishing, Oxford, pp 71–96.

Hammer R (2002) *Antifeminism and Family Terrorism: A Critical Feminist Perspective*, Rowman and Littlefield, Oxford.

Hanmer J (1996) 'Women and violence: Commonalities and diversities' in *Violence and Gender Relations: Theories and Interventions* (Eds, Fawcett B, Featherstone B, Hearn J, Toft C) Sage Publications, London, pp 7–21.

Hearn J (1996a) 'Men's violence to known women: Historical, everyday and theoretical constructions by men' in *Violence and Gender Relations: Theories and Interventions* (Eds, Fawcett B, Featherstone B, Hearn J, Toft C) Sage Publications, London, pp 22–38.

—— (1996b) 'Men's violence to known women: Men's accounts and men's policy developments' in *Violence and Gender Relations: Theories and Interventions* (Eds, Fawcett B, Featherstone B, Hearn J, Toft C) Sage Publications, London, pp 99–114.

—— (1996c) 'The organization(s) of violence: Men, gender relations, organizations and violences' in *Violence and Gender Relations: Theories and Interventions* (Eds, Fawcett B, Featherstone B, Hearn J, Toft C) Sage Publications, London, pp 39–60.

Hoff Sommers C (1994) *Who Stole Feminism: How Women Have Betrayed Women*, Touchstone, New York.

Hunter R (2006) 'Narratives of Domestic Violence'. *Sydney Law Review* 28, 733–76.

Johnson H (1998) 'Rethinking survey research on violence against women' in *Rethinking Violence Against Women* (Eds, Dobash RE & Dobash RP) Sage Publications, California, pp 23–52.

Johnson H & Sacco V (1995) 'Researching violence against women: Statistics Canada's national survey'. *Canadian Journal of Criminology* 37, 281–304.

Johnson MP (1995) 'Patriarchal terrorism and common couple violence: Two forms of violence against women'. *Journal of Marriage and the Family* 57, 283–94.

Johnson MP & Ferraro KJ (2000) 'Research on domestic violence in the 1990s: Making distinctions'. *Journal of Marriage and the Family* 62, 948–63.

Kaganas F (2006) 'Domestic violence, men's groups and the equivalence argument' in *Feminist Perspectives on Family Law* (Eds, Diduck A & O'Donovan K) Routledge-Cavendish, Oxford, pp 139–64.

Kelly L (1987) 'The continuum of sexual violence' in *Women, Violence and Social Control* (Eds, Hanmer J & Maynard M) Macmillan, Basingstoke, pp 46–60.

—— (1996) 'When does the speaking profit us? Reflections on the challenges of developing feminist perspectives on abuse and violence by women' in *Women, Violence and Male Power* (Eds, Hester M, Kelly L, Radford J) Open University Press, Buckingham, pp 34–49.

Koss MP, Gidycz CA, Wisniewski N (1987) 'The Scope of Rape: Incidence and Prevalence of Sexual Aggression and Victimization in a National Sample of Higher Education Students'. *Journal of Consulting and Clinical Psychology* 55, 162–70.

Kurz D (1989) 'Social Science Perspectives on Wife Abuse: Current Debates and Future Directions'. *Gender and Society* 3, 489–505.

Laframboise D (1996) *The Princess at the Window: A New Gender Morality*, Penguin Books, Toronto.

Liddle AM (1989) 'Feminist contributions to an understanding of violence against women—Three steps forward, two steps back'. *Canadian Review of Sociology and Anthropology* 26, 759–76.

Margolin G (1987) 'The multiple forms of aggressiveness between marital partners: How do we identify them?'. *Journal of Marital and Family Therapy* 13, 77–84.

Melton HC & Belknap J (2003) 'He hits, she hits: Assessing gender differences and similarities in officially reported intimate partner violence'. *Criminal Justice and Behavior* 30, 328–48.

Minnich EK (1998) 'Feminist attacks on feminisms: Patriarchy's prodigal daughters'. *Feminist Studies* 24, 159–75.

Nazroo J (1995) 'Uncovering gender differences in the use of marital violence: The effect of methodology'. *Sociology* 29, 475–94.

Patai D (1998) *Heterophobia: Sexual Harassment and the Future of Feminism*, Rowman and Littlefield, Lanham, MD.

Pence E and Paymar M (1993) *Education Groups for Men who Batter: The Duluth Model*, Springer Publishing, New York.

Piispa M (2002) 'Complexity of patterns of violence against women in heterosexual partnerships'. *Violence Against Women* 8, 873–900.

Ptacek J (1990) 'Why do Men batter their wives?' in *Feminist Perspectives on Wife Abuse* (Eds, Yllö K & Bograd M) Sage Publications, California, pp 133–57.

Radford J, Kelly L, Hester M (1996) 'Introduction' in *Women, Violence and Male Power: Feminist Activism, Research and Practice* (Eds, Hester M, Kelly L, Radford J) Open University Press, Buckingham, pp 1–18.

Ramazanoglu C (1987) 'Sex and violence in academic life or you can keep a good woman down' in *Women, Violence and Social Control* (Eds, Hanmer J & Maynard M) Macmillan, Basingstoke, pp 61–74.

Reece H (2006) 'The end of domestic violence'. *Modern Law Review* 69, 770–91.

Roiphe K (1994) *The Morning After: Sex, Fear and Feminism*, Hamish Hamilton, London.

Stark E (2006) 'Commentary on Johnson's "Conflict and Control: Gender Symmetry and Asymmetry in Domestic Violence"'. *Violence Against Women* 12, 1019–25.

Stark E & Flitcraft A (1985) 'Woman-battering, child abuse and social heredity: what is the relationship?' in *Marital Violence* (Ed, Johnson N) Routledge & Kegan Paul, London, pp 147–71.

Swan SC & Snow DL (2006) 'The development of a theory of women's use of violence in intimate relationships'. *Violence Against Women* 12, 1026–45.

Tapp P & Taylor N (2007) 'Protecting the family' in *Family Law Policy in New Zealand*, 3rd edition (Eds, Henaghan M & Atkin B) Lexis Nexis, Wellington, pp 81–166.

Worcester N (2002) 'Women's use of force: Complexities and challenges of taking the issue seriously'. *Violence Against Women* 8, 1390–415.

Yllö KA (1993) 'Through a feminist lens: Gender, power, and violence' in *Current Controversies on Family Violence* (Eds, Gelles RJ & Loseke DR) Sage Publications, California, pp 47–62.

Legislation

Domestic Violence Act 1995 (NZ).

4

Relational Autonomy and Rape

JONATHAN HERRING

I. INTRODUCTION

JACK BAUER, JAMES Bond, Jason Bourne: these are the male icons of our age. These rugged isolated conquerors struggle against the powers of the anonymous authorities. Bravely putting love of country before love of women, against insurmountable odds, they battle through. Leaving broken hearts wherever they go, they emerge bloodied, but victorious at the end of the day. Such men are seen by some as the epitome of the modern autonomous hero. Fighting free from the strings that bind and the forces that oppress, they emerge free men. Yet this image of 'Super-Detached Man' is a fiction (Chen-Wishart, 2006). More than that, he is a 'thoroughly noxious concept' (Hoagland, 1989, p 144).

This chapter will be in two halves. The first will seek to consider the notion of relational autonomy. It will explain how this approach to autonomy grew out of a perception that many forms of liberal autonomy were overly individualistic and thereby failed to accord sufficient weight to the fact that decisions are taken within the context of relationships. Relational autonomy requires that people's decisions are understood in the context of the relationships they live in and that the obligations that flow from those relationships are given due weight. The chapter will seek to explore the strengths and weaknesses of the writings about relational autonomy. One particular difficulty with it is that much of it has been at an abstract level, with few attempts being made to apply it in a concrete setting. Hence, in the second half of this chapter an attempt will be made to apply relational autonomy to the law of rape. Central to the law on rape is the requirement that the victim did not consent to the act. This chapter will critique the use of consent in sexual offences for failing to place the sexual act within the context of the relationship between the parties. It will suggest that consent must be understood in the context of the interactions between the parties prior to the event, the relationship between the parties, and the wider social setting.

II. DIFFERENT VERSIONS OF AUTONOMY

Relational autonomy is a concept that flows from a rejection of the traditional liberal interpretations of autonomy. It regards them as being atomistic (McClain, 1992) and sees the need to reconceptualise autonomy in a way that appreciates values based on care, responsibility and interdependence. It has been developed by a number of writers, particularly, though not exclusively, by those writing from a communitarian or feminist perspective (Barclay, 2000). Some of those who have been persuaded by the kind of criticisms of individualistic autonomy we shall discuss have rejected the language of rights of autonomy altogether and sought alternative approaches, such as an ethic of care (Kiss, 1997). Others, however, believe that it is possible to reconceive autonomy in a way that can take account of the concerns.

A. Individualistic Autonomy

There is much debate over whether or not many of the writers on relational autonomy have misunderstood traditional liberal autonomy (Friedman, 2006). There is much truth in the claim that relational autonomy is based on a rejection of a caricature of liberal autonomy, rather than the real thing. Therefore, in this chapter the term 'individualistic autonomy' will be used to describe the vision of autonomy which is rejected by relational autonomists.

Autonomy in much legal and philosophical writing has obtained a 'sacred status' (Chen-Wishart, 2006, p 231). At the heart of individualistic autonomy is the argument that each individual should be able to choose how to live out their life in whatever way they wish, as long as others are not harmed. Linked to the notion of individual autonomy is a whole set of other ideas: self-sufficiency, self-sovereignty, moral independence, self-government, pluralism and liberty (Fineman, 2005). Autonomy is about living a self-authored life: living according to values that are one's own. This means that the rights attached to individualistic autonomy are all about fighting off unwanted intrusions into an individual's freedom of choice (Donchin, 2001).

B. Relational Autonomy

Relational autonomy is not a 'single unified conception' (Mackenzie & Stoljar, 2000, p 4) but rather an umbrella term with a range of related perspectives. At their heart is a

> shared conviction ... that persons are socially embedded and that agents' identities are formed within the context of social relationships and shaped by a complex

of intersecting social determinants, such as race, class, gender, and ethnicity. (Mackenzie & Stoljar, 2000, p 4)

As will be suggested later, the fact that it has attracted support from a wide range of different perspectives might be explained by the fact that most of the writing on it has been at an abstract level. When it is applied in concrete settings, differences between its adherents may become clearer.

Relational autonomy is based on a reconceptualisation or reconfiguration of the notion of individualistic autonomy. Although its supporters are sympathetic to many of the points made by the notion of autonomy, they argue that traditional liberal autonomy is too individualistic. Lorraine Code (1991, p 78) argues that for supporters of individualised autonomy:

Autonomous man is—and should be—self-sufficient, independent, and self-reliant, a self-realizing individual who directs his efforts towards maximizing his personal gains. His independence is under constant threat from other (equally self-serving) individuals: hence he devises rules to protect himself from intrusion. Talk of right, rational self-interest, expedience, and efficiency permeates his moral, social, and political discourse. In short, there has been a gradual alignment of autonomy with individualism.

Supporters of relational autonomy argue that basing autonomy on a conception of an isolated individual pursuing his own version of life fails to recognise that, in fact, most people live their lives in a complex web of relationships and connection.

Individualistic autonomy emphasises the values of independence and self-sufficiency, while it is inter-dependence and connection which are the values at the heart of many people's lives. An individualistic model of rights presents many legal cases as involving a clash of individual rights and it is the state's job to mediate between these conflicting claims A relational autonomy model argues that such an image misconceives how people understand their lives, especially when in close emotional relationships. We are not constantly clashing rights with those we live with; rather our interests are intertwined. People in close relationships seek a compromise which is good for 'us' and do not see it as a matter of weighing up competing interests. Relational autonomy, therefore, is attractive to communitarians who seek to emphasise the values of community (McIntyre, 1981) and to feminists seeking to emphasise the importance of care and relationships of dependence (Ball, 2005). There can be tensions between those approaching relational autonomy from these two perspectives (Bridgeman, 2007).

Six linked themes which are at the heart of relational autonomy will now be presented.

(i)   Relational Life is Inevitable

We live our lives in relationships with others and those relationships are an important aspect of who we are and how we live. Our characters and understandings of ourselves from the earliest days are charted by our relationships with others (Carle, 2005). The experiences of caring for dependants and the benefits and sacrifices of friendship, are, whether we like it or not, part of our lives (Sevenhuijsen, 2003). We are not free to 'live our lives as we choose' in an isolated way. Our decisions are constrained by the responsibilities and realities of our lives and the relationships within which we are embedded (Nedelsky, 1989). The important decisions we make are, in fact, rarely just about us. They impact on our families, friends and those we are in relationships with. And their decisions impact on us. Hence Allan Johnson (1997, p 30) has called our culture's insistence that we are separate and autonomous as patriarchy's 'Great Lie.'

In fact the point is broader than this. It is not just that our decisions affect those we are in relationship with, but that our relationships enable us to make autonomous decisions. Linda Barclay (2000, p 57) notes that

> our ongoing success as an autonomous agent is affected by our ability to share our ideas, our aspirations, and our beliefs in conversation with others. It is unlikely that any vision or aspiration is sustained in isolation from others. To be autonomous a person must be able to reflect critically on their life and the values underpinning it. But that is only possible with the help and support of those around them (Mackenzie, 2000). For many people their definition of themselves is based on relationship, be it as a mother, a Muslim or a Millwall Football Club fan (Barvosa-Carter, 2007). Our sense of self is a mixture of interlocking and sometimes conflicting social identities (Donchin, 2000). Therefore the obligations, responsibilities and restrictions of relationship are not antithetical to being autonomous. Quite the reverse; they are essential to it.

(ii)   Relational Life is Good

Living in the context of these relationships is good (Groenhout, 2004). Many relationships are to be valued, recognised and indeed treasured by the law. The traditional liberal visions of autonomy, keeping relations hidden and not recognised, result in relationships being devalued and ignored by the law (Herring, 2007). Relationships of care and dependency need to be supported, nurtured and upheld, not hidden and downplayed (Verkerk, 1999).

However, a crucial point must be made here. Supporters of relational autonomy do not have an idealistic view of relationships. Although beneficial relationships are an important part of people's lives and essential to autonomy, relationships and social structures can be oppressive and destructive of autonomy. A central aspect of relational autonomy must be in protecting people from the harms that abusive relationships can cause (Chen-Wishart, 2006).

(iii) Decisions must be Understood in a Social Context

A person's autonomy can only be understood within the personal relationships and social structures that form an agent's desires, beliefs and emotional attitudes (Mackenzie & Stoljar, 2000). Taking these into account may mean that a decision is, in fact, not autonomous, or its meaning may not be the apparent one. The social background may mean that an agent's capacity for self-reflection, self-knowledge or choice can be restricted and inhibited. Inevitably, there is much disagreement between those supporting relational autonomy about when a person's social situation may be so oppressive that they lack autonomy (see Friedman, 2006, and MacKenzie & Stoljar, 2000).

The impact of this is especially important when considering the responsibility the state might have to promote autonomy among its citizens. In promoting autonomy the state must ensure not only that an individual is protected from improper threats from others, but that the social and community structures are such that a person is free to enter into a set of relationships with others within which to develop a vision of the good life. In other words, maximising autonomy does not require giving people the time and space to sit quietly and reach decisions for themselves free from outside disturbance, but rather developing social and community-based structures which will enable human interactions to flourish. Autonomy then is not a psychological state so much as a social one (Oshana, 1998).

(iv) Emotions are Part of Autonomy

A fourth theme in the writings of relational autonomy is that individualised autonomy tends to emphasise our rational side. The ideal decision maker is 'judge-like', weighing up the rational arguments and reaching a 'balanced decision'. Mackenzie and Stoljar (2000, p 21) argue for:

> the need to think of autonomy as a characteristic of agents who are emotional, embodied, desiring, creative and feeling, as well as rational, creatures.

This means that we need to recognise that issues of memory, imagination and emotional disposition are important aspects of autonomy (Friedman, 2000).

This argument is based, in part, on a rejection of the dichotomy between reasons and emotions. For example, Martha Nussbaum (2001, p 22) rejects an argument that emotions do not involve judgement, saying that

> emotions are forms of evaluative judgment that ascribe to certain things and persons outside a person's own control great importance for the person's own flourishing.

Marilyn Friedman (2006) argues that a person's emotions can produce a coherent picture of who a person is. This can therefore be reflective of autonomy. Attitudes and emotional reactions should not therefore be regarded as necessarily lesser when determining what is required to respect a person's autonomy.

(v) The Importance of Other Values

Supporters of relational autonomy emphasise that although autonomy is very important there are many other values that need to be respected such as trust (O'Neill, 2002), responsibility, care (Franke, 2001) and attention to the needs of others. These values are seen as essential to the maintenance of relationships, which are themselves essential to autonomy. Hence, while individualistic visions of autonomy might regard notions of responsibility and trust as antithetical to autonomy, relational autonomy would see them as essential to it.

(vi) Autonomy as a Fluid Concept

Relational autonomy is not treated as a state you either have or do not have, but rather as a state you acquire (Meyers, 1989). Jennifer Nedelsky (1989, p 10) writes:

> I speak of 'becoming' autonomous because I think it is not a quality one can simply posits about human beings. We must develop and sustain the capacity for finding our own law, and the task is to understand what social forms, relationships, and personal practices foster that capacity.

For many of us, the goals for our lives depend upon co-operation with each other. This means that our autonomy ebbs and flows with the changing of relationships. Indeed, it is in and through relationships that the skills needed to exercise autonomy are learned and developed.

III. CRITICS OF RELATIONAL AUTONOMY

We have already mentioned one prominent criticism of relational autonomy, which is that it has misunderstood the traditional liberal idea of autonomy. Much writing in liberal autonomy has emphasised the importance of relationships in individual lives (for example Raz, 1986). It may be said that relational autonomy is not truly criticising autonomy as it has been promoted by academic philosophers and lawyers. Rather it is criticising the popular image of 'self-sufficient autonomous man'. Notably, for example, Martha Fineman (2004) in her criticism of autonomy starts with its dictionary definition rather than the way it has been developed by academic commentators. Indeed, a supporter of liberal autonomy might respond that relational autonomy is telling us how we should exercise our autonomy. It is not, therefore, a critique of liberal autonomy at all. Supporters of liberal autonomy have always accepted that people can use their self-determination to make bad decisions as well as good ones. People can use their autonomy to live isolated individualistic lives, but that is not necessarily a criticism of liberal autonomy.

There is some force in these objections. Certainly it is not always clear in the writing on relational autonomy what is being attacked: whether it is the academic notion of liberal autonomy or the cultural image of the autonomous man. While this is true, it would be wrong to categorise relational autonomy as simply advice on a good life, rather than a challenge to traditional liberal autonomy. First, traditional liberal autonomy values choice and disapproves of restrictions on choice. Yet, by entering relationships our choices are to some extent inevitably limited. That, however, should not be regarded as undesirable. Secondly, while liberal autonomy does not per se promote the image of the isolated individual, it needs to be seen as part of the larger picture. Mary Becker (1999, p 22) writes

> patriarchy values power, control, autonomy, independence, toughness, invulnerability, strength, aggressiveness, rationality, detachment (being non-emotional), and other traditionally masculine attributes that have proven effective in the battle against other men.

Once it is put in the context of other values upheld by society and law, autonomy can be said to play its part in promoting individualism.

Another significant objection is that relational autonomy, in emphasising the importance of interdependent relationships in an individual's life, has overlooked the importance of the 'self' and the importance we attach to self-determination. In other words, if traditional liberal versions of autonomy have been too ready to view individuals as isolated, relational autonomy has over-emphasised the importance of community and relationship and has ignored the importance of the private life of the self. Although relationships do play an important part in people's lives, most people have an inner life and sense of self which is not dependent upon their relationships with others. Indeed, it might be argued that a self-vision which is entirely constructed upon relationships with others is unhealthy (de Botton,

2004). We have dignity and worth in ourselves as people, and not just in our relationships with others. The isolated loner is of no less value or worth than the person with over a thousand friends on Facebook. John Christman (2004, p 157) argues:

> Just as conceiving of persons as denuded of social relations denies the importance of such relations to the self-understandings of many of us at various times in our lives, to define persons as necessarily related in particular ways similarly denies the reality of change over time, variability in self-conception, and multiplicities of identity characteristic of modern populations.

While accepting that there is a danger that relational autonomy can lead to insufficient weight being placed on the self, it need not. As Elizabeth Frazer and Nicola Lacey (1993, p 178) argue:

> The notion of the relational self, in contrast to both atomistic and inter-subjective selves, nicely captures our empirical and logical interdependence and the centrality to our identity of our relations with others and with practices and institutions, whilst retaining an idea of human uniqueness and discreteness as central to our sense of ourselves. It entails the collapse of any self/other or individual/community dichotomy without abandoning the idea of genuine agency and subjectivity

A rather different complaint is that, by emphasising the importance of family and community, there is a danger that relational autonomy too readily allows an individual's rights to be overridden in the name of the family or community (Binder, 1994). There is certainly a concern with the way that relational autonomy is sometimes presented. Friedman (2000, p 47) makes an interesting point with this in mind. She argues:

> Although women still have occasion to fear men's autonomy, it seems that many women have good cause to welcome our own.

Her point is that although women can legitimately be concerned by the way that men's autonomy might be used to justify an adjuration of responsibility for children or other family dependants, women must treasure their own freedom to, for example, leave an oppressive relationship. Feminists should be wary of any suggestions that in the name of relational autonomy an individual's autonomy should be sacrificed for the 'greater good'. History suggests that the 'greater good' tends to require the sacrifice of the rights of women, rather than those of men. Further glorifying values of caring and dependency might reinforce the traditional roles of women (McClain, 1992). The roles of carer, nurse, mother become idealised, thereby reinforcing the model of behaviour from which feminists have been attempting to break free for decades.

There are, therefore, some genuine concerns over the misuse of relational autonomy. However, that is true of many, if not all, concepts at this level of abstraction. With a proper awareness of its dangers, relational autonomy can be developed to be a powerful alternative to the traditional understanding of autonomy.

IV. CONSENT AND RAPE

It has been suggested that the concept of relational autonomy is 'hopelessly vague' (Verkerk, 1999, p 363). There is, it must be admitted, some fairness in these remarks. Proponents of relational autonomy have been eloquent on the description of the concept at a theoretical level, but surprisingly reluctant to move to more concrete implementation of the theory. What follows is an attempt to use insights from relational autonomy to examine the law of rape. For reasons of space and clarity this part of the chapter will focus on rape where the victim is a woman. Many (but not all) of the points made could apply equally if the victim were a man.

The offence of rape requires proof that there was penile penetration of the victim without her consent and that the defendant knew or ought to have known that the victim did not consent. Consent is therefore a key element of rape. As Richard Posner (1994) starkly puts it, 'all that distinguishes [rape] from ordinary sexual intercourse is lack of consent'. Consent is seen as essential because it is at the heart of a liberal approach based on autonomy (Roberts, 2001): I should be allowed to permit another to touch me in any way I like. Some people may not like the way others touch me, but if I am competent and have consented to the touching then my decision must be respected. Hence where there is consent there should be no crime. David Archard (2007, p 210) writes:

> The giving and withholding of consent fixes what is permissible and impermissible in our relations to others, and has this power as an expression of our fundamental moral status as independent, self-governing agents entitled to determine what may and what may not be done to us.

Hence sexual penetration with consent is permissible and sexual penetration without consent is rape.

A. Defining Consent

Despite the popularity of placing great weight on the notion of consent, the concept is in fact extremely difficult to define. The fact that several books have been written on the meaning of consent in the arena of sexual relations (for example Archard, 1998; Wertheimer, 2003; Westen, 2004; McGregor, 2005) indicates how problematic this has been. These writings demonstrate that there is little agreement over questions such as whether consent to sex is to be determined subjectively or objectively; when the use or threat of force negates consent; or when deceptions negate consent.

Overriding all the arguments over consent is whether we should take a strong or weak understanding of consent. We could take a perfectionist view and declare that only the consent of a person with a full range of choices, in possession of all relevant information and with no outside pressures should count as proper consent. But one might conclude that in the sexual context it would be extremely rare that such consent could arise. This would mean that only exceptionally would you be deemed in a position to exercise autonomy. However, relying on a weaker understanding of consent means that a decision is treated as an exercise of autonomy, even where it may not truly be an genuine expression of another's will. Vanessa Munro (2005, p 345) summarises well the tensions between the positive and negative consent:

> While respecting [positive autonomy] entails a wide freedom to seek out, and engage in, intimate relations, respecting [negative autonomy] entails a right to refuse such relations, and to have this refusal taken seriously. Since setting high standards for what qualifies as consent will thus protect negative at the expense of positive autonomy, and vice versa, we must have a clear sense of what is at stake before we can hope to elucidate an appropriate sexual offences framework.

B. A Relational Approach to Consent in Rape

Using an approach based on relational autonomy, it is clear that there are a number of aspects of the current law which are unsatisfactory. Before outlining these, it is striking that even among supporters of a traditional approach to consent, there is clearly some unease and that most of them argue that consent has some special meaning in this context. So, for example, Peter Westen (2004) argues that 'legal consent' is not the same as 'factual consent'. It is hard not to agree with Robin West's (1993, p 1446) analysis that consent is an 'extraordinarily malleable notion'. The suspicion is created that important issues are being hidden behind the label of consent.

A relational autonomy approach could raise the following concerns about the current law's approach to consent.

(i) The Social Setting for Consent

In a rape trial the jury must consider whether or not there is consent. The focus is often on whether the complainant voiced her opposition or consent at the time of the penetration. This can lead to the jury failing to take into account the history of the parties' relationship (Lees, 2002). Notably, violence or threats of violence immediately before the act can create a rebuttable presumption that there was no consent (Sexual Offences Act 2003, s 78). But that presumption only arises where the violence occurs or is threatened immediately before the penetration.

Supporters of relational autonomy would emphasise that a person's consent must be understood in its broader social context and in particular that a woman's consent to sex must be seen in the context of patriarchy. Catherine MacKinnon (2003) argues:

> The problem with consent-only approaches to criminal law reform is that sex, under conditions of inequality, can look consensual when it is not wanted at the time, because women know that sex that women want is the sex men want from women. Men in positions of power over women can thus secure sex that looks, even is, consensual without that sex ever being freely chosen, far less desired.

The claim here is certainly not that women cannot make a rational decision about sex. Rather, the decision must be seen in the surrounding social, economic and relational background. If we are to ascertain whether a person is exercising their autonomy and agreeing to sexual penetration we cannot rely simply on the words used by the parties at the time. There must be consideration of the wider social environment and the influences that will be affecting the parties (contrast Reece, this volume). This will include the paramountcy given to sexual penetration in the heterosexual masculine identity. To many men, sexual penetration is a confirmation of masculinity, and the sexual expectations of women are related to this. Many cultural images reinforce the idea that vulnerability is regarded as 'sexy' in women; whereas strength (manliness) is regarded as sexy for men. These create intense pressures on the parties when decisions are made about sex. In a recent survey for the children's charity, the NSPCC (BBC News Online 2005), it was found that 44% of teenage girls felt guilty saying no to a request for sex from their boyfriends. Of those who had experienced unwanted sex, 55% thought the event was partly their fault.

Further, the economic and social disadvantages that women as a group suffer can be readily exploited to access sex. The narrow approach taken in the law to consent favours those who have the strongest means to acquire it. Robin Morgan (1980) writes:

> [T]he pressure is there, and it need not be a knife blade against the throat, it's in his body language, his threat of sulking, his clenched or trembling hand, his self-deprecating humour or angry put-down or silent self pity at being rejected. How many millions of times have women had sex 'willingly' with men they did not want to have sex with?

Also crucial is the fact that the giving of consent has to be seen within the context of 'rape culture' (Madden Dempsey and Herring, 2007, p 480). This is a culture in which widely available pornography portrays coerced sex as enjoyed by women, and where prosecution and conviction rates for rape are appallingly low. If consent is not provided, the woman can expect little protection from the law and society if the man nevertheless continues with sex. In this light, 'consent' (sic) may be a sensible choice if the man is determined to penetrate whatever happens.

Much more could be said about the cultural background against which sexual encounters take place. What I hope to show is that simply asking the question 'did the victim consent?' closes off the context within which the encounter takes place. An approach which fails to appreciate the pressures on the parties and the relationship between them, the fears of what might or might not happen, the awareness of the lack of effective criminal sanction in cases of rape, is one that cannot claim to be truly seeking to protect sexual autonomy.

(ii) Tokens of Consent

In considering whether or not there was consent, juries inevitably use general social understandings of consent. Widespread attitudes towards women and sexual penetration are built on 'rape myths' (Chapleau, Oswald & Russell, 2007). The myths that women 'like it rough' and that 'unless they say no they mean yes' and 'any woman who is drunk wants to have sex' are barely behind the surface of many commonly expressed attitudes to sex. These myths can, of course, play an important part in jury deliberations. It can be extremely difficult for a woman to show that she did not consent, especially where she has been seen to behave 'foolishly' (for example by inviting a man to her flat after a date). And that is something known by men—and women. Only 'good victims' can hope to receive protection from the criminal law (West, 1996). Even where there are physical injuries, these may be insufficient. In a Home Office Study one victim reported being told by the police that 'your bruises ain't good enough; you've got no case' (Harris & Grace, 1999, p 21). It is not possible to know what factors juries do in fact take into account in jury trials because research into jury deliberations in actual cases is prohibited. However, research projects involving mock juries suggest the rape myths of the kind mentioned in this paragraph do play a central role in their deliberations (Finch & Munro, 2006).

Surveys of public attitudes also appear to back up the prevalence of these rape myths. A survey by Amnesty International (2005) found that 30% of people believed that if a woman had behaved flirtatiously she was partly or completely responsible for a rape; and 26% thought the same if she wore revealing clothing or had been drunk. Astonishingly, 6% thought a woman wearing revealing clothing was totally responsible if she was raped, and 8% that a woman who was known to have had several sexual partners was again totally responsible. As this indicates, there is still within our society credence given to the rape myths that women can generally be taken to agree to sex at any time with any man, unless she dresses in very baggy clothing, stays indoors, is rude and unfriendly, and fights any man who attempts to have sex with her.

(iii) Narrowness of Approach

The notion of consent is too narrow in its time frame. In answer to the question 'did the defendant consent?' the law only permits the answers 'yes' or 'no'. This provides no ready room for the telling of a woman's story of what happened before the sexual incident, or the context within which it took place. As Wendy Brown (2001, p 36) argues, consent is 'a response to power: it adds or withdraws legitimacy but it is not a mode of enacting or sharing in power'.

The story is structured by the 'consent question' as construed by the law: the man wanted to engage in penile penetration and the question for the jury is: did the complainant agree or not? Such a picture reflects images of an active masculinity and passive femininity, but it also closes out the story of what happened before and what was intended to happen after; of how the act was to be understood. Nicola Lacey (1998) has written:

> The victim's consent responds to power by conferring legitimacy, rather than shaping power in its own terms: consent is currently understood not in terms of mutuality but rather in relation to a set of arrangements initiated, by implication, by the defendant, in an asymmetric structure which reflects the stereotypes of active masculinity and passive femininity

This echoes Matthew Weait's (2005) argument that the law tends to isolate criminal offences into a 'discrete and meaningless moment or event'. Consent is focusing on the question: 'was it a "yes" or a "no"?' This decontextualises the event and objectifies the woman in paying no attention to her understanding or experience of the event. It also restricts the woman's role to a legitimising one, rather than regarding her as an equal partner in negotiating how their intimate relationship will develop.

Developing an argument of this kind, Ngaire Naffine (1994, p 20) argues:

> The sexual paradigm of law, the naturalised sex of law, invariably cast the man (never the woman) in the role of initiator (never the negotiator) of a sexual act (a singular, never a plural, thing which never took the form of an engagement)

which always entailed the thrusting of the penis into the vagina (never the lips of a woman on the lips of another, to think of just one of the many other forms that 'the act' might have taken).

Through the consent model, the woman is the respondent to the man's proposal.

> Sex still entails the (unidirectional) proposal of one party to take the body of the other party: the act is lawful when the other party agrees to be taken; it is rape when the other party does not. (p 26)

The significance of this unidirectional approach is extensive. Thus, in the consent model women are the 'passive receptacles of male agency' (Anderson, 2005).

(iv) Overlooking of Other Values

As mentioned earlier, supporters of relational autonomy emphasise the importance of taking into account other values apart from autonomy. By contrast it is a common view among liberal writers on sex that consensual sex cannot be wrong (see also Jenkins, this volume). But this overlooks the ways in which, even in consensual sex, a person can be used.

There is widespread acceptance that in sexual conduct it is particularly easy for one person to use another as a means to an end. Soble (2002, p 226) writes that sexual conduct is all about 'uncontrollable arousal, involuntary jerkings, and its yearning to master and consume the other's body'. That may be philosophers for you, but it is often said that sex is connected to loss of self-control and self-awareness and this readily leads to a loss of regard for the humanity of the other. Germaine Greer (1970, p 250) amply demonstrates the kind of 'sheer use' that can occur too easily in sex when commenting that in many cases the man regards the woman 'as a receptacle into which he has emptied his sperm, a kind of human spittoon, and turns from her in disgust'. Consent supporters claim that where there is consent there cannot be this objectification or use of another person (Wertheimer, 2003, p 128). But Martha Nussbaum (1995) in her seminal article has set out the ways that objectification can occur despite consent. These include instrumentality (where the objectifier treats the other as a tool for his or her purposes); violability (where the objectifier treats the other person as something that lacks boundary integrity and that it is 'permissible to break up, smash, break into' (Nussbaum, 1995, p 357)) and denial of subjectivity (where the objectifier treats the other as something whose experiences and feelings do not need to be taken into account). The fact that the victim may have consented should not lead to a conclusion that therefore she has not been wronged.

V. SUMMARISING AN ALTERNATIVE APPROACH TO CONSENT

An approach based on relational autonomy would seek to improve on the law's current approach. Respecting another's autonomy requires not just asking whether or not there was 'consent' (whatever that means) but looks to enabling people to have autonomy and a careful analysis of the circumstances in which a choice was made. This requires, therefore, a far greater awareness of the social context in which a decision is made, the relationship between the parties, and the transactions between them prior to any consent being given. Respecting autonomy is not the same as respecting choice. It means respecting the other person's right to make their own decisions as to how they wish to develop their version of their good life. It means appreciating that individuals exist in their social context and in the network of relationships. In this context it means a recognition of the patriarchal forces within which women 'consent' to sexual intercourse. No one adopting such an approach would give any credence, for example, to the rape myths mentioned above.

Secondly, a relational autonomy approach would emphasise not simply the point in time at which the sexual penetration took place. It should not be seen as an act which 'man proposes and woman disposes'. The law should expect there to be a mutual agreement between the parties. Where the approach towards sexual penetration is all one way (that is, the man is 'making all the moves') there should be a suspicion as to whether the sexual penetration was the result of a mutual agreement. The law should be looking at the actions, behaviours and attitudes of both parties leading up to the penetration.

Thirdly, sexual partners owe each other responsibilities and in particular responsibility to respect the other party's sexual autonomy. Respect for your partner's humanity requires more than obtaining 'consent'. Onora O'Neill (1985, p 253) writes:

> I shall argue that an adequate understanding of what it is to treat others as persons must view them not abstractly as possibly consenting adults, but as particular men and women with limited and determinate capacities to understand or to consent to proposals for action. Unless we take one another's limitations seriously we risk acting in ways which would be enough to treat 'ideal' rational beings as persons, but are not enough for treating finitely rational, human beings as persons.

This argument does not regard obtaining consent as some kind of a game where the man wins if he gets the woman to say 'yes'; rather it involves a respect for each other with limited capacities and with finite rationality. Developing this theme, the current law fails to properly acknowledge the responsibilities that people have when they engage in sexual penetration.

The responsibility is to respect the other's autonomy. Lying to a partner, pressurising them, threatening them—these things cannot be part of respecting another person's autonomy. Listening to them; removing any pressures; giving time, care and support—these are the things that involve respecting another's autonomy.

VI. CONCLUSION

This chapter has examined the concept of relational autonomy. Writers adopting this approach have found the traditional individualised approach to autonomy thin, inaccurate and dangerous. The law should not be built around a world of individuals pursuing self-interest, with their right to do so being protected from the needs or obligations of others unless absolutely necessary. Rather it should be based on an acknowledgement that individuals are embedded in relationship with others.

Using this concept, this chapter has criticised aspects of the law's approach to consent in rape. The law has failed to show sufficient appreciation of the social and cultural context in which sexual penetrations take place. It reduces consent largely to an isolated event, rather than a fuller consideration of the relational context in which the event takes place. It fails to appreciate the responsibilities that are undertaken between parties who engage in sex.

Relational autonomy provides a richer and a more nuanced way of understanding our lives, our decision-making and our choices. To be autonomous is to not to be isolated and free of responsibility, but to be in a network of relationships, with their dependent responsibilities. As Marilyn Friedman (2006) suggests, it enables us to see that the true picture of an autonomous man is not our Jack Bauer figure riding off into the sunset in a blaze of smoke; but the man at home changing a nappy.

BIBLIOGRAPHY

Amnesty International (2005) *Sexual Assault Survey*, London: Amnesty International.

Anderson M (2005) 'Negotiating sex'. *Southern California Law Review* 78, 1401–89.

Archard D (1998) *Sexual Consent*, Westview, Boulder, CO.

—— (2007) Book Reviews. *Journal of Applied Philosophy* 24, 209–20.

Ball C (2005) '"This is not your father's autonomy": lesbian and gay rights from a feminist and relational perspective'. *Harvard Journal of Law and Gender* 28, 345–79.

Barclay L (2000) 'Autonomy and the social self' in *Relational autonomy* (Eds Mackenzie C & Stoljar N) Oxford University Press, Oxford, pp 52–71.

Barvosa-Carter E (2007) 'Mestiza autonomy as relational autonomy: Ambivalence and the social character of free will'. *Journal of Political Philosophy* 15, 1–21.

BBC News Online (2005) 'Girls reveal abuse by boyfriends', 21 March.

Becker M (1999) 'Patriarchy and inequality: Towards a substantive feminism'. *University of Chicago Legal Forum* 21–61.

Binder N (1994) 'Taking relationships seriously: Children, autonomy, and the right to a relationship'. *New York University Law Review* 69, 1150–75.

Bridgeman J (2007) 'Review'. *Medical Law Review* 15, 144–7.

Brown W (2001) *Politics out of History*, Princeton University Press, Princeton, NJ.

Carle S (2005) 'Theorizing agency'. *American Universities Law Review* 55, 307–62.

Chapleau K, Oswald D, Russell B (2007) 'How ambivalent sexism towards women and men supports rape myth acceptance'. *Sex Roles* 53, 1–23.

Chen-Wishart M (2006) 'Undue influence: Vindicating relationships of influence' in *Current Legal Problems* (Eds Holder J & O'Cinneide C) Oxford University Press, Oxford, pp 231–66.

Christman J (2004) 'Relational autonomy, liberal individualism, and the social constitution of selves'. *Philosophical Studies* 117, 143–64.

Code L (1991) *'Second persons' in What Can She Know? Feminist Theory and the Construction of Knowledge* (Ed, Code L) Cornell University Press, Ithaca, NY, pp 78–98.

de Botton A (2004) *Status Anxiety*, Pantheon, London.

Donchin A (2000) 'Autonomy, interdependence, and assisted suicide: Respecting boundaries/crossing lines'. *Bioethics* 14, 187–201.

—— (2001) 'Understanding autonomy relationally'. *Journal of Medicine and Philosophy* 26, 365–84.

Finch E & Munro V (2006) 'Breaking boundaries? Sexual consent in the jury room'. *Legal Studies* 26, 303–30.

Fineman M (2004) *The Autonomy Myth*, New Press, New York.

—— (2005) 'The social foundations of law'. *Emory Law Journal* 54, 201–37.

Franke K (2001) 'Taking care'. *Chicago-Kent Law Review* 76, 1541–56.

Frazer, E & Lacey N (1993) *The Politics of Community: A Feminist Critique of the Liberal Communitarian Debate,* Harvester Wheatsheaf, Hemel Hempstead.

Friedman M (2000) 'Autonomy, social disruption, and women' in *Relational Autonomy* (Eds, Mackenzie C & Stoljar N) Oxford University Press, Oxford, pp 35–51.

—— (2006) *Autonomy Gender Politics*, Oxford University Press, Oxford.

Greer G (1970) *The Female Eunuch,* McGraw-Hill Co, New York.

Groenhout R (2004) *Connected Lives: Human Nature and an Ethics of Care,* Rowman & Littlefield, Lanham, MD.

Harris J & Grace S (1999) *A Question of Evidence?,* Home Office, London.

Herring J (2007) 'Where are the carers in healthcare law and ethics?'. *Legal Studies* 27, 51–3.

Hoagland S (1989) *Lesbian Ethics: Toward New Values*, Institute of Lesbian Studies, Palo Alto, CA.

Johnson A (1997) *Gender Knot*, Temple University Press, Philadelphia.

Kiss E (1997) "Alchemy or fool's gold? Assessing feminist doubts about rights" in *Reconstructing Political Theory* (Eds, Shanley M & Narayan U) Polity Press, Cambridge, pp 1–24.

Lacey N (1998) *Unspeakable Subjects*, Hart Publishing, Oxford.

Lees, S (2002) *Carnal Knowledge*, Women's Press, London.

McClain L (1992) '"Atomistic man" revisited: Liberalism, connection, and feminist jurisprudence'. *Southern California Law Review* 65, 1171–264.

McGregor J (2005) *Is it Rape?*, Ashgate, London.

McIntyre A (1981) *After Virtue: A Study in Moral Theory*, University of Notre Dame Press, Indiana.

Mackenzie C (2000) 'Imagining oneself otherwise' in *Relational Autonomy* (Eds Mackenzie C & Stoljar N) Oxford University Press, Oxford, pp 124–50.

Mackenzie C & Stoljar N (2000) 'Autonomy refigured' in *Relational Autonomy* (Eds Mackenzie C & Stoljar N) Oxford University Press, Oxford, pp. 3–31.

MacKinnon C (2003) 'A sex equality approach to sexual assault', *Annals New York Academy of Sciences* 989, 265–75.

Madden Dempsey M & Herring J (2007) 'Why sexual penetration requires justification', *Oxford Journal of Legal Studies* 27, 467–91.

Meyers D (1989) *Self, Society, and Personal Choice*, Columbia University Press, New York.

Morgan R (1980) 'Theory and practice: Pornography and rape' in *Take Back the Night: Women on Pornography* (Ed Lederer L) William Morrow & Co, New York, pp 134–40.

Munro V (2005) 'Concerning consent: Standards of permissibility in sexual relations'. *Oxford Journal of Legal Studies* 25, 335–52.

Naffine N (1994) 'Possession: Erotic love in the law of rape'. *Modern Law Review* 57, 10–37.

Nedelsky J (1989) 'Reconceiving autonomy: Sources, thoughts and possibilities'. *Yale Journal of Law and Feminism* 1, 7–36.

Nussbaum M (1995) 'Objectification'. *Philosophy and Public Affairs* 24, 249–91.

—— (2001) *Upheavals of Thought: The Intelligence of Emotions*, Cambridge University Press, Cambridge.

O'Neill O (1985) 'Between consenting adults'. *Philosophy and Public Affairs* 14, 252–77.

—— (2002) *Autonomy and Trust in Bioethics*, Cambridge University Press, Cambridge.

Oshana M (1998) 'Personal autonomy and society'. *Journal of Social Philosophy* 29, 81–102.

Posner R (1994) *Sex and Reason,* Harvard University Press, Cambridge, MA.

Raz J (1986) *The Morality of Freedom*, Oxford University Press, Oxford.

Roberts P (2001) 'Philosophy, Feinberg, codification, and consent: A progress report on English experiences of criminal law reform'. *Buffalo Criminal Law Review* 5, 173–206.

Sevenhuijsen S (2003) 'The place of care: The relevance of the feminist ethic of care for social policy'. *Feminist Theory* 4, 179–99.

Soble A (2002) 'Sexual use and what to do about it: Internalist and externalist sexual ethics' in *The Philosophy of Sex* (Ed Soble A) Rowman & Littlefield, Lanham, MD.

Verkerk M (1999) 'A care perspective on coercion and autonomy'. *Bioethics* 13, 358–71.

Weait M (2005) 'Harm, consent and the limits of privacy'. *Feminist Legal Studies* 13, 97–122.

Wertheimer A (2003) *Consent to Sexual Relations*, Cambridge University Press, Cambridge.

West R (1993) 'Legitimating the illegitimate: A comment on "Beyond Rape"'. *Columbia Law Review* 93, 1442–63.

—— (1996) 'A comment on consent sex and rape'. *Legal Theory* 2, 233–251.

Westen P (2004) *The Logic of Consent: The Diversity and Deceptiveness of Consent as a Defense to Criminal Conduct*, Ashgate, Aldershot.

Legislation

Sexual Offences Act 2003

5

Rules for Feeding Babies

ELLIE LEE AND JENNIE BRISTOW

I. INTRODUCTION

It's not a thing [bottle feeding] that you can do unthinkingly without being concerned about how others will respond to you. It's almost like you've got to play a part, and take on a role of, 'I am the formula feeding mum and here's why' ... you have to defend your actions.

When I went to the clinic to get him weighed I used to hide the bottle in my bag and if there was no one there then I'd give him a quick sip and then if someone came, I'd put the bottle away. I think now why didn't I just say 'I'm bottle-feeding and I'm proud', but no.

When you read magazines, you read books, it's like 'breast is best', you must breastfeed, breastfeed ... it was baby magazines, they used to freak me out ... It's that kind of pressure that just sticks in head ... They made me so paranoid.
    (Experience of mothers who had decided to bottle-feed their babies.
        From Lee, 2007a, 2007b and 2007c respectively)

FOLLOWING BIRTH, THE activity of feeding is central to the relationship between a mother and her baby. In most societies, including Britain, one issue to confront mothers is what feeding strategy they will adopt, and in practice this is reducible to making a decision about the use of formula milk: whether to formula feed at all, whether to formula feed as well as breastfeed (mixed feeding) or whether from the outset or at some later point to feed a baby only with formula milk.

Unlike other relationships examined in this volume, that between a mother and her new baby in this regard is not directly regulated by law. At a formal level the freedom of the mother to make decisions in this area of private life—her decisional autonomy—is upheld. How she feeds her baby is deemed a decision for her to make. Yet evidence suggests it can *feel* as though decision-making in infant feeding is far from autonomous; despite the differences in how mothers *actually* feed their babies, the common experience of mothers is, 'an acute sense of being watched by the world' (Knaak, 2005, p 201). Findings of qualitative studies (detailed further below) suggest that feeding a baby formula milk is associated, in particular, by many mothers with experiencing 'pressure', and feeling that their decisions are monitored by others. The aim of this chapter is to explore this experience and in so doing contribute to discussion of decisional autonomy.

Criticisms of policies and practices that undermine decisional autonomy have been widely articulated in discussion of reproductive choice and sexual conduct. Much attention has been paid to the role of law in this regard, a body of scholarship extended by chapters in this volume. The abrogation of parents' decisional autonomy in the conduct of everyday family life has, however, been the subject of far less critical attention (Reece, 2005). Further, the interaction between the law and the approach it takes to parental autonomy, and wider cultural developments, have been the subject of relatively limited consideration. In what follows, we therefore use the example of infant feeding to discuss these issues.

Our account will contend that the activity of infant feeding is surrounded by conventions and culturally powerful precepts about what are and are not appropriate maternal decisions. We will emphasise that while these precepts do not yet take an explicit legal form, they nevertheless operate as rules that powerfully impact on mothers' experiences of decision-making. We will also indicate that these precepts have been formalised in policy and, to some degree, in law. The chapter will conclude that while it remains to be seen whether the process of rule development highlighted will find reflection in the further juridification of this area of family life, what we are seeing in the present is, at the very least, the development of a context of *pre-juridification* as decisional autonomy in this area of private life becomes more and more culturally problematised.

II. CHOICE AND DECISION-MAKING

The context in which women feed their babies is of course that which tells them 'Breast is Best'; this message is communicated to them by a wide range of agencies (Murphy, 1999). This statement reflects evidence that has shown that exclusive breastfeeding in the early months is associated with a lower incidence of ear infections, chest infections and stomach upsets than found in babies who are given formula milk. Evidence about many aspects of the longer-term health effects of breastfeeding, such as on obesity (Michels *et al*, 2007) and IQ (Der *et al*, 2006), is mixed, but the authors of this chapter do not refute the general position that breast milk is a good food for babies. However, from a socio-cultural perspective, Breast is Best and the wealth of associated schemes that seek to increase breastfeeding rates constitute something other/more than a neutral reflection of the content of breast milk. They comprise a discursive context for motherhood.

This context is one in which the idea of 'choice' in infant-feeding methods is defined in a particular way. It is not constructed as something which is 'actual', where individual mothers might legitimately decide between two alternatives each with benefits. There is, rather, a context of 'moralised and constrained choice' because the alternative to breastfeeding is predominantly represented in very negative ways (Knaak, 2005). The bulk of this chapter considers some aspects of the evolution of this context of 'constrained choice' over the past 30 years.

Ultimately the importance of this context, however, is its effect for mothers' experience of decision-making and, as Knaak explains, it is one which influences this experience in important ways. It 'contextualises mothers' experiences in relation to infant feeding ... and organizes everyday experience, including decision making' (Knaak, 2005, p 198). Detailed studies of mothers' everyday experience confirm this observation and indicate maternal experience is strongly influenced by a culture in which choice is not 'actual'. In particular, decisional autonomy has been shown to be compromised, as many mothers find themselves having to struggle to defend the feeding strategy they adopt, and consequently they experience infant feeding as a fraught, demanding and difficult experience.

Murphy, for example, interviewed women who expressed an intention to formula feed. She explains they had to perform 'identity work' to defend their decision, since the woman in this situation found herself needing to find ways of responding to 'the charge that she is a "poor mother"', a task that poses her with significant 'interactional challenges' (Murphy, 1999, pp 187–8). The extracts that appear at the start of this chapter are taken from a study of the experiences of women who decided to use formula milk for infant feeding wholly or in part in the first three months following birth, and they point to a similar experience.

Mothers in this study reported that while they fully appreciated Breast is Best they made the decision to formula feed for a range of reasons relating to personal circumstances in their lives. These included wanting to share baby care with other people, addressing fatigue, returning to work, and disliking breastfeeding because of pain or because of the demands that very regular breastfeeding placed on them. These pragmatic motivations for formula feeding, based on often unforeseen experiences, led mothers to describe feeding a baby this way as helpful to them; they did it because it was 'easy', most said. Yet many also recounted often very negative experiences, including feeling variously defensive, angry, guilty and anxious, and having to respond to implicit or overt criticism. Their own reasons for formula feeding based on their decision-making process, it seemed, were often not enough to trump the idea that mothers should decide to breastfeed.

That mothers can feel this way about their decision to formula feed is interesting given its continuing normality. Statistics from the UK Department of Health's 2005 Infant Feeding Survey show that 76% of women initiate breastfeeding (defined as any contact between mother's nipple and baby's mouth following birth), an increase in the rate since the 2000 survey. By six weeks after birth, 52% of these mothers have stopped breastfeeding however, meaning that from this point the majority of mothers feed their baby formula milk at least in part (and 25% exclusively bottle-feed from the outset). While the Department of Health recommends that mother exclusively breastfeed for 26 weeks (six months) only 2% follow this advice and only one quarter breastfeed at all by this point (ONS, 2007). Yet the fact that most women formula feed their babies appears to offer a relatively limited sort of defence against what Murphy (1999) terms a position of 'moral jeopardy' generated by mothers' 'mundane deviance' Maternal experience points to the presence of influential rules for infant feeding, albeit of a non-legal sort, and suggests mothers' decisional autonomy is compromised in practice (if not in law) by a climate of constrained choice.

Rules of this kind have been identified and analysed elsewhere in relation to pregnancy. In most Western societies there are no laws that regulate the conduct of the pregnant woman (Jackson, 2005). Nevertheless, it has been shown that the pregnant woman *is* monitored and regulated.

> At the end of the twentieth century [the pregnant woman] is surrounded by a complex network of discourse and practices directed at the surveillance and regulation of her body (Lupton, 1999, p.59).

The rule-bound nature of pregnancy is such that, in the US at least, according to Armstrong, a

> 'preconception' movement ... is gaining momentum ... exhorts women to begin changing their diets, taking vitamin supplements, and avoiding alcohol, tobacco and other substances when they are *considering* becoming pregnant (Armstrong, 2003, p 197)

These analyses also suggest rules for pregnancy are strongly medicalised; it is in the language of health that messages about appropriate decisions and choices are communicated.

The following discussion will show how rule-construction of this sort has come to stretch forwards in a similar way. Maternal decision-making in the postnatal period is increasingly defined as critical on health grounds. Indeed, it could be argued that infant feeding is now just one part of a picture in which mother–child relationships in general, not just those between mother and baby, are being reconstructed, with rules for food and feeding at their centre. The 'good mother' of the early twenty-first century is one who demonstrates her fitness to mother in relation to her concern over what her child ingests and in turn the size and shape of her child's body. The mother is defined more and more (and defines herself) by what she feeds her child (Kukla, 2007).

III. THE 'TANGLE OF MEDICALISATION'

Part of the discursive context for infant feeding is provided by the work of moral entrepreneurs; social actors who seek to alert society to dangers posed by certain behaviours or customs (Jenkins, 1992). Moral entrepreneurs who champion breastfeeding are not a new phenomenon (Kukla, 2005). In recent decades, however, their number has expanded and they have become a key reference point in discussion about feeding babies. While their case is often presented in the language of medicine, these moral entrepreneurs have wider concerns.

Breast is not only deemed 'best' for infants, but also for 'the environment and global economy' (Schmeid & Lupton, 2001, p 234). Environmental concerns are, indeed, currently often very near the surface of breastfeeding advocacy. Patti Rundall is Policy Director at Baby Milk Action, the influential UK wing of the pro-breastfeeding campaign International Baby Food Action Network (IBFAN) formed in 1979. She argues that breastfeeding is a 'unique health intervention' since there is no other food which is

> more locally produced, more sustainable or more environmentally friendly than a mother's breast milk- a naturally sustainable renewable resource which requires no packaging or transport, results in no wastage and is free. (Thomas, 2006, p 23)

The support offered to breastfeeding by environmentalists indicates that its perceived 'naturalness' strongly confirms their pre-existing convictions about what is 'best' for the future of society as a whole. A high degree of importance is thus frequently attached to breastfeeding; the practice matters because it is perceived to form a central part of a wider project.

Validation of 'the natural' is also a feature of another aspect of the advocacy of breastfeeding, which in recent decades grew out of campaigns to limit the 'medicalisation' of childbirth by modern medical practice (Carter, 1995). Just as childbirth was viewed by some as a potentially fulfilling experience, at its most empowering for women when freed from the influence of medical technology and doctors, so it was considered that breastfeeding could provide an expression of women's 'natural power'; as Van Esterick put it, breastfeeding, 'confirms a women's power to control her own body and challenges medical hegemony' (1989, p 70). The campaign to 'de-medicalise' childbirth found expression in Britain in the form of the National Childbirth Trust (NCT). This organisation promotes breastfeeding as an integral part of the natural process of birth and motherhood, and represents formula feeding as one of several 'interventionist' techniques promoted by the medical profession and society at large (NCT, 2007).

That breastfeeding is a route to women's empowerment is, indeed, perhaps the most commonplace conviction held by breastfeeding advocates. 'Breast is best' claimed Stanway in her book of that name from the 1970s, since breastfeeding is 'symbolic of her [a woman's] womanliness' (Stanway, 1978, p 3), and the association of breastfeeding mothers La Leche League (LLL), established in 1956 by seven Catholic women in Illinois, US, describes the practice as a 'womanly art'. This mother–child interaction, contends LLL, allows women to reclaim their bodies, boost their sense of self-esteem, and resist conventional authority in all its forms (Blum, 1999). Interestingly, some who present this sort of account of how women's power can increase also contest other ideas about women's liberation. Feminism in the 1960s, according to influential breastfeeding advocate Mary Renfrew, 'encouraged women to get away from their babies and start living their lives', contributing in her view to female loss of confidence in the empowering capacity to breastfeed (Thomas, 2006).

This means of empowering women, however, is also considered to be the route to strong families and so a strong society. For LLL 'good mothering' is achieved through breastfeeding:

> [M]othering through breastfeeding deepens a mother's understanding and accep-
> tance of the responsibilities and rewards of her special role in the family. As a
> woman grows in mothering she grows as a human being and every other role she
> may fill in her lifetime is enriched by the insights and humanity she brings to it
> from her experiences as a mother (LLL GB, 2007).

In turn, as Weiner notes, LLL's 'maternalist' outlook implies that 'an empowered motherhood defined by "female" qualities would improve society' (Weiner, 1994, p 1358). In this framework, there can be nothing more important for the good of women, families and the wider society than breastfeeding.

Perceptions of how to create a better society have impelled modern breastfeeding advocacy. Yet it is most often in the language of medicine that the case for breastfeeding is now communicated. Ward (2000) describes how LLL was established as a movement privileging the expertise of mothers over that of the medical profession, and the 'natural' qualities of breast milk over the scientific claims made by formula manufacturers. Yet as LLL's influence grew through the 1970s and 1980s, its claims about the superiority of breastfeeding and breast milk took on more and more of the language of medicine. The NCT (like LLL, established in 1956) has come to marry claims regarding maternal self-esteem it believes are accrued through rejecting 'medicalisation' with medical-sounding references.

> The benefits of breastfeeding for both mum and baby are not just measured in
> health terms, but in the pride a mum feels when she looks at her healthy, grow-
> ing breastfed baby. Just one day of breastfeeding makes a difference to a baby's
> health by stabilising their blood sugars, protecting their gut and providing natural
> antibodies against disease (NCT, 2007).

This outcome is what the US scholar Bernice Hausman terms the 'tangle of medicalization' (2003, p 25); she claims those whose concern is with promotion of 'the natural' and who appear in many ways hostile to modern medicine have adopted the language of medicine to make their case. This contradiction in breastfeeding advocacy has arguably intensified recently in a particular way. Some analyses of relevant literature have noted how increasing recourse is made to the notion of *danger* associated with formula feeding, with claims made that medical evidence attests to this proposition (Wolf, 2007). Through the activity of pro-breastfeeding organisations the medicalisation of social life moves forward apace, in line with the wider imperatives of a 'risk society' (Murphy, 2004).

Communication about the risks of formula feeding is sometimes implicit. 'Benefits' are deemed to accrue only with breastfeeding, implying any alternative must carry risk. Claims regarding 'bonding' exemplify this approach. 'Breastfeeding, by its very nature, requires the sort of skin-to-skin contact that babies need. It is a uniquely bonding experience' claims the NCT (2007). From its inception LLL has claimed, 'among other things, that because the breastfed baby is held more by the mother, it is psychologically closer to her' (Eyer, 1992, p 175). The risk of 'impaired bonding' that confronts mothers who formula feed is, however, one of many. Explicit claims about the dire physical health risks that damage formula-fed babies are rife in statements of the relevant moral entrepreneurs.

'Fourteen Risks of Formula Feeding' is the title of a leaflet distributed by INFACT Canada, a longstanding campaign group opposed to 'artificial feeding'. The risks this group attributes to formula feeding include infant death, childhood cancer, diabetes, reduced cognitive development, and obesity. Some speaking for the newly formed alliance of UK-based pro-breastfeeding groups, the Breastfeeding Manifesto Coalition, utilise similar language. Professor Louise Wallace of Coventry University, speaking in support of the coalition[1] claims,

---

[1] The Coalition's membership includes pro-breastfeeding advocacy groups, environmentalist groups, health professionals' organisations and other non-governmental organisations. At the time of writing the membership is listed as Amicus the Union, Association of Breastfeeding Mothers, Baby Feeding Law Group, Baby Milk Action, Best Beginnings, Biological Nurturing, Birthlight, BLISS, Bosom Buddies, Breastfeeding Network, Childfriendly Places, The Community Practitioners' and Health Visitors' Association, Friends of the Earth, Independent Midwives Association, La Leche League Great Britain, Little Angels, The Midwife Information and Resource Service, National Childbirth Trust, National Obesity Forum, Royal College of General Practitioners, Royal College of Midwives, Royal College of Nursing, Save the Children, The Baby Café Charitable Trust, The British Dietetic Association, The Food Commission, The Mother and Infant Research Unit, The Royal College of General Practitioners, The Royal College of Paediatrics and Child Health, The United Kingdom Association for Milk Banking, UNICEF UK, UNISON, WOMB, Women's Environmental Network.

It's not only that breastfeeding is good, it's that formula is bad. It causes asthma, allergies, gut problems, a propensity to diabetes and obesity. The list goes on (cited in Hopkinson, 2007).

'Breastmilk vs Formula: No contest' claims breastfeeding advocate Pat Thomas in *The Ecologist*, since the former 'provides active immunity [and] every time a baby breastfeeds it also receives protection from disease'. Of formula milk, a food she labels 'junk food', she further claims,

newer data from the West clearly show that babies in otherwise affluent societies are also falling ill and dying due to an early diet of convenience food ... the health effects of sucking down formula day after day early in life can be devastating in both the short and long term (Thomas, 2006, p 24).

Death caused by bottle-feeding is thus not a risk only for children living in the developing world, from this perspective.

These messages about infant feeding mostly do not include overt advocacy of laws against formula feeding per se (although some do argue that formula milk should be illegal). They do, however, communicate to mothers a sort of rule about infant-feeding decisions; they should place a large cross against the risky option of bottle-feeding.

Some studies have detected that fear about the effects of formula feeding is shared by some mothers; mothers who formula feed do worry, sometimes to a great degree, about the harm they have done to their child and feel very unconfident about the decisions they make (Lee, 2007a). On its own, however, the discursive context provided by moral entrepreneurs is insufficient to fully account for this sort of maternal experience. The cultural authority of the groups and individuals referred to above is considerable; their pronouncements are rarely challenged on the basis of their accuracy, and their right to speak on behalf of 'mothers' goes mostly uncontested. Yet the extent to which experience can be explained as a result of their activity is limited, not least because the vast majority of mothers have no direct involvement with them. Wider socio-cultural developments, with which contemporary pro-breastfeeding claims largely resonate, play an important part in generating the rules for infant feeding.

IV. PARENTING CULTURE

Intensive mothering ideology remains, despite cultural contradictions and diverse arrangements, the normative standard ... by which mothering practices and arrangements are evaluated (Arendell, 2000, p 1195).

Infant-feeding practice in the contemporary context has been conceptualised as a 'measure of motherhood'. Those who observe mothers and comment upon what they do, and indeed mothers themselves, perceive this area of baby care as a 'signal issue'. Infant-feeding decisions provide a means to assess and 'box off' a woman as a particular type of mother (Kukla, 2007).

Most obviously this can be a 'good mother' who may be lauded for the effort and self-sacrifice she puts into the hard work of breastfeeding. Mothers who formula feed may, in contrast, be defined as simply 'poor mothers' who must be, in the face of the barrage of information that proves to them that it is dangerous to formula feed, selfish, lazy, or 'irredeemably uneducable' (Kukla, 2006). Alternatively (and perhaps more commonly in Britain) they appear in many representations of them as 'mother-victims'. They are mothers who feed their babies formula milk because they are unsupported by family who have undermined their aspiration to breastfeed, poorly served by health service providers who have not funded enough lactation consultants, and misled by the wider 'bottle-feeding culture'. As such they should be sympathised with and pitied, for the 'unhealthy choice' they have had no option but to make.

Their decision to bottle-feed, however, is still one that is considered problematic and symptomatic of less-than-ideal mothering.

In regard to the definition of infant feeding as a 'signal issue' in this way, some have noted the resonance of aspects of breastfeeding advocacy with the wider socio-cultural development labelled by Sharon Hays as 'intensive mothering'. Hays claimed that intensive mothering is a culturally specific ideology, which advises mothers to 'spend a tremendous amount of time, energy and money in raising their children' (1996, p x). Its power, she argued, draws on the perception that mothering in its 'intense' form is perceived as 'the last best defence against what many people see as the impoverishment of social ties, communal obligations, and unremunerated commitments' (Hays, 1996, p xiii). Mothering is considered—albeit to a lesser or greater degree—both the origin of, and solution to, social disintegration and anomie. Hays developed this concept through her study of the experience of motherhood and work, but it has influenced numerous subsequent studies of contemporary experience of many aspects of motherhood in industrialised countries. These studies find that, despite some cultural variation, motherhood is defined by some interrelated features.

Successful child-rearing is centrally defined as that which is 'child-centred'. It requires that the mother becomes absorbed in maximising her child's potential, and so embraces taking individual responsibility for her child's development (Knaak, 2005). Mothering defined this way ideally absorbs the personality of the mother, and to this end culture holds out the promise of child-centred mothering as a uniquely rich source of personal fulfilment. Intensive mothering ideology also, however, constructs mothering as an activity that, because of its significance for the development of the child, is too important to be left to mothers alone. A key characteristic of intensive motherhood is for this reason the cultural validation of expert guidance over the minutiae of child-rearing.

These characteristics of intensive mothering—child-centredness and acquiescence to expert guidance—have also been considered strongly resonant with a risk-averse approach to child-rearing. In risk society, argues Furedi (2001) child-centredness and the professionalisation of parenthood in general have gained increasing strength. This is because the parent–child dyad has come to be more and more constructed around the idea of the 'vulnerable child' and the 'God-like parent'. The former is widely considered at risk from an ever-expanding range of threats to well-being posed by everyday life, and the latter considered central—more central than any other influence over a child—to determining whether the child becomes in some way damaged.

Cultural norms, this analysis suggests, thus construct the 'good parent' (mother especially) as alert to the manifold risks posed to her child(ren) by contemporary society, and it is considered her job to manage these risks through reference to expert advice and 'support'. Parents, mothers in particular, emerge in this circumstance as people who no longer simply 'child rear'; rather, they 'parent'. This definition of parental activity as 'parenting' requires that responsible parents accept they should pay attention to what is said by experts about their children and seek help with any and every aspect of child-rearing. Parental interaction with the child is considered decisive for their future, and the responsible parent is the one who recognises great costs are incurred for individuals and society when parenting is performed in a less than ideal way. Parents in this context play the role of risk manager.

These core aspects of intensive motherhood have been detected in messages about infant feeding in our culture. On the basis of her content analysis of the parenting manual Dr Spock from 1946 to 1998, for example, Knaak (2005) suggests that the turn to intensive motherhood explains why advice to women has shifted in notable ways over the past 40 years, from a position where formula feeding and breastfeeding were presented both as valid options with pros and cons, to one where the former is degraded as best avoided altogether. 'Choice in infant feeding has become constrained discursively to the point where it has become more a directive than a choice', she notes (Knaak, 2005, p 212). This discursive constraint cannot be accounted for simply through reference to the findings of scientific research about infant nutrition, she further argues, but rather, this shift appears reflective of a ideological move expressing power of a 'broader child-centred mothering ideology'. As a result, possible advantages of bottle-feeding, since these are deemed to accrue mostly to the mother, are now, in contrast to the past, largely not mentioned or are clearly relegated to second place. Such child-centred messages about feeding babies are thus about more than just infant feeding. They are also about women's 'capacity as mothers', she concludes (Knaak, 2005, p 201). Wall notes similarly, on the basis of her analysis of parenting guides and information provided to mothers about infant feeding: 'A child-centred focus pervades current understandings.' She quotes one popular text, which states: 'Disadvantages to breastfeeding are those factors perceived by the mother to be an inconvenience since there are no known disadvantages for the infant', suggesting that the decisions to formula feed must imply a clash of maternal and child interests, with the latter losing out (Wall, 2001, p 601).

According to some there is a further, newer component to parenting culture, however, namely the politicisation of parenting. Parent–child interaction in all respects has, over the past decade especially, become more central to politics and policy-making than in the past (Furedi, 2001; Reece, 2005). Greater government involvement in the project of modifying infant-feeding practices is one aspect of this development. This area is of particular interest and import because of state involvement in maternal decision-making, and constitutes the form in which the undermining of decisional autonomy is made more formal and more powerful.

V. THE RISE OF 'INFORMED CHOICE'

No society to date has imposed a maternal duty to breastfeed, for example as part of children's rights law, and sought to compel individual women to breastfeed. Some pro-breastfeeding campaigners do, however, suggest that infant feeding should be a legal matter, arguing that the child has the 'right to be breastfed', and the government should take measures accordingly.

Those who advocate this 'right' tend to frame their case in a particular way. First, they represent the mother as also in need of new rights (rather than duties). 'Infants have a human right to be breastfed, and women have the right to be empowered to fulfil this duty', claims one pro-breastfeeding campaigner (Mahabal, 2004). The legal means advocated through which such 'empowerment of women' is to be enacted are usually measures that purport to 'protect' women from damaging influences. These are primarily laws to restrict/ban advertising of formula milk, and to promote breastfeeding 'in public'. Both these measures are part of law. In Britain, companies that make formula milks have for many years been prohibited from advertising this product through a Code drawn up by the World Health Organization, and supported by the UK government (and more recently by European directives). In Scotland, the 'right to breastfeed' in public places is enshrined in law, and a similar legal arrangement has been proposed for England (Department for Communities and Local Government, 2007).

The 'right to be breastfed' is also construed as a type of health imperative. Citing the World Health Organization/Unicef's 1990 Innocenti Declaration on the Protection, Promotion and Support of Breastfeeding, the US-based

Human Rights Education Association (HREA) claims: 'This declaration asserts that women have the right to breastfeed their babies, and infants from birth to 4–6 months have the right to be breastfed' (HREA, 2007). Whilst this may be an accurate summary of the Innocenti Declaration's meaning, the document itself in fact frames the issue not in terms of rights, but in terms of 'enabling' women to do what is 'healthy': 'All women should be enabled to practise exclusive breastfeeding and all infants should be fed exclusively on breast milk from birth to 4–6 months of age' (WHO/ UNICEF, 1990). It is in this form that more formal rules for infant feeding most often appear. The UK government states, for example, that UK women should exclusively breastfeed for 26 weeks, and has recently innovated more and more policy measures to 'enable' women to do so, and so to 'choose health'.

While government activity in this area has notably increased in recent years, interest in infant feeding from this quarter dates to the start of the twentieth century (Murphy, 2003). Its course has been documented by Carter, who notes that:

> From about 1900 onwards infant feeding in many industrialised and industrialising countries became a issue for the state as well as experts as part of broader population policies, with official pronouncements drawing attention to the alleged 'carelessness' of mothers (Carter, 1995, p 51).

Of the post-Second World War period, she highlights an 'intensification of state interest in family life and the child'. In a context of the growth of both psychological theories of 'maternal deprivation', and increasing employment rates for women outside the home from the 1970s, interest grew in the "natural" now more fundamentally child centred mother' (Carter, 1995, p 56). Policy attempts to encourage breastfeeding in response specifically to 'low' breastfeeding rates date from the 1920s, and concerns about the numbers of women not breastfeeding appear in policy statements from the 1940s.

Carter notes that it is, however, since the 1970s that 'breastfeeding seems to have been revived as an important part of government health policy' (1995, p 60). She draws particular attention to new developments of the 1980s that further encouraged this trajectory, noting in particular the rise of 'health inequality' as a policy concern:

> The political agenda around nutrition has become increasingly polarised between those who see structural and material causes of poor diet, and those who see these things as a result of the of the 'carelessness and ignorance' beloved of policy makers earlier in the century. Although non breast-feeders are not explicitly labelled as ignorant, breast-feeding must nevertheless be seen as a relatively safe political issue ... Instead of focusing on these broader health issues

[associated with feeding patterns] the policy agenda is limited to feeding habits and attitudes. (Carter, 1995, p 61)

There is not space here to detail the outcome of this health inequalities debate for breastfeeding promotion, but 'feeding habits' and 'attitudes' have remained central to policy-making, and activity seeking to change both has expanded in a marked way. The project of modifying mothers' infant-feeding practices and attitudes has come to feature prominently in public health policy. Breastfeeding rates now form a key measure of the 'health of the nation' and 'raising awareness' of the benefits of breastfeeding, and increasing breastfeeding rates, especially amongst socially deprived and low income groups, are stated aims of the Department of Health's public health agenda (2004a; 2004b; 2005a; 2005b; 2005c). State advocacy of breastfeeding in this way can be considered part of the wider outcome of the 'health inequalities' debate referred to by Carter above.

This outcome has been described elsewhere as the 'new paradigm of health', the 'new public health' and a 'new morality of health' (Burrows *et al*, 1995; Fitzpatrick, 2001; Nettleton, 2006). This approach to health focuses policy development on behaviour modification in individuals since 'health behaviours' have come to be defined as a primary cause of ill health. In sociological terms, significance has been attributed to the definition of 'health' that results as a matter of choice; 'health is increasingly understood as something that can be chosen' notes Murphy (2004, p 203). Disease is no longer considered a cruel act of nature that humane medicine seeks to address and confront. Rather a new definition has attained dominance, in which disease is defined as the product of the actions of the individual, and in turn, 'health' as no longer simply the absence of disease, but a project with which we are to be 'fully engaged' in the course of everyday life; a definition of 'health' expressed in the ubiquitous advocacy in policy of 'healthy lifestyles'.

In this circumstance, efforts to encourage people to 'choose health' have been conceptualised, in part at least, as a sort of moral project. 'Health' has come to operate as a 'moral framework' for society, emphasising 'individual responsibility and ... compliance with the appropriate medically-sanctioned standard of behaviour', explains Fitzpatrick (2001, p 70). At the same time, however, it has been noted that people choose health not simply by merit of their own volition, but through being 'engaged' by a wider range of actors and agencies often supported by the state: a development that has been termed not the 'nanny state' but the 'therapeutic state'. It is in this form that the state enacts the project of 'empowerment' (Nettleton, 2006).

Health promotion in this form is reflected in schemes about more and more aspects of what have been termed the 'big four': diet, exercise, smoking and alcohol (Fitzpatrick, 2001). Growth of government activity in the area of breastfeeding promotion forms part of this development, since how a baby is fed is understood increasingly as part of the wider social problem of what people (especially children) eat. In 'Choosing a Better Diet: a food and health action plan', a plan developed on the basis of New Labour's flagship health policy, 'Choosing Health', the Department of Health thus draws attention to the importance of breastfeeding. It also notes the set of policy innovations of which 'Choosing a Better Diet' forms one part, namely the National Service Framework for Children, Young People and Maternity Services (Department of Health, 2004a) which sets standards that maternity services must achieve to support breastfeeding; National Breastfeeding Awareness Week, the NHS campaign begun in 1993 to increase breastfeeding rates; and programmes that aim to increase rates of breastfeeding amongst low income groups in particular, for example 'peer support' programmes often run by breastfeeding advocacy groups, antenatal and postnatal support groups, and 'targeted education' of health professionals. 'Choosing a Better Diet' also notes the introduction of a new scheme, 'Healthy Start'. In this case, it is not just that policy seeks to encourage breastfeeding, but acts to discourage formula use, as 'Healthy Start' ends all provision of infant formula from healthcare premises.

Notable as part of this policy approach is the way in which 'choice' is defined. The term 'choice' now litters health policy documents; the phrases 'responsible choice' and 'informed choice' make frequent appearances. 'Informed choice' policies are in place for maternity care in general, and they purport to increase women's ability to choose throughout the antenatal and postnatal periods. These policies, according to Wray (2005), should mean that women are provided a fair and honest account of alternatives, to assist the individual to come to a decision about a course of action. The facilitation of 'informed choice' in infant feeding appears, however, to take place in a way that departs from this definition of it. 'Informed choice' in infant feeding is more and more defined as a choice made only if women fully appreciate that formula milk use is a health risk for babies. It is by becoming aware of risk that they are deemed empowered to make 'real' decisions.

The currency of this definition of choice has been noted in a particularly extreme form in the US (Kukla, 2006) and also in the Canadian context (Wall, 2001; Knaak, 2006). Knaak, on the basis of her reading of official Canadian information about breastfeeding, thus asks whether these materials are 'educating or advertising'. 'In general there is a failure to appropriately contextualise risk and benefit', she explains. The overriding emphasis, according to Knaak, is rather on the drawbacks for young babies of formula feeding, with almost no consideration given to '[mothers'] many other health and mothering considerations' (2006, p 413). In Britain this definition of informed choice is currently transmitted less overtly than is the case in North America, but it is nonetheless apparent.

One example where a risk-aware version of informed choice is promoted in Britain is through the UNICEF scheme the Baby Friendly Initiative (BFI). BFI is a programme that began in 1992 worldwide and in 1994 in the UK. While it is non-governmental in origin, its work (like that of a wide range of pro-breastfeeding advocacy groups) is now officially endorsed by the National Institute of Clinical Excellence (NICE) and the Department of Health; the BFI standard is defined as the 'gold standard for maternity care' that all UK hospitals should achieve. Maternity services in NHS hospitals can be accredited as 'Baby Friendly' if they adopt the BFI's Ten Steps to Successful Breastfeeding. Steps include prohibition on hospital premises of provision by health professionals of any food or drink for newborn babies other than breast milk unless 'medically indicated', and adherence to the mandate that 'no group demonstration on the use of infant formula' be provided as part of antenatal care. Where mothers themselves choose to give their babies 'supplementary feed' (formula milk), the Baby Friendly Hospital must take on the responsibility of ensuring they only do so 'after being fully informed of the benefits of exclusive breastfeeding and the risks of supplementary feed' (UNICEF, 2005). Under this programme, mothers should thus be 'counselled correctly and enabled to make and carry through informed choices' (Saddeh & Akre, 1996, p 155) and, as Murphy notes, 'correct counselling' is defined as that which will encourage a 'positive attitude' towards breastfeeding (Murphy, 1999, p 247).

The climate of 'constrained choice' surrounding maternal decision-making identified by Knaak is thus clearly identifiable in the approach of BFI, since only one 'correct' approach to infant feeding is posited. The developing relationship between the state and non-governmental organisations like UNICEF evident in this example also adds a further dimension to the 'tangle of medicalisation'. Organisations that claim to 'empower' mothers by 'de-medicalising' maternity care in hospitals come themselves to represent the state-supported source of expert knowledge, allegedly verified by evidence, about how best to feed babies (Murphy, 2004).

In sociological terms, this definition of choice, now institutionalised in the National Health Service, is important for the social construction of mothering. As Kukla notes, in the modern era our culture has tended to assume mothers' responsibility for 'nutrition, basic care, fostering appropriate self-care practices and protecting children from the risks and harms of everyday life' (Kukla, 2006, p 157). Contemporary health promotion in general has been analysed as having the effect of intensifying and further individualising this already taken-for-granted maternal responsibility (Nettleton, 1998). In the age of 'informed choice' the responsibility of mothers for ensuring the health of future generations is elevated further still, as the state does more and more to alert women to the dangers of making the 'uninformed choice'. In this form the rules for infant-feeding 'choices' are cemented and formalised.

VI. CONCLUSIONS

This chapter has sought to explain why infant-feeding decisions are experienced, by many mothers, as a 'measure of motherhood', whereby their autonomy in this area of family life is compromised. It has been argued that this experience reflects a context where formula feeding is culturally problematised as risky. The past decade in particular has, however, witnessed the development of interaction between culturally supported precepts which de-legitimise formula feeding and the more formal sphere of regulation. The imperative of health has turned 'Breast is Best' into a dominant aspect of policy, and law to some degree, and hence the state plays an important role in compromising decisional autonomy in infant feeding. The dynamic in place may suggest that the role of the law itself will become more significant in the near future.

Our final point concerns the outcomes of the process described above. Breastfeeding promotion currently sits upon the moral high ground. Yet it has outcomes which are negative. These include an increased psychological burden for individual mothers, in the form of guilt, disorientation and anxiety, associated especially (although not only) with infant feeding with formula milk. Further the current context may have divisive consequences for informal networks. An outcome identified anecdotally, and in research studies, is that it is encouraging tension between mothers as maternal identity becomes more and more bound up with decisions mothers make about infant feeding (Lee, 2007a). Paradoxically while the ideology of intensive mothering emerges as a response to the perception that the social fabric is disintegrating, this outcome suggests it may make the situation worse, encouraging strains and tensions in the informal networks on which vibrant, dynamic communities are built.

BIBLIOGRAPHY

Armstrong E (2003) *Conceiving Risk, Bearing Responsibility*, John Hopkins University Press, Baltimore, MD, and London.
Arendell T (2000) 'Conceiving and investigating motherhood: the decade's scholarship'. *Journal of Marriage and the Family* 62, 1192–207.
Blum LM (1999) *At the Breast, Ideologies of Breastfeeding and Motherhood in the Contemporary United States*, Beacon Press, Boston, MA.
Burrows R, Nettleton S, Bunton R (1995) 'Sociology and health promotion: health, risk and consumption under late modernism' in *The Sociology of Health Promotion* (Eds, Bunton R, Nettleton S, Burrows R), Routledge, London and New York, pp 1–9.
Carter P (1995) *Feminism, Breasts and Breast-feeding*, Macmillan, Basingstoke.
Department for Communities and Local Government (2007) *Discrimination Law Review. A Framework for Fairness: Proposals for a Single Equality Bill for*

Great Britain, Department for Education and Skills, Department of Trade and Industry, Department for Work and Pensions, Ministry of Justice, Department for Communities and Local Government, London.

Department of Health (2004a) *National Service Framework for Children, Young People and Maternity Services*, Department of Health, London.

—— (2004b) *Choosing Health*, Department of Health, London.

—— (2005a) *Maternal and Infant Nutrition*. http://www.dh.gov.uk/PolicyAnd Guidance/HealthAndSocialCareTopics/MaternalAndInfantNutrition/fs/en (accessed 7 December 2005).

—— (2005b) *Choosing a Better Diet*, Department of Health, London.

—— (2005c) *National Breastfeeding Awareness Week*. http://www.dh.gov.uk/ PolicyAndGuidance/HealthAndSocialCareTopics/MaternalAndInfantNutrition/ fs/en (accessed 7 December 2005).

Der G, Batty DG, Dreay I (2006) 'Effect of breast feeding on intelligence in children: prospective study, sibling pairs analysis, and meta-analysis'. *British Medical Journal* 333, 945–8.

Eyer D (1992) *Mother–Infant Bonding: A Scientific Fiction*, Yale University Press, New Haven, CT, and London.

Fitzpatrick M (2001) *The Tyranny of Health*, Routledge, London and New York.

Furedi F (2001) *Paranoid Parenting*, Penguin, London.

Hausman BL (2003) *Mother's Milk: Breastfeeding Controversies in American Culture*, Routledge, London.

Hays S (1996) *The Cultural Contradictions of Motherhood*, Yale University Press, New Haven, CT, and London.

Hopkinson C (2007) 'It's not that easy, Jemima'. *The Daily Telegraph*, 21 May, p 27.

HREA (Human Rights Education Association) *Study Guides: Food and Water*. http://www.hrea.org/learn/guides/food.html (accessed 9 July 2007).

Jackson E (2005) *Regulating Reproduction: Law, Technology and Autonomy*, Hart Publishing, Oxford.

Jenkins P (1992) *Intimate Enemies, Moral Panics in Contemporary Great Britain*, Aldine de Gruyter, New York.

Knaak S (2005) 'Breast-feeding, bottle-feeding and Dr Spock: The shifting context of choice'. *Canadian Review of Sociology and Anthropology* 42, 197–216.

—— (2006) 'The problem with breastfeeding discourse'. *Canadian Journal of Public Health* 97, 412–14.

Kukla R (2005) *Mass Hysteria, Medicine, Culture and Women's Bodies*, Roman and Littlefield, New York.

—— (2006) 'Ethics and ideology in breastfeeding advocacy campaigns'. *Hypatia* 21, 157–80.

—— (2007) 'Philosophical and sociological perspective in intensive mothering: measuring motherhood'. Paper presented at Monitoring Parents: Childrearing in the Age of 'Intensive Parenting' conference, University of Kent, 21–22 May. Abstract available at www.parentingculturestudies.org.

Lee E (2007a) 'Health, motherhood and morality: women's experiences of infant feeding with formula milk in the early weeks'. *Sociology of Health and Illness* 29, 1–16.

—— (2007b) 'Infant feeding in risk society'. *Health, Risk and Society* 9, 295–309.

—— (2007c) 'Living with risk in the age of "intensive motherhood": maternal identity and infant feeding'. *Health, Risk and Society* 10(5), 476–7.

LLL GB (La Leche League Great Britain). 'La Leche League Philosophy'. www .laleche.org.uk (accessed 4 July 2007).

Lupton D (1999) 'Risk and the ontology of pregnant embodiement' in *Risk and Sociocultural Theory: New Directions and Perspectives* (Ed, Lupton D) Cambridge University Press, Cambridge, pp 59–85.

Mahabal KB (2004) 'Infants have a right to be breastfed'. *Healthcare Management Express*, 1—15 January, http://www.expresshealthcaremgmt.com/20040115/ humanrights01.shtml (accessed 9 July 2007).

Michels KB, Willett WC, Graubard BI, Vaidya RL, Cantwell MM, Sansbury LB, Forman MR (2007) 'A longitudinal study of infant feeding and obesity throughout life course'. *International Journal of Obesity* 31, 1078–85.

Murphy E (1999) '"Breast is best": infant feeding decisions and maternal deviance'. *Sociology of Health and Illness* 21, 187–208.

—— (2003) 'Expertise and forms of knowledge in the government of families'. *Sociological Review* 51, 433–62.

—— (2004) 'Risk, maternal ideologies, and infant feeding' in *A Sociology of Food and Nutrition* (Eds Germov J & Williams, L) Oxford University Press, Oxford, pp 200–19.

NCT (National Childbirth Trust). 'History of the NCT'. http://www.nct.org.uk/ about/history (accessed 9 July 2007).

Nettleton S (2006) *The Sociology of Health and Illness*, Polity Press, Cambridge.

—— (1998) 'Women and the new paradigm of health and medicine'. *Critical Social Policy* 16, 33–53.

ONS (Office for National Statistics) (2007) *Infant Feeding Survey 2005*, ONS, London.

Reece H (2005) 'From parental responsibility to parenting responsibility'. *Current Legal Issues* 8, 459–83.

Saadeh R & Akre J (1996) 'Ten steps to successful breast feeding: a summary of the rationale and scientific evidence'. *Birth* 23, 154–60.

Schmeid V & Lupton D (2001) 'Blurring the boundaries: breastfeeding and maternal subjectivity'. *Sociology of Health and Illness* 23, 234–50.

Stanway P (1978) *Breast is Best*, Pan Books, London.

Thomas P (2006) 'Suck on this'. *The Ecologist*, www.theecologist.co.uk (April). (accessed 5 May 2007).

UNICEF (2005) UNICEF UK Baby Friendly Initiative. www.babyfriendly.org.uk (accessed 7 December 2005).

Van Esterick P (1989) *Beyond the Breast–Bottle Controversy*, Rutgers University Press, New Brunswick, NJ.

Wall G (2001) 'Moral constructions of motherhood in breastfeeding discourse'. *Gender and Society* 15, 592–610.

Ward J DeJ (2000) *La Leche League: At the Crossroads of Medicine, Feminism, and Religion*, University of North Carolina Press, Chapel Hill & London.

Weiner LY (1994) 'Reconstructing motherhood: the La Leche League in post war America'. *Journal of American History* 80, 1357–81.

WHO (World Health Organization)/UNICEF (1990) Innocenti Declaration on the Protection, Promotion and Support of Breastfeeding. www.unicef.org/programme/breastfeeding/innocenti.htm (accessed 5 May 2007).

Wolf, J (2007) 'Is breast really best? Risk and total motherhood in the National Breastfeeding Awareness Campaign'. *Journal of Health Politics, Policy and* Law 32, 595–636.

Wray, J (2005) 'Choice: fad or fashion?' *The Practising Midwife* 8, 4–5.

6

Legal Representation and Parental Autonomy

The Work of the English Family Bar in Contact Cases

MAVIS MACLEAN AND JOHN EEKELAAR

I. INTRODUCTION

THIS VOLUME ADDRESSES the complex and demanding question of how far individual autonomy is, or should be, limited by state regulation. The extent and character of such regulation becomes visible in the family setting mainly when there is conflict that cannot be resolved by the parties themselves or with informal help. In this chapter we look at disputes between parents about how their children will maintain a relationship with a non-resident parent, and how these matters are managed within the justice system in England and Wales.

The paramount consideration for any court in deciding a matter relating to the care and upbringing of a child is the 'welfare' of that child (Children Act 1989, section 1). But invariably, parents who are in conflict both believe that they are acting in their child's best interests. Furthermore, each is likely to seek to maintain their individual autonomy and to oppose any threat to that freedom posed by the actions of the other. It is then hard for the law to allow complete autonomy to two people in dispute who are party to a joint enterprise—parenting—when not only are they in conflict, but the interests of the child and the state have also to be taken into account. Nevertheless, although complete autonomy for each parent cannot be achieved, the system can seek a resolution that gives as much scope as possible to the autonomy of each, consistent with protecting the interests of all other parties concerned. It will be our contention that, in conflicted cases, the work of the family barrister is central to achieving that objective.

Family law in England and Wales is characterised by flexibility, discretion and concern for the future welfare of children. This fluidity makes possible individually tailored outcomes but has given rise to criticism about the failure of law to provide certainty for those involved in family disputes. There have been calls for more openness and accountability, and new ways of managing family disputes outside the adversarial court system, away from advocacy and adjudication, have emerged. Family courts are now characterised as a service of last resort. The preference is for settlement to be reached through negotiation and mediation, with individuals empowered to make their own decisions and to acquire the necessary skills to manage conflict in the future. But this emphasis on enhancing autonomy in decision-making is always constrained by the overriding need to protect the vulnerable.

This chapter presents some early findings from our study of the work of the Family Bar in England. Our research explores how families experience regulation, and demonstrates the contribution made by their legal representatives in their search for freedom from interference in parents' relationships with their children, parental autonomy. We challenge the view that lawyers and courts inevitably limit the freedom of those they serve and ask whether they may, on the contrary, be empowering the vulnerable to enjoy the entitlements the law gives them as far as is consistent with the entitlements of others.

II. THE POLICY LANDSCAPE AND ATTENDANT MYTHS

The dissatisfaction amongst policy makers with the part played by lawyers in family matters in our adversarial system and the search for new forms of professional intervention to support men and women through divorce and separation are well documented. Philip Lewis (2000) has shown how lawyers are described in government documents as standing between parties, making negotiation more difficult, while courts are held to disempower the individuals who come before them through the process of adjudication. At the same time, however, public demand for the help of family lawyers remains high (see Genn, 1999; Pleasence, 2006). The new or alternative dispute resolution services, which emphasise the autonomy of the individual and the desirability of enabling conflicted couples to reach their own agreements, have been slow to attract clients. These alternative interventions are beginning to be more rigorously researched and evaluated (see Davis *et al*, 1999; Genn, 2007). But the work of the traditional legal profession—that is, the work to which alternative dispute resolution (ADR) is the alternative—has received little recent attention. There is increasing evidence (Enterkin & Sefton, 2006) that those using mediation may not understand the process, may feel pressured to agree and may have no access to appeal or enforcement of the agreement reached.

What, then, do men and women seek from the traditional forms of intervention? Building on our previous research on the work of family solicitors

(Eekelaar *et al,* 2000), data from the OXFLAP study of the work of the English Family Bar (which looked at the work done and the skills employed by family barristers) suggests that, in contact cases, parents are finding in the justice system the means to promote their individual parental autonomy. Further, the framework of the Children Act (1989) enables them to be supported in seeking to pursue what they believe to be in the best interests of their child.

Family lawyers are no more popular with policy makers (both politicians and officials) in other common law jurisdictions (Canada Department of Justice, 2003; Rhoades, 2007) than they are in England and Wales. Moreover, the lack of trust between a British government department and the professionals providing the service for which it has responsibility is not confined to the area of law. The Department of Health takes a poor view of doctors, and the Department for Education and Skills is highly critical of teachers. This lack of trust is not surprising, given the tendency of the professionals who provide a service to be critical of departmental policy ideas which often involve changes in established practices, increased bureaucracy and demands for harder work combined with cuts in resources. But the Ministry of Justice (MoJ) in London (formerly the Department of Constitutional Affairs (DCA) and, before that, the Lord Chancellor's Department (LCD)) seems particularly hostile towards the role of the legal profession with respect to family matters (see Lewis, 2000), and has put a great deal of effort into seeking alternatives. Government has continued to support alternative methods of dispute resolution, usually described as mediation, despite the hesitation of consumers in using the services, and despite continuing public commitment to the legal profession. The use of mediation by divorcing separating couples remains below 15% (see Maclean, 2004), and Genn (1999) found that 80% used solicitors, and that 80% of those who did found them helpful.

The MoJ regards the law and the courts as the service of last resort for those who have been unable to resolve their family disputes in any other way, such as through the advice of family and friends, advice services or dispute resolution agencies. The family justice system has recently come under criticism from the Constitutional Affairs Select Committee, which expressed concern about the lack of transparency in the family courts in England and Wales (see CASC, 2005) This 'secrecy' has been construed, on the one hand, by fathers' groups as concealing poor decision-making and bias in favour of women, and, on the other hand, by women's groups as indicating a lack of willingness to confront issues of safety. On the subject of continuing parenting, policy papers refer to the relative satisfaction of parents who have made arrangements privately for ongoing contact with their children without the help of the courts, and compare this with the high levels of dissatisfaction among those who have been to court to seek an order (DCA and DfES, 2004). The possibility of a reverse direction of causality, namely, that it is unhappy, angry people who go to court, rather than that it is the courts that make people angry and unhappy, is seldom discussed (Trinder & Kettle, 2007).

Research suggests that the small group of parents who go to court about contact after separation are seriously distressed (see Buchanan *et al*, 2001) and have exhausted all other sources of help. Children involved in conflicted contact cases have been found to experience levels of distress comparable with those of children in care and protection cases. When we use the term 'alternative dispute resolution', we might wish to consider the possibility that courts are not necessarily primarily an unwelcome alternative to the empowering interventions of ADR/mediation, but may be a valuable alternative to potential domination of the weaker party, and better able to take care of the best interests of the most vulnerable parties involved, the children.

The lawyers who work in the courts, the family solicitors and barristers, are presented in policy documents (for example, LCD, 1995) as obstructing face-to-face negotiation and agreement between parties, and tend to be attributed with the responsibility for making disputes aggravated and protracted, although the study commissioned by the DCA from Philip Lewis (2000) found little empirical support for these claims. The high level of public expenditure on family legal aid, now under review, and concerns about the regulation of the profession, have also contributed to the unpopularity of the legal profession in policy circles.

III. THE SEARCH FOR DATA

This anti family lawyer policy came to a head some years ago during the preparation of the Family Law Act (1996) (LCD, 1995), which sought to replace lawyers with mediators as the primary mode of professional intervention in divorce.

At that time, we became concerned about the lack of data available to support this view. We therefore set out to examine the divorce work of family lawyers, beginning with the solicitors who are the first point of contact for clients (Eekelaar *et al*, 2000). We found a profession which could be divided into three groups according to the type of client: those doing big money cases, involving large trusts and tax matters; those doing legal aid work with publicly funded clients on low incomes with more debt than property to sort out; and those working with middle-income clients struggling to find a way of organising two households instead of one without extra resources. But although the work settings looked different, the same tasks and skills could be clearly seen. We used and added to the typology for legal work developed by Lewis and Abel (1995). We observed solicitors endlessly collecting, checking and updating information, sorting a mass of conflicting and changing detail into a narrative which would be meaningful to a court. But, at the same time, they worked hard to avoid going to court. They were committed to achieving settlement, which they perceived to be usually better for their clients, and which was in line with their financial incentives, as court actions impeded their ability to increase throughput of cases in the firm which was the key to maintaining a regular income.

As the client's story was pieced together and issues giving rise to conflict identified, the solicitors were negotiating with their clients to reach a position which a court would find acceptable. When this stage was reached, the solicitor would be ready to talk to the solicitor for the other party, who had been engaged in a similar exercise, so that with the adoption of two reasonable positions, a settlement should be reachable. Adjudication was rare. The culture of settlement was all-pervasive. Cases where adjudication was needed were often those where one side was unrepresented or poorly represented, and there was no way of bringing the party into a negotiable position. This has been confirmed by research in New Zealand (Barwick *et al*, 2003). Partly because solicitors in Britain were so averse to going to court, this earlier work did not enable us to comment on the work of the barristers, the advocates who appear in court. We are therefore (again with gratitude for the support of the Nuffield Foundation) carrying out a study of the Family Bar. In this chapter we present some preliminary findings.

IV. A METHODOLOGY FOR STUDYING THE FAMILY BAR

Our methodology follows the design developed for the solicitor study. We began by collecting all available statistical data on the barrister workforce, including age, gender, geographical distribution and specialisation. We then spent 20 days with individual barristers from different parts of the country, at different levels of seniority and with different special interests in order to observe the tasks carried out and skills employed. The barristers were encouraged to help us by an editorial in the Family Law Bar Association Bulletin (*Family Affairs*, Winter 2006) and were contacted mainly through this request. This is a purposive sample, and may be biased towards those who are confident about their work, or concerned about the public image of the profession. To reach a more representative sample and to understand the contribution of a barrister to a particular case we have approached members of the Bar Council Directory who are listed as doing family work (excluding family trusts and probate).

Unlike the solicitor, who is the first point of contact for the client and stays with the case throughout its course, the barrister is instructed by the solicitor when a court hearing appears unavoidable. The barrister will then work to a particular hearing, and may not be involved with the case throughout its course. The barrister comes in to do a specific task, and then returns the papers to the solicitor who may or may not need to call on the barrister again. To get a picture of this 'job' we have secured a response from 38 barristers describing themselves as doing family work in the General Bar Council Directory and collected information from them about their most recent hearing (even if the case was settled and did not in fact have a day in court). We asked what kind of case it was (divorce finance, child contact and residence, or child protection), whom they represented, what work was done (for example, reading papers, attendance in court, preparing written arguments, meetings with clients and solicitors), the time spent and fee charged and whether this had been paid and by whom. This information proved extraordinarily difficult to obtain, mainly due to the unpredictability of the barristers' diaries (cases are settled or postponed, another taken, and while in court the barrister is unavailable). However, we have been greatly helped by research assistance from a former solicitor, who is skilled in tracking down members of the bar, and on analysing the data we are finding a wide range of interventions and remuneration.

V. WHAT DID WE FIND?

A. The Workforce

The lack of clear and accessible information about the Family Bar has contributed to the pervasive stereotype of family barristers as articulate, affluent 'fat cats', usually male. This has been challenged by some of the fathers' rights groups, who argue that the profession is dominated by feminist man-haters (CASC, 2005, see evidence 49, Coe). Using the Bar Council Directory we found just over 200 sets of chambers where family work is carried out. These were largely concentrated in London (126 sets), and in a small area within London (47 fall within the single postcode area surrounding the Inns of Court, EC4) although some of these chambers have branches outside London. The most common size of 'firm' is between 20 and 50 barristers, although we found one set in Birmingham with 150 barristers 'hot-desking' in a modern paper-free building, a long way from the leather armchairs and dusty legal volumes traditionally associated with the bar.

Using data collected by the Family Law Bar Association in 2002 we found that half of the 1,600 barristers specialising in family work were women, as compared with a third of the bar as a whole (14,350). This shows gender balance but hardly a feminist conspiracy. Just under 5% of family barristers were at the most senior level, Queen's Counsel, and over 20% of the total had been called to the bar and begun work over 20 years ago. A specialist in family law was defined as someone who spends at least 50% of their time on family work. Of these specialists, 60% were general family lawyers but 14% specialised in the financial aspects of divorce and 24% specialised in child protection cases. There was also a small group who specialised in combining family work with welfare or housing expertise, and immigration work. This group represents an interesting response to the need of many people for help with a cluster of problems (see Moorhead & Robinson, 2006; Pleasence, 2006) such as a mental health problem leading to unemployment, debt, housing problems and relationship breakdown.

There is concern in the profession about the lack of young recruits, and this is attributed to the recent and forthcoming changes to legal aid funding which will make it difficult for young barristers to begin a career in family work, especially child protection (see LCD, 1998; DCA and LSC, 2006). Legal aid expenditure doubled between 1990 and 1995, reaching a total of £1.4 billion in 1995/96. With a cap on the total budget it became difficult to prevent expenditure on criminal defence work (where the Human Rights Act (1998) requires proper representation for someone at risk of losing their liberty) from eating into family law provision.

The policy response of trying to privatise family disputes (apart from domestic violence and child protection proceedings) by diverting cases to mediation, which was expected to be cheaper and better, has not been successful. The bar has become demoralised. In the 2002 Survey, 75% reported that their morale was low and 20% were contemplating giving up family work. There is particular concern about child protection cases, where the interests of vulnerable children are at stake. Under the new graduated fee scheme in 2002, 20% of barristers were being paid less than £20 per hour. Although there are arguments for making the division of assets after separation or divorce a private responsibility, it is hard to justify withdrawing support for any service which seeks to do what is best for children in need of care or protection.

B. Tasks and Skills in Contact Work

(i) What do Family Barristers do?

The barrister's clerk will advise the barrister of an approach from a solicitor and then book the case into the electronic diary. The clerk takes responsibility for negotiating the fee and collecting payment.

Papers on the case will be sent by the instructing solicitor, often not arriving until late on the day before a court hearing, often incomplete, and without page numbers. Pagination might seem a minor irritation, but in practice it is a major concern as it affects the ability of counsel to direct the judge to a particular point, or refute a claim by the other side during a hearing. Papers are in heavy lever-arch files, ranging from 3 to sometimes 30 per case, to be carried by the barrister to the hearing. Barristers type every word they produce, are responsible for all travel arrangements, and their own tax liability. They are basically self-employed lone operators sharing offices with a group with whom they are in competition for work.

The barrister may speak to the solicitor on the phone, but not to the client, or may hold a 'con' (shorthand for 'conference'), a meeting with the client and solicitor, usually at 5 pm after courts rise at 4.30 pm. He or she will not see a client alone except at court if there is no attending solicitor.

Perusing documents in divorce cases is almost an accounting or auditing exercise. The barrister will be looking for figures which fail to add up, looking for missing information, considering pursuing discovery of documents, finding out about house prices in relevant areas, and access to schools. In child protection cases, the reading is mainly of statements and reports, which are almost always delivered late, (the researcher saw 40 pages received by email at midnight for a 10 am hearing), the expert reports are often medical and technical, and social work reports are lengthy and sometimes repetitive.

After reading the papers in chambers or at home, the barrister will draft a skeleton argument, setting out a chronology and identifying key issues. This may be sent to the other side or to the judge in advance or handed up to the bench at the hearing. On the day of the hearing, the barrister may have been up till the early hours of the morning preparing his or her case; he or she will then travel to the court bringing the papers. He or she then meets the client, often for the first time, by calling out the name in the crowded court corridor. The barrister has to form an instant rapport, gain trust and confidence, and provide emotional support throughout the day, sometimes but not always supported by a solicitor. He or she may need to clarify some points with the client, and then begin to negotiate with the other side. At the same time he or she may be negotiating with the judge through the clerk for extra negotiating time. The judge has a list of cases to get through and has to be convinced that altering the timetable will be productive. Everyone is seeking settlement rather than adjudication.

Court time is very precious. Courts can be very crowded and there are few rooms for meetings. Negotiation and final preparation often take place in crowded corridors, sometimes shared with a criminal court. On arrival the barrister takes the papers out of the case on wheels, puts his or her coat inside the case, and hunts for a room. If he or she fails to find one he or she becomes a mobile and self-sufficient workstation.

The main task of the day for the barrister is client and judge management, grounded in close attention to the detail in the papers, which leads to negotiation and settlement. All those with whom he or she deals are highly stressed. The only friendly face is likely to be the barrister for the other side who will be a colleague or friend, and the only person in court who understands what the day is like ... lack of sleep, no food, no personal space—physical or emotional. And at the end of the day he or she faces the final authority of the judge to make decisions, which he or she may find satisfying or profoundly unhelpful. In the lower courts (family proceedings courts staffed by lay magistrates with legal advisers) the barrister is subject to the decisions of people who know far less about family law then he or she does.

When the court rises, the barrister will need to explain to the client what has happened, before travelling back to chambers where a new set of papers will probably have just been delivered.

(ii) What Skills and Qualities does a Barrister Need?

These are: charm, quick intelligence and articulacy, but above all, stamina! Like an actor, counsel is only as good as his or her last performance. Very little of the performance takes place in the courtroom in the form of legal argument, and even when he or she is in court, a good part of the time is spent on administrative matters and case management. Nevertheless, as soon as he or she stands up in court, counsel is exposed to the arguments of the other side and subject to the authority of the judge. All barristers have 'court nerves' even though only parts of the family jurisdiction resemble a trial where a finding of fact is needed, such as in domestic violence or child protection hearings, where there may be examination and cross-examination of witnesses. The barrister basically deals with the people whom the solicitors have been unable to bring to settlement; that is, the very angry or distressed.

The workload is heavy and unpredictable. Even the experience of shadowing was exhausting For example, the researcher received text messages at 11 pm saying: 'we are not in Portsmouth at 10 am tomorrow but Coventry at 9 am'. The inability to plan ahead puts pressure on the barrister's own family life. A successful mid-career barrister doing big money cases said: 'I can't ever say to my wife, yes, I can come out to dinner ... a case might settle, it might overrun ... and a day in court is like taking an exam every day ... but you have the think of the questions as well as the answers.'

VI. WHAT CONTRIBUTION DO FAMILY BARRISTERS MAKE TO CLIENT WELFARE IN CONTACT CASES?

In the following section we give an example of the work done by two barristers on a single day in two contact cases, both acting for mothers. We observed them doing the same tasks, using the same skills, and moving distressed and angry clients towards a way out of their unhappy situation. But while revealing the commonality of the tasks done and skills employed, the very different circumstances raise questions about why men and women in contact disputes sought the help of the court. What did they expect from the court? What model of the family justice system did we observe in action? Were we seeing top-down dispute resolution—adjudication—or professional dispute management by legal advisers in the shadow of adjudication? Were these perhaps cases of professional and institutional support for a way of coping with problems already chosen and defined by the client? The evidence points to the last. In both these cases all the parties had agreed that contact should continue; the dispute was limited to how this should happen. And all those represented believed that only the court could help them to be responsible parents, and relied on their counsel to bring this about. They were not so much seeking dispute resolution but rather actively using the court to achieve the freedom to do what they thought was best for their child; that is, seeking parental autonomy through the justice system.

Case 1—Court as a Safe Place: Mary, Using the Court to Manage her Ex-husband, with her Barrister as Enabler/Facilitator

In this case we observed a barrister in his late thirties, specialising in work with children, practising in a town in the South West. In this case, he had been involved with the family for about a year, representing the mother, Mary, and was paid from public funds (legal aid). The parents had separated over a year ago, and had a three-year-old son who lived with his mother, and saw his father at weekends in a contact centre in the presence of his mother's sister. The father was seeking unsupervised contact, and overnight contact. Mary wanted the child to see his father, and indeed had an older child by a previous partner who had always spent weekends with his dad. But the three-year-old had a mild speech disorder that made it difficult for him to express himself, and if frustrated, he tended to have a tantrum. Mary believed that the father, who also had 'a short fuse', overreacted to this kind of behaviour, and she was afraid that the resulting confrontations would damage the boy's confidence and development. Mary wanted her ex-husband to manage the boy better and had been resisting his demands for unsupervised contact. But both parents wanted the child to have a worthwhile long-term relationship with both parents.

We arrived at court at 9.30 am and spent the day until 2 pm in the court building, moving from small meeting room to coffee bar to waiting area, in constant negotiation and persuasion before going in to see the judge. The barrister's view was that a judge would order unsupervised contact at some stage and possibly now. Therefore, his strategy was to persuade the other side to accept the need for some way of increasing the mother's confidence in the father's parenting ability, suggesting that a short parenting course would achieve this. He gently led the mother towards this view (fetching cups of tea for mum and her sister, sitting cross-legged on the floor, talking about his own children and the judge's child). He then persuaded the father's counsel to move away from a demand for immediate overnight access to agreeing that the father would take part in a parent education course, found a place on the course, and secured agreement from the organiser that a record of the father's attendance and development could be brought back to the court welfare officer (CAFCASS officer) for a report to be made to the court. His hardest task was persuading the hard-pressed CAFCASS officer to take on this responsibility. Following this there would be a hearing where the interim order would be finalised.

Counsel for the father was a member of the mother's barrister's chambers, and with support from the District Judge, who permitted a number of delays, he and his colleague dashed across the road to their chambers to type up an agreed form of words which was taken into the judge before he began his afternoon list, to be made into an order of the court by consent. No adjudication was required. The judge congratulated everyone on being so helpful. The barrister's ability to see the issues, identify his client's concerns and find a way both to gain her confidence and meet her needs within the parameters of what a court would decide if adjudication was reached, made this agreement possible. This all took place within the framework of the Children Act 1989, and everyone was united in seeking the best interests of the child. Mary was relieved that she had achieved what she wanted, that is, time for the child to develop, and a chance that the father's parenting skills would improve. She had the confidence to accept the proposals because of the forthcoming welfare report on father's progress, and the judge's assurance that she could come back to him if at any time she was not happy with the gradual move towards full unsupervised access. The court had in effect protected her parental autonomy.

What might have been the alternatives to a court hearing? Mary had previously seen a welfare officer, who had not offered this degree of support, and she had not wanted to see a mediator. The barrister's empathy and intelligence had relieved her anxiety in a way other professionals had failed to do. These personal qualities were combined with his use of the court, not to seek adjudication, but to ensure parental confidence and compliance with an agreement reached by the parties. The court also provided authority to ensure that the father went on the course and made progress. If he failed to make progress, the matter would be reopened. Very little judicial time or input had been required. The main activity was well-orchestrated bilateral negotiation with the client and welfare service, and then with the other side, who were also talking with the welfare officer. Nine such meetings took place in that half-day. The court provided a safe and efficient location for this flurry of activity, and the framework to inspire confidence and deliver an enforceable plan for action.

Case 2: Martha, Using the Court as a Power-base to Protect her Children, with the Barrister as a Reluctant Champion

This case also concerned a father's request for unsupervised contact, but this was being opposed on serious grounds by the mother, Martha, who alleged that the father had sexually abused the two boys, now aged four and six. The barrister was representing the mother and was publicly funded. In these proceedings, the role of the court is closer to the criminal model, in that the mother had asked for a finding of fact that the abuse had taken place, while the father sought the opposite finding. This case was, in its structure, a trial, with oral evidence being presented and examination and cross-examination of witnesses taking place before a judge who was then required to reach a 'verdict'.

Martha had been happily married to an older man, who was a loving and attentive father, at the time the incident allegedly occurred. She went upstairs to call her husband while he was putting the boys to bed, and she was convinced that when she saw him lying on the bed with them reading stories that he was touching them inappropriately. The police were called the next day, and the children interviewed by specialist child protection officers. As often with young children, it was difficult to piece together a reliable account, and during the months between the alleged incident and the court hearing it was argued by the father that the mother, with whom the children lived, had been influencing their evidence. Meanwhile, Martha was taking the children to see their father every weekend, but she was not willing to leave them alone with him.

Martha was very anxious and afraid of the court hearing, but determined to proceed. The barrister, however, spent a great deal of time trying to persuade her not to go ahead. He suggested that it would not be possible for a judge to make the finding she wanted on the basis of uncorroborated evidence, particularly in the light of the case *Re H and R* (1996) which established that the more unlikely an action appeared to be the greater the degree of proof was to be required. Furthermore, he argued that going ahead could make matters worse: the experience of giving evidence in court against her husband, and his evidence against her, would only inflame the hostility between them and make it even more difficult to manage a worthwhile ongoing relationship between father and sons, which she valued and wanted to continue. The barrister put forward all the arguments which those who are critical of the family justice system use, but to no avail. This mother believed that in some ways her husband was a good father. But she also believed that he had a specific problem and should not be left alone with the boys. She wanted the day in court, not because she expected a judgment in her favour, but because 'I owe it to my boys ... even if they don't say he did it this time he will never ever dare do it again'. For her, the only way she could think of to prevent further abuse was to bring it out into the open and have her husband face the accusations and be frightened off. She wanted to use the power of the court to protect her ability to bring up her children free from fear.

The barrister did his best to support her through an extremely distressing day, using his best arguments, but focusing always on the welfare of the children and the inadequacy rather than criminality of the father, and resisting any attempt to widen the area of dispute. It was a solemn and impressive process, and when written judgement was given the following week it was critical of the evidence and unable to make any finding of fact. Martha's strategy may well, however, have been effective. It is hard to see what else she could have done to protect her children according to her belief in what had happened, as neither police nor social services had been willing to take any action on the basis of her concerns.

VII. CONCLUDING OBSERVATIONS

What did these women seek from the justice system? What did the barristers do for them? In these two contact cases all four parents agreed that an ongoing relationship between children and both parents was their aim. Their disputes were limited to how that should be achieved. Both fathers sought relief from the controls over their access to their children, while both mothers sought to protect their children by maintaining the status quo. Both mothers had anxieties about the fathers' parenting abilities to the extent of being willing to go to court over the issue. The barristers who helped these mothers through the court experience shared the expectation that unsupervised contact would eventually be granted if the matter reached adjudication, but saw it as their task to provide the mothers with sufficient support and safeguards to be able to accept a move in that direction. Both were anxious to reach settlement or restrict the scope of the dispute. Although representing the mothers, both barristers worked within the overarching framework of the Children Act 1989, which states that in any matter concerning the care and upbringing of a child, the court must have as its paramount consideration the welfare of that child. It is this framework which helps those representing parents to work for the best interests of the child, and use the power of the court to provide support while a transition is made, or to discourage bad parenting in the future.

The mothers did not seek dispute resolution in the sense of a decision, or adjudication, on a single day. They were pursuing the freedom to raise their children without fear of harm from the other parent, and access to a way of enabling them to protect their children for the foreseeable future. Family law, despite the trial-like mode of the fact-finding procedure, looks to the future rather than the past. The court at present is the only source of clear authority backed up by sanctions. These parents were brought to the court by the demands of their former partners which they found unacceptable, but found a way, with the skilled support of their legal representatives, to resist them, and to achieve parental autonomy through the justice system.

Although ADR is widely held to promote individual autonomy and individual decision-making, it seems to us that legal representation too can be used to buttress freedom from interference in parenting and can do so not only at the point of decision-making in a dispute, but can provide safeguards for the future. Courts can provide not only resolution of the immediate dispute, but also the tools for at best avoiding or at least managing future difficulties. Whatever new professional interventions develop, it seems foolish to underestimate the power of the court to protect the vulnerable, or to undervalue the contribution of the Family Bar in supporting those who need this help. The observations reported here show how the court-based process is capable of, and can be essential to, providing a service which the 'alternative' procedures cannot provide.

It might be argued that the increasing dominance of the welfare discourse as opposed to the language of justice in family courts may be eroding the autonomy not only of the parties but also of their lawyers. But, as can be seen from our second case in particular, the barrister takes instructions from his or her client and attempts to follow them, even where he sees no chance of success or even any merit, within the confines of the law. This must remain the entitlement of each individual, if the law is to respect autonomy at all. Where statute as voted by the legislature, or precedent as established by the judiciary, sets a framework, the barrister will follow that path while seeking to achieve his or her client's goals. But in doing that, he or she will try to avoid conflict that is widely believed to be unnecessary and damaging. We should not forget, however, that in the end, in these areas of deep personal conflict, allowing people any degree of autonomy risks hurt and conflict. We cannot always blame the messenger.

BIBLIOGRAPHY

Barwick H, Gray A, Macky R (2003) *Characteristics Associated with Early Identification of Complex Family Court Cases*, Department of Courts, Wellington, New Zealand.

Buchanan A, Hunt J, Bretherton H, Bream V (2001) *Families in Conflict*, Policy Press, Bristol.

Canada Department of Justice (2003) *Managing Contact Difficulties*.

CASC (Constitutional Affairs Select Committee) (2005) *Family Justice: The Operation of the Family Courts*, 4th Report of 2004/5, vol 2, House of Commons, London.

Davis G, Bevan G, Dingwall R, Finch S, Fenn P *et al* (1999) 'Monitoring publicly funded mediation'. *Family Law* 29, 625.

DCA (Department for Constitutional Affairs) and DfES (Department for Education and Skills) (2004) *Parental Separation: Children's Needs and Parents' Responsibilities*, Cm 6273, Norwich, Stationery Office.

DCA and LSC (Legal Services Commission) (2006) *Legal Aid Reform: The Way Ahead*, Cm 6993, The Stationery Office, London.

Eekelaar J, Maclean M, Beinart S (2000) *Family Lawyers*, Hart Publishing, Oxford.

Enterkin J & Sefton M (2006) *An Evaluation of the Exeter Small Claims Mediation Scheme*, Research Report, Department for Constitutional Affairs, London.

Genn H (1999) *Paths to Justice*, Hart Publishing, Oxford.

—— (2007) *Court Referred and Court Related Mediation under Judicial Pressures*, Ministry of Justice, London.

Lewis P & Abel R (1995) *Lawyers in Society*, University of California Press, Los Angeles, CA.

Lewis P (2000) *Assumptions about Lawyers*, Research Report, Department for Constitutional Affairs, London.

LCD (Lord Chancellor's Department) (1995) *Looking to the Future: Mediation and the Grounds for Divorce*, Cm 2799, LCD, London.

—— (1998) *Striking the Balance: The Future of Legal Aid in England and Wales*, Cm 3305, LCD, London.

Maclean M (2004) *Together and Apart*, Joseph Rowntree Foundation, York.

Moorhead R & Robinson M (2006) *A Trouble Shared: Legal Problem Clustering in Solicitors and Advice Agencies*, Department for Constitutional Affairs, London.

Pleasence P (2006) *Causes of Action*, Legal Services Commission, London.

Rhoades H (2007) *Family Lawyers and Family Dispute Resolution Services*, University of Melbourne, Melbourne.

Trinder L & Kettle J (2007) *The Longer Term Outcome of In Court Conciliation*, Research Report, Ministry of Justice, London.

Legislation

Children Act 1989
Family Law Act 1996
Human Rights Act 1998

Cases

Re H and R [1996] AC 563.

7

Regulating Step-parenthood

JAN PRYOR

I. INTRODUCTION

T**O SPEND SOME** part of one's life living in a step-family household is to experience what is fast becoming a normative situation. Step-families are increasingly ubiquitous, not only statistically but also in terms of public and official acknowledgement. It is evident that they have always existed, and the main change between now and a hundred years ago is in the pathways by which they are formed. The word 'step' derives from 'stoep', an old English word that in turn is related to the word 'astieped', meaning bereaved. It is perhaps significant that still in some societies—notably Japan—there is not a word in the language for step-families (Nozawa, 2006). This may reflect a fundamental reluctance to acknowledge families that do not have biological or adoptive links. Alternatively, the lack of a distinguishing word for step-families may indicate a desire to regard the newly formed household as both legitimate and indistinguishable from its biologically based predecessor.

Step-families exemplify, perhaps to a greater extent than other family structures, the complexities of families in the twenty-first century. The variance and diversity they display may partially explain why the law has, internationally, dragged its feet in addressing the regulation of relationships within this family form. It is undoubtedly challenging for any legal system to develop laws to address every permutation that exists. Whatever the cause of this legal foot-dragging, perspectives on whether or not legal systems should involve themselves, and to what extent, in regulating the relationships in step-families, range from the frequent plaint that step-parents and their step-children are legal strangers, to calls for caution in deciding to intervene legally (Agell, 1993; Bainham, 2006). In fact, Bainham goes as far as to suggest that 'we should be vigorously defending the parental status of the divorced parent ... and not pretending that a stepparent is a parent' (Bainham, 1999).

There are, however, other possible explanations for the apparent reluctance to bring step-parent–step-child relationships into the ambit of the judiciary. First, step-families themselves may resist legal intervention in their social arrangements, given the frequently cited desire by such families to be 'just like normal families', and to be seen as being as similar as possible to first families.[1] Calls from families themselves for legal recognition of their relationships are not heard as frequently as those from lawyers and social scientists (Mason *et al*, 2002).

Conversely, it may be that step-parents and stepchildren suffer from 'status anxiety' (Bainham, 2006), and that step-parents want at least the choice whether or not to legitimise the status of their relationship. This wish is illustrated by the New Zealand case where lobbying by gay and lesbian advocates resulted in the passing of the Civil Union Act (2004). To date, a scant 6% of same-sex couples, with or without children, have chosen to have a civil union,[2] suggesting that while families want to be able to choose, they may not exercise the choice. We might also note that in the US, 50% of step-families are cohabiting families—the parents are not married to each other. This choice, or a failure to legitimise their relationship, may denote low commitment; alternatively it may indicate a perceived lack of relevance of the law for their relationships.

A second, oft-cited cause of the slowness of jurisdictions to enact laws relating to step-families is the perceived conservatism of law-makers, who see biological and adoptive relationships as proper and are reluctant to legitimise social parents (especially if the parents are not married). This privileging of biological links may be particularly evident in the US, where children have been removed from the long-term care they have known with social (step-)parents, to that of biological parents who were comparative strangers to them.

This position is reinforced by another concern: the likelihood that legitimising step-parenting relationships through adoption will jeopardise or displace the roles of a child's birth parents. Indeed, an arguably anachronistic aspect of adoption by a step-parent of his or her step-child in New Zealand is that the *resident* biological parent, as well as the non-resident biological parent, loses their legal parenthood status when the step-parent adopts. This means that the resident biological parent must in turn adopt his or her own child. (This is not the case in most other countries, however, where the rules have recently been modified with regard to the resident biological parent). In most jurisdictions, however, the legal rights and duties of the non-resident biological parent are terminated. Again, in

[1] In this chapter the term 'first families' will be used to denote those in which the parents are the biological or adoptive parents of the children who subsequently enter a step-family household.

[2] Figures calculated from New Zealand census reports, and data from Statistics New Zealand.

some countries grandparents (parents of the displaced parent) are allowed visiting rights (Sosson, 1993).

II. AUTONOMY AND REGULATION IN STEP-FAMILIES

It is somewhat incongruous to talk about autonomy in the step-parenting relationship, in a context that is clearly at variance with the concept of autonomy as a characteristic of an individual. Not only does this relationship involve two people of unequal power status; it is also embedded in a wider family context that includes people both within and outside the household. Herring's discussion (this volume) of relational autonomy, acknowledging that people make decisions in a social context that takes account of obligations to others, is much more relevant than a notion of individual autonomy.

More salient to this chapter, however, is the question of regulation and in particular the legitimisation of the step-parent–step-child relationship along with the associated rights and responsibilities. And, as in other instances of regulation, the legal legitimisation of this relationship has its proponents and its opponents.

In this chapter, arguments for and against legitimising the step-parenting relationship are discussed, and comparisons made amongst the ways that several countries attempt to regulate step-parenthood (or not). Children's rights and perspectives in regard to step-families are addressed, and the implications for step-parenthood regulation discussed.

III. THE REGULATION OF STEP-PARENTING

A. Why might Legal Recognition of the Step-parenting Relationship be Important?

Ambiguity of legal status is not confined to step-family relationships; it is apparent in several other family constellations including those formed through artificial reproductive technologies, cohabitation and adoption. Step-families represent a particularly high degree of complexity, including, as they often do, issues of social and biological parenthood, legal and de facto parental unions, same-sex and heterosexual unions, and the likelihood of fluidity given their comparatively high levels of instability. These factors render them especially challenging in regard to legitimisation of relationships. Nonetheless, there are several aspects of step-parenting that lead to a consideration of involving the law in some capacity.

(i) Day-to-day Decision-making

Step-parents are often involved in the day-to-day care of their step-children, especially if the children are young (Edwards *et al*, 1999; Mason *et al*, 2002). Yet unless they have some legal status, they do not have the authority to make simple authorisations such as permission for health checks, authority for school trips, and other issues that legal parents are able to address.

(ii) Inheritance

In the US, the UK, New Zealand and Australia step-children are not entitled to inherit from their step-parents (and vice versa) unless stipulated in wills. In situations of intestacy, if there is not a legal relationship between step-parent and step-child then step-children have no claim on step-parents' estates, in contrast to biological children and spouses.

(iii) Economic Support for Step-children

Some but not all countries enforce an obligation on step-parents to support their step-children. In both New Zealand and Canada step-parents can be declared liable. However, there are no guidelines for support should the marriage to the biological parent fail.

(iv) Continuation of the Relationship when the Partnership with the Child's Biological Parent Dissolves

The rights to apply for custody or visitation vary according to the country and to the legal status of the step-parent. In the US, for example, there is a three-step process involved in trying to obtain custody of a step-child, and the success of the application appears to depend to a large extent on judicial discretion (Hans, 2002). This is an obvious concern where long-established and significant relationships between step-parents and their step-children exist.

(v) Symbolic Meaning

The legalisation of the step-parenting relationship may, in many cases, confer a symbolic and emotional legitimacy that denotes (on the part of the step-parent) commitment to the child and his or her family. It may, too, confer a legal status and respectability that ameliorates the status anxiety described by Bainham (2006).

In all these respects, it can be argued that some form of legal structure might enable step-parents and their step-children to function more effectively than they do as legal strangers. Conversely, there are voices of caution. Bainham, for example, points out that the diversity in step-parenting relationships calls, at the least, for careful scrutiny of the extent to which a social parent is, in fact, parenting a child. He suggests that

> before concluding that a full legal status ought to be conferred on all those who can lay claim to be in familial relationships, there surely needs to be some investigation of whether there is *in fact* a functional equivalence between, for example, married and unmarried cohabitation or legal and social parenthood. (Bainham, 2006, p 50)

Moreover, the variation in step-parent–step-child relationships is enormous; a child may have been raised from infancy by a man who is not their biological parent, or the step-parent may be one of several partners of a mother who enter and leave the household. The dangers, then, of a 'one-size-fits-all' legal structure are apparent.

Bainham also argues that the fundamental aspects of legal parenthood include in particular the fact that legal parenthood makes the child a member of a family with all the appurtenances of that—for example, the law of succession, liability for child support, the right to object to a change of surname or removal from jurisdiction, an automatic right to go to court, and the presumption of contact. The concept of legal parenthood also emphasises (where it exists) a genetic connection that is increasingly being regarded as a right of the child, and as important to physical and emotional well-being.

It is, however, argued in regard to the UK (Edwards *et al*, 1999) and the US (Malia, 2008) that the law privileges the original families of children at the expense of step-families, by making it difficult for social parents to obtain legal recognition. In both countries this is underpinned by an emphasis on the continuing responsibility of biological parents to parent and to support their children after relationship dissolution. In the UK the Children Act (1989), Edwards and her colleagues argue, diffuses power across households by upholding parenting rights of non-resident parents. This is reinforced by the Child Support Act 1995, which imposes financial responsibilities on non-resident biological parents often without regard for the actual situations of the families involved. Legal adoption, however, which is available to step-parents in the UK and elsewhere, severs all ties with non-resident parents by removing their legal parenthood status. We can perhaps assume that step-parent adoption occurs in the majority of cases when the non-resident parent is dead or completely absent from the child's life. The diversity of situations in which children and their families live suggests that there will be some situations where the legal termination of the child–non-resident parent relationship is appropriate and many more where a continuing relationship of some kind is desirable.

In the US the parental rights doctrine upholds the fundamental right for 'fit' parents to make all decisions regarding their children. In order for the status quo to be changed, strict scrutiny is required before step-parents, for example, can successfully challenge these rights. The emphasis is on the abilities and rights of biological parents to make all decisions regarding their children, and interference by the state or other third parties is resisted as far as possible.

These two positions (emphasis on the rights and responsibilities of the biological parents versus the needs of step-families) reflect a pervasive conflict between the need for children to retain relationships with their original families, and the need for step-families to carry on their lives without undue interference (see Golombok, this volume, for a discussion of biological ties). In most countries the legal system is responsible for this because of the law's insistence that children can have only two legal parents (in the US, this is through the rule of parenthood as an exclusive status (Malia, 2008)). Adoption by a step-parent invariably terminates the child's relationships with at least one former legal parent (and as noted above, the resident biological parent may have to apply to adopt his or her own child at the same time as the step-parent).

This reflects the tension between the two positions Edwards *et al* (1999) describe as 'children need biological parents' versus 'children need social families' (p 80). As they point out, in first families these two needs are met simultaneously, with biological parents being also social parents; however, in step-families they are partially contradictory since both biological and social parenting is in place. Edwards *et al* point out that the law, at least in the UK, has been constructed in a 'top-down' manner that privileges biological parenthood.

The reality for most children who live in step-family households is that they have dual households, as ongoing contact with non-resident parents both is encouraged and has increased (Pryor, 2008), both in person and through other channels such as e-mail, telephone, and texting.

It is also increasingly acknowledged that children have a constitutional right to ongoing contact with their biological parents and that parents have right of contact (see Bainham, 2003, and later in this chapter for a discussion of children's rights). In many cases, ongoing contact with both parents after separation and divorce is demonstrably beneficial for children; it is something that they clearly want, and depending on the levels of involved parenting on the part of the non-resident parent, is linked with favourable outcomes (Amato & Gilbreth, 1999). Any legislation, then, that has the effect of diminishing or eliminating a child's relationship with his or her family of origin is arguably not to be encouraged. As Malia (2008) points out:

> The law faces the challenge of determining how it might honor a psychological attachment that may exist between a stepparent and a stepchild, while not denying the biological parents' constitutional and legal rights to their child.

In the following sections, the ways in which specific countries attempt (or not) to legitimise step-parenting relationships are described, and parallels and differences between them examined.

B. The (Non-legal) Status of Step-parents

Step-parents who have not sought or achieved any legal status in relation to their step-children hold very few rights or responsibilities. At the most basic level, they are not authorised to sign forms for children's day-to-day activities such as school trips or health checks. They have no power to make decisions in these areas on behalf of their step-children, and in many countries they are also not liable for providing financial support either during or after the marriage to the child's biological parent. Exceptions to this are in 17 states of the US where step-parents are obliged to support step-children financially (Funder, 1998; Hans, 2002), and in Australia (Funder, 1998), Holland (Sosson, 1993), New Zealand and Canada (Atkin, 2008). Step-parents do, however, hold the general responsibilities of any person caring for a child to ensure that they are properly cared for. As Sosson states,

> the stepparent ... does not legally have any powers over the child, even if, in actual fact, he or she plays a major role in the child's upbringing because they live under the same roof. Similarly, he or she has no legal responsibility for the child, this being fully assumed by the guardian parent. (Sosson, 1993, p 396)

Step-parents with no legitimised status have no rights of custody or access, or responsibilities of support, when a marriage ends (exceptions to this are in France and Switzerland, where step-parents can be granted visiting rights). This situation may disadvantage children severely if they have established a close affectional bond with their step-parents. Multiple transitions from one family structure to another increase the risk for poor psychological and emotional outcomes for children (Pryor & Rodgers, 2001); one of the reasons for this can be the loss of a significant relationship, which occurs if a beloved step-parent is unable to maintain contact.

There are, too, no rights of inheritance when step-parents and step-children do not have a legal relationship. Even when the step-parent's will stipulates that a step-child inherit from them, biological children may have a stronger claim. In France, in fact, step-parents face tax penalties if they leave their step-children a legacy (Mignot, 2008).

C. When Step-parents Become Legal Parents: Step-parent Adoption

Legal adoption by a step-parent is the most unambiguous way in which they can obtain full legal parenthood, and many adoptions in the US, the UK and New Zealand are step-family adoptions. However, legal adoption is not encouraged in either the UK or Australia (Bainham, personal communication; Parkinson, personal communication). Although traditional adoption severs legal ties with both biological parents, in some instances step-family adoption can avoid this in relation to resident biological parents (the step-parent's spouse). This is the case in the US, where the step-child adoption rule applies (Wendel, 2005), and in the UK where the Adoption and Children Act 2002 enables step-parents to adopt without terminating the legal status of the resident parent. In these cases, the non-resident parent must either consent to this adoption, or be declared absent or unfit. And in all cases, he or she loses a legal relationship with the child. Similarly, in some European countries full adoption does not nullify the rights of the resident parent, and may even allow visiting rights to extended family members such as grand-parents of the disenfranchised biological parent. In France, however, full or plenary adoption cannot take place if the child has any affiliation with the non-resident biological parent (Mignot, 2008), but there is the option of simple adoption. This creates a legal relationship between step-parent and step-child but leaves intact the relationships with both biological parents and their families. It also encompasses a maintenance obligation (*obligation alimentaire*). The non-resident biological parent, however, has a duty to support his or her child if the step-parent cannot.

It is apparent that many countries, albeit reluctantly, have acknowledged the complex realities of step-family life by modifying adoption statutes to allow continuing relationships to some degree with hitherto disenfranchised non-resident parents and their families. It is not clear why some take this further than others; it may be that Western countries in particular have been forced to acknowledge the situation for step-families by dint of the sheer numbers of parents divorcing and repartnering. This is some concession to the fact that in many cases children have important relationships with (usually) paternal extended family members, and the severance of these entails a loss for both parties. This concession may be insufficient for those scholars whose concern is for the preservation of genetic relationships (for example, Agell, 1993; Bainham, 2006). Indeed, one wonders about the extent to which a non-resident parent's family may be discouraged from contact when the step-parent is the legal parent in place of the biological father.

Agell notes that a consideration of adoption should hinge on the well-being of the child; in this regard, there is an absence of research examining children's views on step-parent adoption and of their well-being or otherwise in that situation. Agell notes, too, the relative instability of step-families. Given the irrevocability of adoption, a situation in which a second marriage ends might pose particularly incorrigible legal issues.

In contrast, Edwards and colleagues make the argument that in many instances preserving the non-resident parent–child relationship is not helpful for the stepamily household, suggesting that co-parenting across households 'can be regarded as desirable but unrealistic' (Edwards *et al*, 1999, p 98). In practice, there are many variations in the nature of the links children have with non-resident parents after divorce and step-family formation, and social science evidence suggests strongly that when a lone custodial parent repartners, the levels of contact between children and their non-resident parents do not change. Total absence of a relationship through death or disappearance might be seen as justification for a step-parent adoption that severs legal ties, although as Agell (1993) points out, in the long term this relationship might be susceptible to restoration. Increasingly, in fact, children do maintain relationships with non-resident parents and, challenging as it is, many step-families manage the combination of social and biological parenting across households, usually to the benefit of children. However, there is a clearly articulated need for some kind of legal relationship that confers strength and cohesion on step-families rather than leaving them in legal limbo.

D. Intermediate Positions: Diluted Legal Statuses

Several countries, and particularly the US, are actively addressing the challenge articulated by Malia (2008), to find ways of preserving biological parents' legal relationships with their children at the same time as recognising the importance of the psychological attachment between the step-parent and step-child. This is done, in the main, by developing legal relationships that fall short of full parental status yet fulfil the perceived need to legitimise the step-parent–step-child relationship.

(i) The United States

The existing avenue to some kind of legal parenthood for step-parents in the US is via de facto parenthood. De facto parents are defined as those who have voluntarily taken on the role of a biological parent in a child's life. It derives from a common law doctrine of *in loco parentis*, and is accompanied by the rights and duties of a parent. It is not legally conferred; rather, it is identified ex post facto, and determined by the step-parents' intent which, in turn, is not necessarily articulated or documented and may be inferred from the actions of the step-parent. De facto parenthood can be relinquished at the step-parent's discretion, and ceases upon the dissolution of the relationship with the child's custodial parent.

De facto parenthood can be seen as a partial relaxation of the exclusive parenting doctrine that holds in the US, declaring that children cannot have more than two parents. However, it does not stray too far into violating that imperative.

There have been, in the US, some significant proposals for alternative legal relationships between step-parents and step-children that go beyond this somewhat vague and post hoc recognition of step-parental status. Mason *et al* (2002) have called for a strengthening of the de facto parenting status to endow it with full rights and duties that might endure beyond the end of the marriage (for example, a de facto step-parent in this situation would have standing to apply for custody or access, *and* would be obligated to continue supporting the child for a certain length of time). De facto status would automatically be conferred at the time of marriage to the custodial parent, and might even be applicable to unmarried step-parents, although Mason *et al* suggest that given possible questions about the strength of commitment to the partner and child, an application process might be recommended in this situation.

Hans (2002) suggests a modification to the above proposal, which is dichotomous (where a step-parent either is or is not a de facto parent), that incorporates *degrees* of parental rights and responsibilities. These would be based on (a) the length of time the step-parent and step-child have lived together; (b) the child's age; (c) the nature of the child's relationship with the non-resident parent; and (d) the nature of the step-parent–resident parent relationship. The determination of degrees of legal relationship might be resource-intensive; however, it does go beyond the somewhat arbitrary acquisition of de facto status on marriage.

Another proposal for considering degrees of legal parenthood arises from the American Law Institute's 'Principles of the Law of Family Dissolution' (2002). As well as full legal parenthood (adoption), two further categories are suggested: parenting by estoppel, and a stronger form of de facto parenthood.

Parenthood by estoppel requires that the step-parent has lived with the step-child(ren) for at least two years. It also requires the agreement of both biological parents. The step-parent must have taken a parenting role for two years and accepted financial and other responsibilities for the child. In addition, a court must recognise that it is in the child's best interests that the step-parent has estoppel parental rights. Parenting by estoppel would also allow the step-parent to be eligible for custody of the child in the event of marriage breakdown.

De facto parenthood in its more rigorous form, according to the Principles, would also require a two-year period of co-residence but the consent of only one legal parent. The step-parent would also have had to assume at least half of the caretaking functions. At marital dissolution, he or she would be eligible for regular access, but not custody.

(ii) The United Kingdom

In the UK, step-parents (and others) can gain the status of parental responsibility. This is defined in the Children Act (1989), section 5(3)(i) as 'all the rights, duties, powers, responsibilities, and authority which by law a parent has in relation to a child and his property'. Parental responsibility must be preceded by the issuing of a residence order, and is conferred by order for a defined period of time. A person must have lived with a child for at least three years, before a residence order may be granted. Parental responsibility status enables the child to have legal relationships with three adults, and requires the permission only of the resident legal parent.

(iii) Australia and New Zealand

In these countries, step-parents can apply for a parenting order that confers parental responsibility. In New Zealand they can also be awarded guardianship of the child, and this remains in place until the child is 18 years old (unlike parental responsibility in the UK that can be more easily revoked) (Atkin, 2008). Guardianship is usually awarded by the court and this can happen without the consent of the non-resident parent. There is, however, a new procedure for appointment as guardian by agreement, without court involvement other than administration. It requires the agreement of both legal parents, and has a fairly minimal threshold for suitability. Step-parents must have shared parenting for a year, and have no convictions for involvement in domestic violence, child abuse or pornography. Also, they must not have been involved in proceedings under the Care of Children Act (2004), or former Acts. Watt (2006) has questioned the appropriateness of the informality of this procedure, arguing that it is open to abuse by being granted with insufficient scrutiny or input from children.

Most countries, then, have made some concessions and gestures towards the reality of the lives of step-family households, without jeopardising the relationships with non-resident biological parents and families, and without conferring full legal parenting status. These compromises vary in their implications for step-parents and their step-children. They also reflect the fact that children are increasingly likely to retain a relationship with both biological parents. They are, however, both piecemeal and non-specific about what responsibilities and rights a step-parent might have and, in the main, they fail to confer stability on that relationship.

IV. CHILDREN'S WISHES AND CHILDREN'S RIGHTS

A notable absence in the literature addressing legal issues around step-parenting is a consideration of children's perspectives. These tend to be subsumed under the well-being of the step-family as a whole. It is well established that children in step-families are at levels of risk for poor outcomes similar to those growing up in lone parent families (Pryor & Rodgers, 2001). Reasons for this are complex and not well understood, and it is equally true that many children in step-families thrive. Yet there is a considerable body of literature that bears on children's rights, and on their experiences of and perspectives on step-parents and non-resident parents.

A. Children's Rights

Children's rights are enshrined predominantly, but not only, in the United Nations Convention on the Rights of the Child, the substance of which is well known. (It remains notable that the US is one of only two countries that are not signatories to the Convention.) Relevant to this chapter, Article 9(3) of the Convention states:

> States parties shall respect the right of the child who is separated from one or both parents to maintain personal relationships and direct contact with both parents on a regular basis, except if it is contrary to the child's best interests.

The crux of the matter is the last phrase, which modifies the obligations of states to ensure that contact continues on a regular basis.

How might we decide whether or not ongoing contact with a non-resident parent, especially in a step-family situation, is in the child's best interests? It is possible, although resource-intensive, to make decisions on a case-by-case basis; fortunately, there is a body of social science research that provides evidence and some guidance when decisions of this nature are being made.

B. Children's Views of Non-resident Parents

There is a burgeoning literature that examines children's views of what constitutes a family, and it is not surprising to discover that they endorse a wide variety of family forms as 'real' families, given the diversity of families they are likely to experience. Of direct relevance to this chapter is the finding in numerous studies that children continue to regard their non-resident parents as members of their families. In one study in which children were given vignettes of groups of individuals and asked to decide whether or not they were families, 99% included a non-resident biological father as a family member (Rigg & Pryor, 2007). In a similar study involving adolescents, 63% included non-resident parents (Anyan & Pryor, 2002). In an Australian sample of 16- to 18-year-olds whose parents had separated, 91% included their non-resident parents in family sculptures (Funder, 1996).

In Canada, Gross (1987) examined the family typologies of children living in step-families. It was found that 33% included only biological parents as family members; while 28% included both biological and step-parents. Only 13% excluded non-resident parents and included step-parents. And in the studies asking children about families mentioned above, step-families were endorsed as 'real' families by 95% of 9- to 13-year-olds if the stepfamily had existed for 10 years and by 85% for new stepfamilies. Adolescents were less likely to endorse step-families as real families with 54% (Anyan & Pryor, 2002), perhaps because of their understanding of the complexities of step-family households in comparison with that of younger children. These findings suggest that children in step-families do not exclude non-resident parents, at the same time as they recognise step-families as 'real' families. They also demonstrate the diversity of children's views and, presumably, experiences.

It is also notable that, when asked what defines a family, the most frequent criterion mentioned is an affective one—families are people who love you (Anyan & Pryor, 2002; Rigg & Pryor, 2007). As one 10-year-old put it, 'Family is people who care for you and love you, and are there for you' (Rigg & Pryor, 2007, p 24). In the adolescent study, biological relationships were mentioned next most frequently, followed by cohabitation.

Children and adolescents, then, do not appear to discount non-resident biological parents in talking about families, and a substantive body of research also indicates that children want ongoing contact with non-resident parents when their parents separate. Loss of the day-to-day relationship with that parent is often cited as the worst aspect of their parents' separation (Pryor & Rodgers, 2001). Clearly there are exceptions to this, where a child has dim or no memories of living with their other parent because of their age at separation or the fact that their mother never lived with their father, or when the other parent is violent or abusive. In these cases the absence of a second biological parent in their lives can be positive or, at the least, not a loss.

C. Children's Views of Step-parents

The majority of children, and especially adolescents, view their step-parents as friends rather than parenting figures (Buchanan & Maccoby, 1996). This is especially true of adolescents, who are typically engaged in developing their own autonomy and relationships. Younger children find it easier, overall, to accept the step-parent as an involved parent carrying out discipline and monitoring roles. Young children, too, will have spent less time with their non-resident biological parent and so may not be so likely to see that parent as their 'real' parent. The onus, clearly, is on the resident biological parent to be the main parenting figure for their children in the step-family household with, ideally, the support of their partner, who takes the role of friend and supporter to their children.

In sum, social science evidence suggests that children whose parents separate want to retain a relationship with their non-resident parents, and include that person in their 'nominative' family (Finch, 2006). At the same time, children and adolescents regard step-families as 'real' families and are very likely to include step-parents *and* non-resident parents in their nominated families. They are less likely, however, to accept the step-parent as a parenting figure, and this is salient for our discussion of the legitimisation of that relationship.

D. Who Benefits Children Most—Step-parents, Non-resident Parents, or Both?

There is a large body of research that examines the potential benefits of relationships with non-resident parents for children, and the consensus is that contact itself, although often desirable, appears to confer little advantage. The *closeness* of the relationship is associated with child well-being, but the most salient factor is the extent to which the non-resident parent is actively involved in parenting (Amato & Gilbreth, 1999). Most studies, however, do not distinguish between children living in lone parent households and those where their resident biological parent has repartnered. We might expect that the involvement of another potential parenting figure in the child's life would reduce the level of contact and involvement of the non-resident parent, given the possibility of dilemmas for children between resident and non-resident parents of the same sex. Perhaps surprisingly, then, the available evidence suggests that when a step-family is formed, there is no reduction in the frequency or quality of contact between the child and the non-resident parent (Maclean & Eekelaar, 1997; Dunn *et al*, 2004; Flouri, 2006). In one study (Blackwell & Dawe, 2003), contact decreased if the mother had both repartnered *and* had another child, and another reported *increased* contact when the resident mother repartnered (Aquilino, 2006). If the non-resident parent repartners there is some indication, however, that contact reduces (Blackwell & Dawe, 2003), especially if the non-resident parent has further children. There is little overall support for the suggestion, then, that repartnering by parents reduces contact for children with their non-resident parents.

If we are concerned with children's well-being in step-families, it is important to know whether it is to their benefit or detriment to sustain relationships across households. White and Gilbreth (2001) suggest three possible models: an accumulation model in which both non-resident and step-parents contribute to the child's well-being; a substitution model where (usually) the relationship with the step-parent replaces the non-resident parent relationship; and a loss model where both non-resident parent and step-parent are irrelevant to the child's well-being. King (2006) has extended this to incorporate five possibilities:

(i) An additive model where closeness to both resident and non-resident parents contributes to child well-being (the same as White and Gilbreth's accumulative model);
(ii) A redundancy model in which it does not matter which parent is close to the child as long as one is;
(iii) Primacy of the biological parent, where closeness to the non-resident parent but not the step-parent is important;
(iv) Primacy of residence, where closeness to the step-parent matters but not closeness to the non-resident parent;
(v) Irrelevance—neither makes a contribution to well-being (similar to White and Gilbreth's loss model).

Six recent studies have addressed the question of the comparative contributions to children's well-being of the relationships with non-resident and step-parents. Dunn *et al* (2004) found evidence for the primacy of biology—step-parents in their study did not contribute to well-being, but contact with the non-resident parent did. Five others found evidence for the additive or accumulative model, where relationships with both step-parents and non-resident parents made contributions to outcomes for children (White & Gilbreth, 2001; Berg, 2003; Falci, 2006; King, 2006; Schenck *et al*, submitted).

In the Resilience in Stepfamilies study in New Zealand, we found that the quality of relationships with step-parents as reported by children was lower than with resident and non-resident biological parents (Pryor, 2008). We also found that if children reported feeling close to the step-parent, they were also likely to report feeling close to their non-resident parent—in other words children did not appear to trade one relationship for another. Importantly, we also found that relationships with non-resident parents and step-parents predicted *different* outcomes; closeness to step-parents was associated with a strong self-concept, and closeness to the non-resident parent was associated with fewer behaviour problems.

V. CONCLUDING THOUGHTS

The debate about the regulation of step-parenting relationships resides predominantly in the spheres of parental rights and family rights, with remarkably little attention given to the perspectives of children. The struggle to reconcile the law with the realities of step-families is considerably complicated by the diverse situations that step-families are in at any one time, as well as the fact that, like any families, but perhaps particularly so, their relationships change over time. It is relatively straightforward to make decisions about legalising the relationship when the non-resident parent has died or is permanently absent; beyond that, the appropriate degrees of legitimisation become far less clear.

The rights, views and perspectives of children give some guidance. Even when there is limited or no contact with their non-resident parent, children not only have a right to potential connection or re-connection in the future, they also, in the main, want that. In a study of adult children of divorce, for example, Laumann-Billings and Emery found that well-functioning college students still reported painful feelings of loss at not having their fathers in their lives (Laumann-Billings & Emery, 2002).

At the same time, in step-family households children need reassurance about the commitment and stability of the relationship with their step-parent. It is perhaps relevant that Buchanan and Maccoby (1996) found in their study of children after divorce that those whose parents were married to their step-parents were doing better emotionally and psychologically than those whose were not, and the authors suggested that the legal status of marriage conveyed some sense of commitment to the household by the step-parent. In the same way, a legal connection to the step-parent may convey the same message to step-children that he or she is committed to the child.

We might, too, ponder the implications of a child having four parenting figures in his or her life. Increasingly, children spend equal or nearly equal amounts of time in two households and it is entirely possible that both step-parents will seek a legal status with regard to them. In the best scenarios, multiple parents can only be an advantage for children since they have several adults committed to their well-being. The danger in this instance lies in the increased possibility of losing a relationship that has become significant for the child, as one or other parental marriage dissolves. Edwards *et al* (1999) also point out the potential problems in diluting parental responsibility across households.

The semi-legal statuses of parenthood described in the first section of this chapter, and put in place in many countries, go some way to providing a framework of commitment. Most, however, do not go sufficiently far in conferring stability and continuity on the relationship. The existing parental responsibility (the UK, Australia) and de facto (ex post facto, in the US) statuses are particularly perilous if the remarriage or repartnership ends. Guardianship in New Zealand goes a few steps further in being less easily revoked or relinquished. In this regard, Bainham (2006) has suggested that an irrevocable status that falls short of adoption might be considered. And parenthood by estoppel, proposed by the American Law Institute, goes some way to maintaining stability by giving a step-parent standing to apply for custody when a marriage ends.

An important consideration is how the step-parent status is perceived, by non-resident parents and their extended families, and step-parents and *their* extended families. Step-grandparents can and do form close relationships with step-grandchildren; they may, however, feel constrained from letting those relationships develop if they do not feel entitled to do so through some sort of formal recognition of their adult child's relationship with the step-children. Terminology might be an issue here; 'parental responsibility' whilst clumsy is unlikely to be threatening to non-resident parents and their families. It is, however, a somewhat cold and unappealing appellation for step-parents and step-children. A term is needed that conveys involvement and responsibility but not full parenthood. A simile for simple adoption might be worth consideration.

Another potentially negotiable aspect of this relationship is the degree of responsibility involved, with a great deal being appropriate for some situations and rather less for others. Is it possible to match levels of social parenting with degrees of legal responsibility? Problems with this include the changing nature of the parenting involvement by the step-parent with the length of time spent living with the child (likely to increase), and the age of the child (involvement is likely to decrease the older the child, especially at time of step-family formation). Nonetheless, it might be possible to assess appropriate degrees of parenting involvement in specific situations, and this would make possible more flexibility in conferring legal rights and responsibilities. The suggestions proposed by Hans (2002) might be helpful in this regard.

It is also evident that for many step-families, regulation of this relationship is neither beneficial nor desired. An optimal situation, and one that exists at least in part in some jurisdictions, is the *availability* of regulation (as with civil unions in New Zealand) without its imposition.

This chapter has documented the somewhat half-hearted efforts of jurisdictions to address the issues facing step-families who in many ways would benefit from legal recognition of the status of the step-parenting relationship. The efforts walk the thorn-strewn path of dilemmas and positions and, to date, have not developed ways of legitimising this relationship that cover all contingencies and situations. Of all those canvassed, an equivalent of the French model of simple adoption might be the most promising. However, it, and any other models developed, would benefit from taking heed of the body of evidence that documents children's perspectives on their families. In the end, it is their lives with which we are concerned. As one 15 year old boy in a recent interview said, 'Try to take into account the kids' views because the kids know what they want more than the parents do because they're them' (Gollop *et al*, 2000).

BIBLIOGRAPHY

Agell A (1993). 'Step-parenthood and biological parenthood: Competition or Co-operation?' in *Parenthood in Modern Society. Legal and Social Issues for the Twenty-first Century* (Eds, Eekelaar JS & Dortrecht P) Martinus Nijhoff, The Netherlands, pp 407–20.

Amato P & Gilbreth JG (1999) 'Nonresident fathers and children's well-being: a meta-analysis'. *Journal of Marriage and the Family* 61, 557–73.

American Law Institute, The (2002) *Principles of the Law of Family Dissolution: Analysis and Recommendations*, American Law Institute, Philadelphia, PA.

Anyan S & Pryor J (2002) 'What is a family? Adolescent perceptions'. *Children & Society* 16, 1–12.

Aquilino WS (2006) 'The noncustodial father–child relationship from adolescence to young adulthood'. *Journal of Marriage and Family* 68, 929–46.

Atkin B (2008) 'Legal structures and reformed families—The New Zealand Example' in *International Handbook of Stepfamilies. Policy and Practice in Legal, Research, and Clinical Environments* (Ed, Pryor, J) James Wiley, New York, pp 522–44.

Bainham A (1999) 'Parentage, parenthood and parental responsibility: subtle, elusive yet important distinctions' in *What is a Parent? A Socio-legal Analysis* (Eds, Bainham A, Day Sclater S, Richards M) Hart Publishing, Oxford, pp 25–46.

—— (2003) 'Contact as a right and obligation' in *Children and Their Families. Contact, Rights and Welfare* (Eds, Bainham A, Lindley B, Richards M, Trinder L) Hart Publishing, Oxford, pp 61–88.

—— (2006). 'Status anxiety? The rush for family recognition' In *Kinship Matters* (Eds, Ebtehaj F, Lindley B, Richards M) Hart Publishing, Oxford, pp 47–66.

Berg EC (2003) 'The effects of perceived closeness to custodial parents, stepparents and nonresident parents on adolescent self esteem'. *Journal of Divorce & Remarriage* 40(1/2), 69–86.

Blackwell A & Dawe F (2003) *Non-resident Parental Contact*, London, Office for National Statistics.

Buchanan CM & Maccoby EE (1996) *Adolescents after Divorce*, Harvard University Press, Harvard, MA.

Dunn JH, Cheng H., O'Connor T, Bridges L. (2004) 'Children's perspectives on their relationships with their nonresident fathers: influences, outcomes, and implications'. *Journal of Child Psychology and Psychiatry* 45(3), 553–66.

Edwards RV, Gillies V, Ribbens McCarthy J. (1999) 'Biological parents and social families: legal discourses and everyday understandings of the position of stepparents'. *International Journal of Law, Policy and the Family* 13(1), 78–105.

Falci C (2006) 'Family structure, closeness to residential and nonresidential parents, and psychological distress in early and middle adolescence'. *The Sociological Quarterly* 47, 123–46.

Finch J (2006) 'Kinship as 'Family' in Contemporary Britain' in *Kinship Matters* (Eds, Ebtehaj F, Lindley B, Richards M) Hart Publishing, Oxford, pp 293–306.

Flouri E (2006) 'Non-resident fathers' relationships with their secondary school age children: Determinants and children's mental health outcomes'. *Journal of Adolescence* 29(4), 525–38.

Funder K (1996) *Remaking Families: Adaptation of Parents and Children to Divorce*, Australian Institute of Family Studies, Melbourne.

—— (1998) 'The Australian Family Law Reform Act 1995 and public attitudes to parental responsibility'. *International Journal of Law, Policy and the Family* 12, 47–61.

Gollop MM, Taylor N, Smith A (2000) 'Children's perspectives on their parents' separation' in *Children's Voices* (Eds, Smith A, Taylor N, Gollop MM) Pearson Education, Auckland, NZ.

Gross P (1987) 'Defining post-divorce remarriage families: a typology based on the subjective perceptions of children'. *Journal of Divorce* 10, 205–17.

Hans JD (2002) 'Stepparenting after divorce: Stepparents' legal position regarding custody, access and support'. *Family Relations* 51, 301–7.

King V (2006) 'The antecedents and consequences of adolescents' relationships with stepfathers and nonresident fathers'. *Journal of Marriage and Family* 68, 910–28.

Laumann-Billings L & Emery RE (2002) 'Distress among young adults from divorced families'. *Journal of Family Psychology* 14, 671–87.

Maclean M & Eekelaar J (1997) *The Parental Obligation: A Study of Parenthood Across Households*, Hart Publishing, Oxford.

Malia S (2008) 'How relevant are US family and probate laws to stepfamilies?' in *International Handbook of Stepfamilies: Policy and Practice in Legal, Research, and Clinical Environments* (Ed, Pryor J) James Wiley, New York, pp 545–72.

Mason MA, Harrison-Jay S, Svare GM, Wolfinger N. (2002). 'Stepparents: De facto parents or legal strangers?'. *Journal of Family Issues* 23, 507–22.

Mignot JF (2008) 'Stepfamilies in France since the 1990s' in *International Handbook of Stepfamilies: Policy and Practice in Legal, Research, and Clinical Environments* (Ed, Pryor J) James Wiley, New York, pp 53–78.

Nozawa S (2006) *Stepfamilies in Japan. Strain and Support*. Florida State University, Tallahassee, FL, and Tokyo, p 21.

Pryor J (2008) 'Child's relationships with nonresident parents' in *International Handbook of Stepfamilies. Policy and Practice in Legal, Research, and Clinical Environments* (Ed, Pryor J) James Wiley, New York, pp 345–68.

Pryor J & Rodgers B (2001) *Children in Changing Families. Life after Parental Separation*, Blackwell Publishers, Oxford.

Rigg A & Pryor J (2007) 'Children's perceptions of families: what do they really think?' *Children & Society* 21, 17–30.

Schenck CE, Braver S, Wolchik SA, Saenz D, Cookston JT, Fabricious WV (submitted) 'Do I matter to my (step- and non-residential) Dad? The relation between perceived mattering and adolescent mental health problems'.

Sosson J (1993) 'The legal status of step-families in Continental European countries' in *Parenthood in Modern Society. Legal and Social Issues for the Twenty-first Century* (Eds, Eekelaar JS & Dordrech P) Martinus Nijhoff, The Netherlands, pp 395–406.

Watt E (2006) 'The DIY procedure for appointing stepparents as additional guardians'. *New Zealand Family Law Journal* 5, 118.

Wendel P (2005) 'Inheritance rights and the step-partner adoption paradigm: shades of the discrimination against illegitimate children'. *Hofstra Law*, Winter, 351–404.

White L & Gilbreth JG (2001) 'When children have two fathers: effects of relationships with stepfathers and non-custodial fathers on adolescent outcomes'. *Journal of Marriage and Family* 63, 155–67.

Legislation

Care of Children Act 2004 (NZ)
Child Support Act 1995 (UK)
Children Act 1989 (UK)
Civil Union Act 2004 (NZ)
UN Convention on the Rights of the Child

8

Internet Sex Offenders: Individual Autonomy, 'Folk Devils'* and State Control

JULIA DAVIDSON AND ELENA MARTELLOZZO

I. INTRODUCTION

THE LAST DECADE has seen attempts to place increasingly punitive controls upon those convicted of sexual offences against children: the debate rages regarding the public identification of registered sex offenders in the community, and the Sexual Offences Act (2003) has introduced a range of new measures and several new internet-related offence categories. Cohen has argued that sex offenders are the 'folk devils' of our time (2002, p 4) attracting constant media focus and condemnation. A large criminal justice industry has developed in the UK around the need effectively to assess risk and to monitor and treat internet and other sex offenders. Proposed measures to monitor, control and treat this group in the community include electronic tagging, polygraph testing, possible use of hormone-suppressing drugs, the regular inspection of offenders' homes and computers, and the introduction of a new probation treatment programme. This chapter explores the extent to which such measures are justified in terms of arguments regarding the need to protect children and young people and to prevent re-offending, set against the need to re-integrate such offenders into the community. This chapter explores the extent to which such measures, which often continue beyond sentence completion, constitute a threat to the individual autonomy[1] and successful social re-integration of such offenders, touching on contentious issues around the right of sex offenders to lead a life that is free from state intervention and manipulation despite the nature of their offending.

---

* A term that Cohen has recently used to describe media representation of sex offenders (2002, p4).

[1] Autonomy is taken here to refer to the extent to which an individual is able to lead their life as they choose to without the constraint of external forces.

II. THE EMERGENCE OF THE INTERNET SEX OFFENDER

Internet use has grown considerably over the last five years; information technology now forms a core part of the formal education system in many countries, ensuring that each new generation of internet users is more adept than the last. Research conducted in the UK by Livingstone and Bober in 2004 suggested that the majority of young people aged 9–19 accessed the internet at least once a day. The internet provides the opportunity to interact with friends on social networking sites such as MySpace and Bebo and enables young people to access information in a way that previous generations would not have thought possible. The medium also allows users to post detailed personal information, which may be accessed by any site visitor, and provides a platform for peer communication hitherto unknown.

There is, however, increasing evidence that the internet is used by some adults to access children and young people in order to 'groom' them for the purposes of sexual abuse. MySpace has recently banned 29,000 convicted sex offenders and is being sued in the US by parents who claim that their children were contacted by sex offenders on the site and consequently abused (*Net Family News*, 2007). Recognition that the internet has the potential to foster the development of international child-abuser rings has begun to filter through to newspaper coverage—the *Guardian*, for example, confirmed this recently in an article reporting on the detention of British offenders participating in a large, international internet sex offender ring involving over 2,000 offenders (Johnson & Connolly, 2007). The *Daily Mail* had reported extensively on this social problem six years earlier, commenting on the discovery of the internet-based 'Wonderland Club', a child-abuser ring involving 180 men operating in different countries and sharing 750,000 indecent images of children (*Daily Mail*, 2001).

The media identified a new category of predatory sex offender, a new 'folk devil' (Cohen, 2002, p 4), and have sought actively to raise public awareness around this issue, suggesting that parents should be wary about allowing their children unrestricted access to the internet. Indeed, the *Daily Mirror* provided advice to parents in the form of a booklet about internet safety ('safety net', 18 January 2007). The government and its criminal justice agencies have responded to the steady trickle of convictions for internet-related child abuse, and to perceived public anxiety, in a number of ways: by commissioning of research in the area; by attempting to address risk; through the creation of a probation treatment programme for internet sex offenders (i-SOTP) in England and Wales; and through the introduction of legislation that seeks to monitor and restrict the movements of sex offenders in the community.

There is however, a certain hypocrisy associated with a society that condones the sexualisation of children appearing in fashion magazines and on the television, but condemns the sexual abuse of children and young people. In a recent paper Emma Rush and Andrea La Nauze (2006) from the Australian Institute suggest that companies which use sexualised images of children to advertise goods are guilty of 'corporate paedophilia'; Rush further claims that such images encourage sex offenders to view children as sexual objects. An inquiry has recently been launched by the British Fashion Council (March 2007) to explore health concerns regarding models in the fashion industry; an ex-model (Clarke, 2007), commenting in the *Daily Mail* newspaper, has claimed that the review, chaired by Baroness Kingsmill, will do little to change entrenched, damaging industry practices and the use of young models. Clarke comments that the industry's obsession with very thin, childlike models, sometimes as young as 12, who are posed in sexualised images, does little to discourage the sexual abuse of young people and serves as an active endorsement of such abuse.

III. LEGISLATION

A. Online Grooming

Recent legislation has sought to protect young people from internet abuse through the introduction of a 'grooming' clause. This new offence category was introduced in the Sexual Offences Act (2003) in England and Wales (this section of the Act also applies to Northern Ireland[2]). Section 15 makes 'meeting a child following sexual grooming' an offence; this applies to the internet, to other technologies such as mobile phones and to the 'real world'.

'Grooming' involves a process of socialisation through which an offender seeks to interact with a child under the age of 18, possibly sharing their hobbies and interests in an attempt to gain trust in order to prepare them for sexual abuse. The concept of 'grooming' is now also recognised in legislation in Scotland, England and Wales, and Northern Ireland. The Sexual Offences Act (2003) in England and Wales, and Northern Ireland and the Protection of Children and Prevention of Sexual Offences Act (2005) in Scotland includes the offence of 'meeting a child following certain preliminary contact' (section 1). 'Preliminary contact' refers to occasions where a person arranges to meet a child who is under 18, having communicated with them on at least one previous occasion (in person, via the internet or via other technologies), with the intention of performing sexual activity on

---

[2] The Sexual Offences Act 2003 (England and Wales) is currently under review in Northern Ireland. Some concerns have been raised regarding a lack of clarity around the age of consent and informed consent. Currently the age of consent is 17 in Northern Ireland (it was raised from 16 to 17 under the Children and Young Persons Act 1950) (Northern Ireland Office, 2006).

the child. The definition of 'grooming' in UK legislation is provided by the Crown Prosecution Service (CPS) (England and Wales):

> The offence only applies to adults; there must be communication (a meeting or any other form of communication) on at least two previous occasions; it is not necessary for the communications to be of a sexual nature; the communication can take place anywhere in the world; the offender must either meet the child or travel to the pre-arranged meeting; the meeting or at least part of the journey must take place within the jurisdiction; the person must have an intention to commit any offence within or outside of the UK (which would be an offence in the jurisdiction) under Part 1 of the 2003 Act. This may be evident from the previous communications or other circumstances eg an offender travels in possession of ropes, condoms or lubricants etc; the child is under 16 and the adult does not reasonably believe that the child is over 16 (CPS, 2007).

Several countries are beginning to follow the UK in legislating against 'grooming' behaviour. Sexual grooming has also recently been added to the Crimes Amendment Act (2005) in New Zealand. In the US it is an offence to transmit information electronically about a child aged 16 or under, for the purpose of committing a sexual offence[3]. The Australian Criminal Code[4] makes similar restrictions, as does the Canadian Criminal Code.[5] The legislation in the UK differs in that the sexual grooming offence applies both to the internet and to the 'real world'; legislation in other countries addresses only electronic grooming via the internet and mobile phones. The concept of sexual grooming is well documented in the sex offender literature (Finkelhor, 1984), and is now filtering into legislation policy, crime detection and prevention initiatives.

B. Indecent Images of Children

The Internet Watch Foundation (IWF) is the IT industry watchdog in the UK. It recently reported a rise in the number of websites containing indecent images of children from 3,438 in 2004 to 6,000 in 2006. Over 90 per cent of the websites are hosted outside the UK (many are hosted in the US and Russia), and are therefore extremely difficult to police and control and there is currently no international agreement on regulation of the internet in respect of online grooming and indecent child images.[6] Many indecent

---

[3] US Code Title 18, Part 1, Chapter 117, AS 2425.
[4] Australian Criminal Code, s 218A.
[5] Canadian Criminal Code, s 172.1.
[6] A breakdown of countries where websites containing child abuse images appear to have been hosted during the period 1996–2006 is provided by the IWF: US 51%; Russia 20%; Japan 5%; Spain 7% and the UK 1.6% (IWF, 2006).

images depict the sexual abuse of children who are victimised both in the creation of the image and in the distribution of the image. It could be argued that a child is re-victimised each time their image is accessed, and images on the internet can form a permanent record of abuse. Whilst there is no doubt that such abuse has a damaging and negative impact upon child victims, particularly where children are abused and the abuse recorded by members of their own family or people known to them (Klain *et al*, 2001), the seriousness and nature of the offending and the *actual* risk posed by perpetrators should be carefully considered in sentencing and treatment approaches. There is a difficult balance to be struck between the measured and reasonable assessment of offender risk and the online protection of vulnerable young people.

Legislation has been introduced in the UK in an attempt to curb the production and distribution of indecent images of children. The legislation in England and Wales (Sexual Offences Act 2003 (England and Wales), sections 45–6)[7] and Scotland (the Protection of Children and Prevention of Sexual Offences (Scotland) Act 2005, section 16) attempts to protect children from abuse in the creation of such images in order to curb circulation. The age of consent is raised from 16 to 18 in both Acts with certain provisions.[8]

In the US the law is similar (Child Online Protection Act 2000 (COPA)); indecent images of children do not have to be overtly sexual, and the possession of suggestive images of children may be prosecuted under the legislation. It is also an offence simply to access images without saving them on a computer. There has been considerable debate in the US regarding the introduction of COPA; the Act has been returned to the Supreme Court several times on the basis of representations made by the American Civil Liberties Union (ACLU) regarding its restrictiveness. The ACLU has argued consistently and fairly effectively that the Act infringes upon civil liberties and individual autonomy, as it is possible accidentally to encounter such images online. In the US under COPA, the making available for commercial purposes on the web of material that is harmful to children is also illegal, unless child access has been restricted. It was argued by the ACLU that more effective, less restrictive mechanisms exist to protect children and that educating children and their parents about internet awareness would be the better approach (Supreme Court Transcripts, *Ashcroft v ACLU* 2/3/04).

---

[7] The Sexual Offences Act 2003 does not create any new offences in this category but raises the age from 16 to 18 by making amendments to the Criminal Justice Act 1991 and the Protection of Children Act 1978.

[8] The provisions allow a defence to the charge if: the picture is of a 16- or 17-year-old; the 16-/17-yearold 'consents'; the pictures of 16-/17-year-olds are not distributed; and the perpetrator and the 16-/17-year-old are in long-term sexual relationship/married/cohabiting: S. 8H 2005.

Legislation in other countries places greater emphasis upon the production of indecent images of children. In Switzerland, Articles 135 and 197 of the Penal Code (The Production and Distribution of Illegal Pornography [Child]), imply that if the indecent material is only to be used for personal viewing, possession is not punishable. But recent research indicates that some federal courts are arguing that the downloading of such material from the internet constitutes *computer storage* rather than possession, which is illegal and therefore contravenes the Articles (Davidson, 2007).

In summary, UK and international legislation seeks to curb the production and supply of and demand for indecent images of children. The position in the US is somewhat different in that an individual may be prosecuted for the possession of 'suggestive' images, and there has been a great deal of debate regarding the interpretation of this term and the implications for sentencing practice. The ACLU also objects to the inclusion in the legislation of the possession of suggestive images. The ACLU has undoubtedly formed a powerful lobby in the US. The autonomy and civil liberties of sex offenders as a group has not been debated in the UK in this way, and such a debate would probably not gain popular support. The child victim's rights lobby has a powerful voice, and it could be argued that key individuals and groups have campaigned very successfully for the rights of child victims of internet abuse and no one has dared to campaign for the rights of convicted sex offenders.

C. Sex Offenders: Sentencing and Control

The use of custody for sex offenders as a group has fluctuated little over recent years in the UK. It rose by five per cent over a ten-year period between 1995 and 2005; 55 per cent were given immediate custodial sentences in 1995 compared with 60 per cent in 2005. The average prison sentence length for all sex offenders increased from 36.8 months in 1995 to 41.5 months in 2005 (Home Office, 2007a). It is, however, too early to comment upon sentencing practice with internet sex offenders as only a small number of cases have been prosecuted under the Sexual Offences Act (2003).[9] In recent research undertaken by one of the authors (Davidson, 2007), police practitioners expressed concern regarding variance in sentencing practice and particularly the ways in which courts view the possession of indecent images of children. It was suggested that sentencers have different views regarding the seriousness of possession, on the basis that no *direct*

---

[9] The Metropolitan Police estimate, for example, that approximately 70 convictions for grooming have been secured since the Act came into force in May 2004, but no national figures are currently available.

victimisation appears to occur. This view was echoed by a psychiatrist working with sex offenders in Switzerland:

> The problem is that federal areas treat the offence differently in that some will remand these offenders into treatment and some will not. Some view this as an offence and some do not. There is no equity and sentencing varies by federal area. (Graf, 2006, cited in Davidson, 2007)

More research is needed into sentencing practice in this area. Punishment of sex offenders does not and should not always involve a custodial sentence. In England and Wales the National Probation Service runs a community treatment programme for sex offenders that allows for diversion from custody for more minor offences. The current legislative framework introduces a range of sentences, including a community order (formally a probation order), which may include a number of requirements (including treatment). Offenders given a community order must agree to comply with any measures imposed; these usually include attending the probation sex offender treatment programme (for those charged with online grooming and other non-internet related sexual offences) or the recently introduced i-SOTP (for those convicted of indecent image-related offences). Other measures may include the use of electronic tagging and, in future, hormone-suppressing drugs (Home Office, 2007a). Although such measures are entered into voluntarily, in reality individuals will have little choice but to comply, as the alternative would be a custodial sentence.

The management of sex offenders in the community is supported by the present legislative framework.[10] All newly convicted sex offenders are required to register under the Sex Offenders Act 1997 (strengthened by Part Two of the Sexual Offences Act (2003), which introduces a number of new orders), including offenders supervised in the community, those cautioned and those released from prison. The duration of the registration requirement depends on sentence length, type of offence, age of the offender and age of the victim. The minimum period of registration is five years and the maximum an 'indefinite period', for sentences of 30 months or more in custody. These arrangements follow automatically on conviction and are not, as such, a part of the sentencing process, but sentencers have a duty to inform offenders about the requirement at the point of sentence. Sentencers may consider extended periods on licence for sex offenders where risk to the public is considered high (Criminal Justice Act 2003, sections 225–9).

Some countries have passed legislation that allows for the detention and supervision of all sex offenders beyond sentence completion. In the UK, the

---

[10] The Sex Offenders Act (1997); the Crime (Sentences) Act (1997); the introduction of Sex Offender Orders under the Crime and Disorder Act (1998) and later under the Sexual Offences Act (2003); the Risk of Sexual Harm Order introduced under the Sexual Offences Act (2003).

Crime and Disorder Act (1998) allowed courts to extend periods of supervision beyond custodial sentences where a person was considered to be at risk of further offending. The Sexual Offences Act (2003) now allows sentencers to pass indeterminate sentences on completion of a custodial sentence for sexual and violent offenders considered to be high risk. In Australia, the High Court, in *Attorney-General v Fardon* (2004), upheld the Queensland Dangerous Prisoners (Sexual Offences) Act (2003), which allows for the detention of sex offenders beyond sentence where offenders are considered to be at high risk of re-offending. In the US, sentencers also have the power to detain sex offenders indefinitely; the system differs from the UK in that the decision to detain indefinitely is made at the end of the period of imprisonment and no minimum term for parole review is set, as the detention takes the form of a civil commitment on mental health grounds. This could lead to incarceration for life with no opportunity to appeal. A US Supreme Court ruling (by a 5 to 4 majority) in June 1997 held that sex offenders could be subject to indefinite civil commitment in a psychiatric institution if, due to a 'personality disorder' or 'mental abnormality', they are deemed to be at a high risk of perpetrating further sexual offences. This ruling constitutes an attack on individual autonomy, effectively placing control of such individuals' right to liberty and autonomy in the hands of the criminal justice system, with no right to appeal.

D. Internet Sex Offenders: Assessing and Managing the Risk

In the UK, all sex offenders are subject to the restrictions placed upon them by Multi-Agency Panel Protection Arrangements (MAPPA).[11] These arrangements require criminal justice, housing, health, local authority, social work and probation services to put into place arrangements for establishing and monitoring risk from sex offenders and violent offenders. The Criminal Justice and Court Services Act (2000) formalised MAPPA arrangements by placing a statutory duty on police and probation services, working jointly as the 'responsible authority' in each area, to establish arrangements for the assessment and management of the risk posed by such offenders. The Criminal Justice Act (2003) (sections 325–7) extends the definition of 'responsible authority' to include the Prison Service, establishes a reciprocal 'duty to co-operate' between the responsible authority and a range of other authorities and social care agencies, and requires the Secretary of State to appoint two lay advisers to assist with the strategic review of arrangements in each area. In Scotland, MAPPAs were introduced in September

---

[11] Established by the Criminal Justice and Court Services Act 2000 and re-enacted and strengthened by the Criminal Justice Act 2003 in England and Wales, and by the Management of Offenders (Scotland) Act 2005 in Scotland.

2006, and legislation which amends the Sexual Offences Act (2003) has now come into force (Police, Public Order and Criminal Justice (Scotland) Act 2006).[12] MAPPAs address several areas of good practice: ongoing risk assessment; the development of risk management plans that focus upon public protection; and service performance evaluation. There are several core functions: identifying MAPPA offenders; sharing relevant information across agencies involved in the assessment of risk; and assessing and managing risk of serious harm. A responsibility is placed upon the Prison Service, the police and local authorities jointly to establish arrangements for the risk assessment and management of sex offenders subject to the notification requirements of Part Two of the Sexual Offences Act (2003).

This collaborative multi-agency response to the monitoring of sex offenders in the community is unusual and has not been adopted as a model by other countries. The advantages of this system are that the responsibility for monitoring is a shared one and that decisions regarding offenders will be taken by a range of agencies represented under the arrangements. The move to monitor this group on release from custody or on community supervision orders is a preferable alternative to extended periods in custody but it could be argued that prolonged monitoring constitutes a threat to individual autonomy and to the opportunity to rebuild lives following a custodial sentence.

In England and Wales and in Scotland violent and sex offenders are divided into three distinct categories under MAPPAs: *Category One* includes all registered sex offenders; *Category Two* includes violent offenders; and *Category Three* includes offenders with previous convictions whose behaviour suggests that they pose a continuing risk. Level 1 offenders (considered to be the least serious group) are overseen by one agency, usually the police or National Probation Service, whilst level 2 offenders are subject to multi-agency oversight. Level 3, high-risk offenders, may be subject to intensive measures, such as monitoring on a daily basis by a private care firm or police surveillance.[13] The Home Office has recently conducted a review of measures to control all sex offenders in the community and plans to legislate to strengthen MAPPAs. Measures include: the use of medication to control offending (chemical castration);[14] compulsory use of polygraph

---

[12] Section 80 of the Police, Public Order and Criminal Justice (Scotland) Act (2006) amends the Sexual Offences Act (2003) by inserting s 96A. Police can apply to a sheriff to obtain a warrant to enter and search a known (registered) sex offender's home address for risk assessment purposes or following failure to gain entry on more than one occasion.

[13] Categories and levels of offending are not mutually exclusive: someone in category 1 on the sex offenders register, for example, could be classed as level 1, 2 or 3.

[14] Drugs have been used in an attempt to control sex offender behaviour, in the UK, other European countries such as France and the Netherlands, the US and Canada for some time. This procedure is often referred to as 'chemical castration' and involves the use of testosterone-reducing anti androgen drugs, administered to control sexual desire. The drugs are synthetic progestins which inhibit hormone development and limit the development of testosterone.

testing; enhanced use of satellite tracking; provision of early treatment for self-referring sex offenders who have not been convicted; expansion of treatment, and a review of the continuity between prison and probation treatment (at present this does not exist) (Home Office, 2007b).

The majority of internet sex offenders using indecent images of children are categorised as low risk (level 1). At present there are no specific MAPPAs for internet sex offenders but measures are planned, which may include: the screening of all sex offenders for internet use in offending; regular inspection of home computers; the installation on home computers of the kind of software currently employed in the US to monitor the internet use of registered sex offenders (Davidson, 2007). In theory it may be easier to control the behaviour of this group as it may soon be possible to monitor their computer use electronically and remotely—this may initially prove costly, but such a move will provide a more cost-effective alternative in the long term than MAPPA officer visits. There is no evidence to suggest that these methods will prevent further offending and it is probable that computers will be used outside the home environment to escape detection.

In terms of judging seriousness and risk when sentencing, the Court of Appeal accepted the advice of the Sentencing Advisory Panel (2002) in sentencing internet sex offenders using indecent images of children, following *R v Oliver, Hartrey and Baldwin* (2003).[15] The offence of possession of indecent images of children is triable either way under the Sexual Offences Act (2003) in England and Wales, and carries a maximum penalty of five years' custody for possession and up to 10 years' custody for production and distribution. Aggravating circumstances include: distribution; evidence of a systematic collection; use of drugs or alcohol; collection stored so that others may view it accidentally; intimidation or coercion; and financial gain. Mitigating factors include: a small number of images held for personal use and images viewed but not stored.[16]

IV. OFFENDER AUTONOMY: PUBLIC NOTIFICATION AND CHEMICAL CASTRATION

Media and public pressure upon the government to disclose sex offender details has become considerable in the wake of highly publicised cases

---

[15] Here the two determining factors of seriousness were taken to be the nature of the material and the degree of the offender's engagement with the material. In considering the custody threshold, the fact that the material upon which the convictions were based constituted a small part of the collection and that the potential for others to access and view the collection was considerable, were considered to be aggravating offence circumstances. The defendants all received a custodial sentence.

[16] The sentencing guidelines may be viewed at http://www.sentencing-guidelines.gov.uk/docs/advice-sexual-offences.pdf (Sentencing Advisory Panel, 2004) p 99.

involving the sexual abuse and murder of children. The Home Office has recently undertaken a review in this area (Home Office, 2007c) and plans to legislate to introduce a watered-down version of the system that operates in the US following the introduction of Megan's Law.[17] The government has probably avoided the introduction of full community notification following vigilante action when the *News of the World* newspaper published photographs and addresses of suspected sex offenders in the wake of the abduction and murder of eight-year-old Sarah Payne by convicted sex offender Roy Whiting in 2000. The proposed legislation will place a legal obligation upon MAPPA panels (including the National Probation Service and the police) to consider disclosure of information to the public about sex offenders in all cases. The disclosure decision will be based upon the offender's perceived risk to children. This is problematic, given the difficulty of accurately predicting risk of re-offending, and it is probable that ad hoc practice will result in the identity of some offenders being subject to community notification and some not, depending upon the policy and practice of different MAPPA panels.

Action Three in the review states that the government plans to

> introduce a legal duty for MAPPA authorities to consider the disclosure of information about convicted child sex offenders to members of the public in all cases. The presumption will be that the authorities will disclose information if they consider that an offender presents a risk of serious harm to a member of the public's children. (Home Office, 2007c, p 13)

The new legislation will also allow a member of the public to register a child protection interest against someone who has previous convictions for sexual offences against children, and the police may disclose such cautions or convictions to a 'relevant' member of the public. This may occur, for example, where an individual with previous convictions becomes involved with a family who have children, but who are unaware of the person's past. A concerned friend or neighbour may register a child protection interest, and the police will have a duty to investigate the basis of the claim and possibly inform the family. This move effectively endows MAPPA agencies with the power to disclose, removing the decision from sentencers and the Home

---

[17] Eight-year-old Megan Kanka was murdered in 1995 by a convicted sex offender. Following the murder of her daughter, Megan's mother campaigned for the public disclosure of sex offenders' home addresses, and succeeded in forcing the New Jersey State Supreme Court to uphold 'Megan's Law' in 1995. Other states soon followed, and on 17 May 1996, the federal version of the law, the Jacob Wetterling Crimes Against Children Law, was passed. This law formed the first part of the federal version of 'Megan's Law'. On 13 September 1996 the 'Megan's Law' notification element of the legislation was passed. All states were given a deadline (September 1997) to pass versions of 'Megan's Law' or risk losing federal aid. Forty-seven states and the District of Columbia passed the legislation.

Office. The basis on which such decisions should be taken is not discussed in the document, but will presumably rest in part upon existing risk assessment tools. It is clear from the review that the Home Office is attempting to gain public support for such measures through greater community engagement under MAPPAs. Just how this might function in practice is unclear. The review also stresses the need to strengthen MAPPAs.

In the US, compulsory chemical castration was introduced for sex offenders in California on 17 September 1996.[18] This legislation required the court to sentence any repeat child abuser whose victim was under 13 years old to drug treatment, and allowed sentencers discretion in sentencing the use of drugs for other sex offenders abusing children (*Harvard Law Review*, 1997). Similar legislation was enacted in Florida six months later (Helm Spalding, 1998). Consequently, all repeat sex offenders (where the victim was under 13) must agree to take drugs as a condition of release from prison. Compliance with the intervention is monitored via the taking of regular blood samples. Chemical castration is compulsory in other states such as: Florida, Washington, Michigan and Texas.

The ACLU opposed the use of chemical castration in 1997, describing the intervention as a 'cruel and unusual punishment' (ACLU, 2002,) and therefore unacceptable under the US Bill of Rights. This term is taken from the Eighth Amendment to the US Constitution (1787), which states that 'cruel and unusual punishments shall not be used' (US Bill of Rights, 2007). This claim was unsuccessful and did not prevent the introduction of chemical castration in other US states. The ACLU also claimed that the drugs would interfere with an offender's right to procreate, an issue that goes to the very heart of the right to autonomy.

It has been claimed that the move to introduce chemical castration in California was never supported by the medical profession, and that the intervention is only effective with offenders motivated to change their behaviour (Berlin, 1997). The Association for the Treatment of Sexual Abusers (ATSA) in the US does not support the widespread use of drugs in controlling sex offender behaviour. In a position paper on the use of anti-androgen therapy, ATSA states that its use should be limited, given individual differences. It is recommended that such drugs should be prescribed by a doctor following an extensive period of evaluation of individual need; there should be ongoing medical supervision due to the possible harmful side effects; administration should occur in the context of a treatment plan (this is usually not the case in the US) and that an offender's informed consent to the administration of such drugs should always be gained (ATSA,

---

[18] See 'Constitutional Law. Due Process and Equal Protection. California Becomes First State to Require Chemical Castration of Certain Sex Offenders': Act of Sept 17, (1996), ch 596, 1996 Cal Stat 92 (To Be Codified at Cal Penal Code Section 645), *Harvard Law Review* 110(3) (January, 1997), pp 799-804 doi:10.2307/1342251.

2007). This point is supported by Harrison (2007) in the UK, who recently conducted a literature review exploring the advantages and disadvantages of chemical castration.

The use of drugs to control offending behaviour has also been criticised on ethical grounds in the light of possible harmful side effects which can include insomnia, depression, hypoglycaemia, blood clots, allergic reactions, diabetes, breast enlargement, liver damage and weight gain (Berlin & Manicke, 1981; Craissati, 2004). Some have suggested that the side effects are particularly pronounced in adolescent sex offenders (Gagne, 1981). Anti-androgen drugs have only recently been used in this way and consequently there is no research exploring the long-term effects.

The employment of drugs to suppress sexual desire assumes that the act of child abuse is entirely physiological, which is a misconception. Rather, research demonstrates that child abusers enjoy the company of children; they enjoy the feeling of power, control and domination that the abuse of a child affords. They are likely to have experienced abuse themselves as well as rejection in past relationships and tend to have low self-esteem (Finkelhor, 1984; Davidson, 2006). Thus the forces that drive an individual to abuse a child are highly complex and not always necessarily predicated only upon sexual desire. It is also apparent that only those individuals motivated to change are likely to benefit. The government is undoubtedly attempting to assuage public outcry through the introduction of a range of measures for which there is very little conclusive research evidence to suggest effectiveness. This would seem to be an attempt to find a 'quick fix' simple solution to a very complex issue, which has serious human rights implications.

It is clear that the introduction of hormone-suppressing drugs and community notification in some cases constitute a real threat to individual autonomy, anonymity and the human right to procreate and that there is in reality little research evidence to suggest that such measures will serve to protect children and young people from abuse, the vast majority of which is perpetrated by people known to victims and often from within their own families.

V. CONCLUSION

The sexual abuse of children is an emotive issue that attracts considerable media attention. Sex offenders are the pariahs of our time: the only group of offenders in British legal history to be singled out with designated Acts and civil orders. The identification of a new category of sex offender—the internet abuser—has prompted a move simultaneously to punish and control this offender group, alongside an effort on the part of criminal justice agencies such as the Prison Service and the Probation Service to provide effective treatment programmes.

The management of internet sex offenders must be viewed within the context of the attempted control of serious offenders. It could be argued that a paradigm shift is occurring within criminal justice, and that a systems analysis approach to danger management of 'high risk' offenders has come to characterise policy and practice (Feeley and Simon, 1992; 1994). In this 'new penology' the focus is actuarial, and concern is not with punishment or rehabilitation, but with the classification of offenders by seriousness of offence and risk posed. This model applies particularly to attempts to manage internet sex offenders in the UK, where the emphasis is upon ways to maximise the control of offenders, and as Garland suggests, (sex) offenders are viewed as 'risks who must be managed'. Instead of emphasising rehabilitative methods that meet the offender's needs, the system emphasises effective controls that minimise costs and maximise security (Garland, 2001, p 175). Actuarial risk assessment tools play a significant part in this process, allowing criminal justice practitioners to calculate the risk posed and determine both sentence and treatment on this basis. It could be argued that the employment of such techniques constitutes a threat not only to defendant/offender autonomy but also to the autonomy of practitioners, as decisions regarding treatment and assessment are predicated upon a risk calculation, rather than upon professional judgement. In the US such tools also serve to justify the long-term incarceration of sex offenders subject to indefinite civil commitment orders.

The difficulty of weighing the individual's right to autonomy in internet sex offender management and treatment against the need to apportion responsibility for harm caused to victims is the difficult issue. Some feminist researchers such as Kelly (2003), commenting on adult rape, have argued that any form of sexual abuse constitutes an affront to victims' individual autonomy.[19] Cohen (2002) has suggested that sex offenders have become the folk devils of our time, describing them as 'candidates for monster status' (2002, p xvi); the question is how far policy makers and sentencers can remain impartial enough to consider the *real* value and effectiveness of legislation and measures designed to control, when faced with offending that constantly attracts media attention and prompts what Cohen describes as a 'primitive' (2002, p xvi) public response. As Downes and Rock suggest:

> A panoply of adverse labelling extends from more severe sentencing of convicted offenders to their lifelong social exclusion. The expansion of preventive measures, due in part to the woeful neglect of child protection in the past, now includes, as well as demands for the publicisation of the addresses of known child sex offenders, such processes as regular checks on the criminal records of all teachers and staff engaged in primary or secondary education. How far this reaction amounts

---

[19] Although Herring argues (ch 4, this volume) that respecting individual autonomy in adult sexual relations is not simply an issue of 'consent', since the social and cultural context in which sexual relations occur is relevant to how far consent was freely given.

to an over-reaction, which has counter-productive implications for the very object of the exercise—the protection of children—is now a pressing issue in public policy debate. (Downes and Rock, 2008, p 4)

The difficulty of weighing the individual's right to autonomy in internet sex offender management and treatment, against the need to apportion responsibility for harm caused to victims is the difficult issue.

BIBLIOGRAPHY

ACLU (2002) *International Civil Liberties Report,* http://www.aclu.org/FilesPDFs/iclr2002.pdf.
Berlin FS & Menicke CF (1981) 'Treatment of sex offenders with antiandrogen medication: Conceptualization, review of treatment modalities and preliminary findings'. *American Journal of Psychiatry,* 138, 601–7.
Clarke G (2007) 'They measured my fingers to see if I was fat'. *Daily Mail,* 29 May.
Cohen S (2002) *Folk Devils and Moral Panics,* 3rd edn, Routledge, London.
CPS (Crown Prosecution Service) (2007) Legal Guidance on Sexual Offences Act 2003—Grooming, http://www.cps.gov.uk/legal/s_to_u/sentencing_manual/s15_grooming/index.html.
Craissati J (2004) *Managing High Risk Sex Offenders in the Community. A Psychological Approach,* New York: Routledge.
Daily Mail (2001) 'Wonderland sentences a joke', 12 February.
Davidson J (2006) 'Victims Speak: Comparing Child Sexual Abusers' and Child Victims' Accounts'. *Perceptions and Interpretations of Sexual Abuse Victims and Offenders* 1(2) 159–74.
—— (2007) *Current Practice and Research into Internet Sex Offending,* Risk Management Authority (Scotland), http://www.rmascotland.gov.uk/ViewFile.aspx?id=235.
Feeley M & Simon J (1992) 'The New Penology: Notes on the Emerging Strategy of Corrections and Its Implications'. *Criminology* 30, 449–74.
Finkelhor D (1984) *Child Sexual Abuse: New Theory and Research,* The Free Press, New York.
Gagne P (1981). 'Treatment of sex offenders with medroxyprogesterone acetate'. *American Journal of Psychiatry,* 138, 644–6.
Garland D (2001) *The Culture of Control: Crime and Social Order in Contemporary Society,* Oxford, Oxford University Press.
Helm Spalding L (1998) 'Florida's 1997 chemical castration law: A return to the dark ages', *Florida State University Law Review,* http://www.law.fsu.edu/journals/lawreview/frames/252/spalfram.html.
Home Office (2007a) Regulatory Impact Assessment: Making Provision in the Management of Offenders and Sentencing Bill for the Mandatory Polygraph Testing of Certain Sexual Offenders, <http://66.102.9.104/search?q=cache:yaX1mUmiqOQJ.www.homeoffice.gov.uk/documents/ria-manage-offenders-bill-060105/ria-offender-polygraphy-060105%3Fview%3DBinary+Home+Office+polygraph+testing+of+sex+offenders&hl=en&ct=clnk&cd=1&gl=uk.

—— (2007a) *Statistical Bulletin Sentencing Statistics 2005*, England & Wales RDS NOMS.

—— (2007b) National Offender Management Service website, http://noms.homeoffice. gov.uk/protecting-the-public/risk-assessment/.

—— (2007c) *Review of the Protection of Children from Sex Offenders 6/2007*, http:// www.homeoffice.gov.uk/documents/CSOR/chid-sex-offender-review-130607.

Johnson B & Connolly K (2007) 'Briton under investigation in global internet pae- dophile ring'. *The Guardian*, 8 February.

Kelly L (2003) *Attrition in Reported Rape Cases: A Forgotten Issue?*, Conference Proceedings, 'Sexual Violence: Issues and Responses Across Europe', Rape Crisis Network, Dublin, 3 October.

Livingstone S & Bober M (2004) *UK Children Go Online: Surveying the experi- ences of young people and their parents* (LSE, 2004).

Net Family News (2007) 'Sex offenders on MySpace', 3 August, http://www. netfamilynews.org/letterindex4.html.

Northern Ireland Office (2006) *Reforming the law on sexual offences in Northern Ireland: A consultation document, Vol 2*, 2006, Northern Ireland Sex Crime Unit.

Rush E & La Nauze A (2006) *Corporate Paedophilia: Sexualisation of Children in Australia*, Canberra: Australia Institute.

'Safety net for families' (no author named) *Daily Mirror* 21/08/2007 web link http://www.mirror.co.uk/news/more-news/technology-gaming/2007/08/21/safety- net-for-families-115875-19665747/.

Sentencing Advisory Panel (2004) *Sexual Offences Act 2003: The Panel's Advice to the Sentencing Guidelines Council*, http://www.sentencing-guidelines.gov.uk/ docs/advice-sexual-offences.pdf.

Legislation

Child Online Protection Act 2000 (COPA) (US)
Crime and Disorder Act 1998 (UK)
Crimes Amendment Act 2005 (NZ)
Criminal Code (Australia)
Criminal Code (Canada)
Criminal Justice Act 2003 (UK)
Criminal Justice and Court Services Act 2000 (UK)
Dangerous Prisoners (Sexual Offences) Act 2003 (Queensland, Australia)
Jacob Wetterling Crimes Against Children Law 1996 (US)
Management of Offenders Act (Scotland) 2005
Obscene Publications Act 1959 (England and Wales)
Obscene Publications Act 1964 (England and Wales)
Penal Code (The Production and Distribution of Illegal Pornography [Child]) (Switzerland)
Police, Public Order and Criminal Justice (Scotland) Act 2006
Protection of Children and Prevention of Sexual Offences (Scotland) Act 2005
Sex Offenders Act 1997 (England and Wales)
Sexual Offences Act 2003 (England and Wales)
US Bill of Rights 2007

Cases

Ashcroft v ACLU 2/3/04, US Supreme Court, transcript available at http://www. supremecourtus.gov/oral_arguments/argument_transcripts/03-218.pdf.

Fardon v Attorney General For The State Of Queensland (2004) *Deakin Law Review*, http://www.austlii.edu.au/au/journals/DeakinLRev/2005/13.html (Australia).

R v Oliver, Hartrey and Baldwin [2003] 2 Cr App R28: (2003) Crim LR 127 (UK).

Part 2

Reproduction

9

Regulation of Reproductive Decision-making

THERESA GLENNON

I. INTRODUCTION

WHEN IS GOVERNMENT justified in interfering with autonomous decision-making about assisted reproduction (AR)? When should individuals be permitted to pursue their private choices about intimate aspects of their lives, including the creation of family, free of government interference? These questions rest upon a conventional understanding of personal autonomy as enhanced by markets and undermined by government regulation. This chapter seeks to unsettle this conventional understanding, and to do so, proceeds as follows. The first section provides a broad overview of the different regulatory approaches taken by the US and UK governments to various issues implicated by AR. The second section analyses the concept of autonomy and the common assumption that government regulation stands in opposition to autonomy while the unfettered market enhances autonomy. The third section identifies several legitimate government and societal interests implicated by individual decisions regarding AR. It focuses on several areas of particular concern: access to treatment; treatment practices that lead to pregnancy with multiples, and the identity rights of children born through gamete donation. For each area, it illustrates policies that governments may choose to further legitimate interests while supporting individual autonomy.

II. BROAD OVERVIEW OF THE US AND UK APPROACHES
TO FERTILITY REGULATION

As demonstrated more fully below, the UK and US have chosen markedly different responses to the 'warp-speed' development of AR. The UK has adopted a centralised regulatory approach, while the US is characterised by a market-based approach. These generalities do not fully capture the complicated picture in each country, but do highlight important regulatory differences. Each approach may restrict personal autonomy in important ways.

This chapter uses the term 'assisted reproduction' (or AR) to refer to a wide range of infertility treatments. These include medications to induce ovulation, donor insemination, egg donation, in vitro fertilisation (IVF), and surrogacy.

The US has enacted little in the way of specific regulation of AR at either the federal or state level (Kindregan & McBrien, 2006; Henne & Bundorf, 2007). US reluctance to regulate may be due to the highly charged debate concerning the status of human embryos and the desire to avoid regulation in areas of rapid technological change (Spar, 2006; Johnson, 2007). In the absence of such regulation, a thriving market-based system of fertility clinics and intermediaries for gamete donation and surrogacy has developed. Patients seeking treatment for infertility do so through this private, mostly for-profit, market. Most patients must use private funds to pay for treatments, which are expensive and beyond the reach of many families (Spar, 2006).

Federal regulation is designed to support this market approach by providing consumers with information about success rates of individual fertility clinics (Fertility Clinic Success Rate and Certificate Act 1992). Physicians at fertility clinics follow only state medical licensing requirements, but face no separate requirements for fertility clinics. Their practices are limited only by medical licensing and general contract, tort and criminal law. In the absence of specific governmental regulation, professional societies such as the American Society for Reproductive Medicine have developed practice guidelines that many clinics follow but which do not carry the force of law (Practice Committee of the American Society for Reproductive Medicine [ASRM], 2006b).

Clinics in most states are free to determine who to accept as patients and what treatments they will offer, including the number of embryos to implant, use of donor gametes and surrogates, and disposition of frozen embryos. Intermediaries for donated gametes and surrogates are not regulated or licensed, need no special qualifications, and are free to charge whatever fees the market will bear. Only a few states have specifically restricted the use of donor gametes or surrogates, and in most states, donors and surrogates are free to enter into contracts as they see fit, although they cannot be sure that the contract will be enforced. Most states have defined the resulting parent–child relationships only for sperm donation, not egg donation or surrogacy (Kindregan & McBrien, 2006). This lack of clear definition has led to several instances of protracted litigation over the legal parentage of children born through surrogacy (*JF v DB*, 2006).

In contrast, the UK has undertaken extensive centralised regulation of fertility treatment. The Human Fertilisation and Embryology Act (HFE Act) (1990) regulates the use of a wide range of AR techniques, including the storage of donated gametes, IVF and surrogacy. It does not regulate the use of fertility drugs (Jackson, 2006). It also identifies the parentage of children born through the use of various reproductive technologies (Jackson, 2006). The HFE Act (1990) established the Human Fertilisation and Embryology Authority (HFEA), to prescribe standards of practice and license fertility clinics. The HFEA does this through its Code of Practice, currently in its seventh edition, which ensures non-discriminatory access to treatment, requires treatment to take account of the welfare of the child, and mandates the offer of counselling to patients, donors and children born through AR.

Although some fertility services are available at no cost through the National Health Service (NHS), limited services have made NHS fertility services inaccessible to many. These restrictions have prompted most patients to enter the private fertility market (Blyth *et al*, 2003; Jackson, 2006).

The HFEA defines the types of fertility services that fertility clinics can offer under various circumstances and restricts compensation for sperm and egg donors and surrogates to 'reasonable expenses' (HFEA, 2007a, para G.9.8.2e). However, in practice, some patients have received 'in-kind' fertility services for their egg donation, and courts have approved significant payments to surrogates well beyond the concept of 'reasonable expenses' (Jackson, 2006). The HFE Act (1990) also requires that the identity of gamete donors be available to children born through donations from April 2005 onwards once they reach the age of 18 (HFEA (Disclosure of Donor Information) Regulations 2004).

Individuals are not necessarily bound by the strictures of their national, state or local governments. Global fertility tourism has become a marked phenomenon in which individuals or couples seeking prohibited or costly fertility treatments travel to obtain desired services elsewhere (Storrow, 2005). While international forms of regulation are beyond the scope of this chapter, it is clear that at least some people will manage to evade their home country's regulation of fertility services through such travel.

The less regulated, market-based approach of the US is often described as having created a greater realm of personal autonomy for those who seek reproductive services, while the UK regulations are viewed as imposing greater restrictions upon individual decision-making and autonomy. Neither country has taken the steps necessary to study the effects of these new forms of reproduction on all affected—and most particularly, those children born through the use of new reproductive technologies. A more complete analysis of the appropriate level of regulation will be possible only if this research becomes a high priority.

III. REALMS OF FREEDOM AND THEIR LIMITATIONS

A. A Complicating View of Autonomy

Individual autonomy in matters concerning reproduction is a central value in both Europe and the US. The US Supreme Court has held that

> If the right of privacy means anything, it is the right of the individual, married or single, to be free from unwarranted governmental intrusion into matters so fundamentally affecting a person as the decision whether to bear or beget a child. (*Eisenstadt v Baird*, 1972).

The European Convention on Human Rights, which has been incorporated into UK law, protects reproductive decision-making as part of the right to respect for 'private and family life' (European Convention on Human Rights, Article 8).

However, the meaning of individual autonomy is often vague. Gerald Dworkin (1988) defines persons as autonomous 'when their decisions and actions are their own; when they are self-determining' (p 13). In order to be self-determining, individual decisions must be free of coercion. In addition, individuals should not act solely on their first order desires—their short-term impulses or desires—but only after critical reflection. This critical reflection enables them to make decisions that reflect their 'true' selves.

Others have challenged the claim that deliberation and self-reflection lead to clear preferences. Sunstein and Thaler (2003) argue that people lack 'clear, stable and well-ordered' preferences (p 1161). Instead, people are 'strongly influenced by details of the *context* in which they make their choice' (p 1161). That context, they argue, is never neutral. One type of context, referred to here as *decisional context*, relates to how choices are offered. Individuals are apt to go along with default rules, and changes in default rules sway individual choices dramatically. Clinic consent forms, for example, often contain default rules which few patients contest.

Starting points are also strongly influential. Individuals given one price as a starting point are likely to reach a different conclusion on what is a reasonable price than those given a different price at the outset (Sunstein & Thaler, 2003). In the context of AR, clinics concerned with high success rates may tell patients that most other patients implant three or four embryos. These numbers become patients' analytic starting point and they are unlikely to vary from that.

The way in which information is framed also affects decision-making. Individuals considering a risky medical procedure reach different conclusions depending on whether they are told the procedure leaves 90% of patients still alive five years later or 10% of patients dead after five years (Sunstein & Thaler, 2003). Fertility patients may be swayed by framing that highlights their chance of getting pregnant rather than their greater chance of not getting pregnant, or framing that emphasises a possible small increase in their chance of becoming pregnant from implanting multiple embryos while downplaying the risks of multiple gestations or the disturbing nature of selective reduction.

Thus, patient treatment decisions are likely to be strongly influenced by their fertility clinic's approach. Patients are unlikely to opt out of default rules established by the clinic, they tend to accept choices listed first, and they are swayed by the manner in which their options are framed. The norms of the particular fertility clinic and the advice of the treating physician carry the weight of expertise, and patients are unlikely to challenge the advice they are given (Gurmankin *et al*, 2002). The decisional context created by the fertility clinic cannot help but affect individual decisions about AR, and any plausible account of individual autonomy must account for this reality.

The *relational context* of decision-making is also important (Clement, 1998). Decision-making regarding AR is influenced by a number of social factors. First, AR often involves joint decision-making by two people, and it is difficult to identify the extent to which such joint decisions reflect the choices of each individual. One partner may defer to the other partner in order to sustain the relationship, avoid conflict, or allow the partner to reach a deeply desired goal. Decision-making may also be constrained by the beliefs of family, friends and religion. Thus, 'individual' choices regarding AR are just as likely to reflect another important aspect of our inner selves: the desire to honour and maintain connections with a partner, family, friends and other important social relationships.

Reproductive decision-making also takes place in a *broader context*: social, cultural and political (Clement, 1998). The desire for offspring and the priority placed on genetic relationships to offspring may depend on the background assumptions embedded within the broader context in which those decisions are made. Individuals' deeply personal desires are powerfully influenced by this broader context. If children are not a high priority in the culture, people with infertility are less likely to seek treatment. If adoption is viewed as an especially honourable way to build a family, it, too, may be preferred to fertility treatments. If genetic connection dominates, then donor egg and sperm become less desirable or shameful facts that need to be hidden. These beliefs may be so deeply embedded that they are experienced as facts, not beliefs, unquestioned because they are not noticed (Berger & Luckmann, 1966).

A variety of other *internal characteristics* bear on the 'autonomy' of individual decisions. For example, people exhibit 'bounded rationality', demonstrating limitations on their ability to obtain, process and interpret information. Instead, they use rules of thumb, or heuristics, that are often biased. For example, the 'availability heuristic' describes the tendency to over-predict a familiar outcome and under-predict an outcome they have never previously encountered (Sunstein, 2004). In addition, individuals often exhibit 'bounded willpower', making decisions that serve their immediate (first order) desires even when they are aware that those decisions undermine their long-term (second order) desires (Jolls *et al*, 1998). Bounded willpower may lead a couple to implant a higher number of embryos because they are so eager to become pregnant in *this* cycle that they undervalue the later stress if too many embryos successfully implant and they are faced with serious health risks or pressure to make the painful decision to abort one or more developing fetuses. Moreover, individuals experience significant limitations in their ability to predict future emotional states, such as happiness or distress. In particular, individuals are inaccurate at forecasting the duration and intensity of future affective states, such as the experience of raising multiple, possibly disabled, children.

Finally, autonomy depends on individuals' power to effectuate their decisions. For those unable to reproduce without assistance, the inability to access such assistance limits their reproductive autonomy (Herring, 2006). Resource limitations may also prevent them from choosing the safest and most effective medical options (Mundy, 2007). A couple may prefer IVF to the use of a hormone to stimulate ovulation. However, if they lack the financial resources to pay for the more expensive procedure, they may be unable to effectuate their decision. Their use of the hormone does not reflect their unconstrained autonomous choice, but rather the material limitations that restrict the range of options available to them (Clement, 1998).

These various factors—including decisional, relational and broader context; internal characteristics such as bounded rationality and willpower and inaccurate forecasting; and material limitations—may all affect our view of the autonomy of the reproductive decisions made by individuals or couples who have trouble conceiving. They suggest that individuals' choices are strongly influenced by the environment in which they are made, and that decisions are never made in a neutral environment.

Unlike some, I do not take these concepts as undermining any possibility of human autonomy. Rather than viewing autonomy as a Platonic ideal, or as an 'all or nothing' proposition, these ideas suggest that autonomy is better understood as occurring along a continuum. It is possible for particular contexts and particular government policies to encourage Dworkin's critical self-reflection or to encourage impulsivity; it is also possible for the context to favour market profitability or long-term societal interests.

Hence, these arguments also suggest deep scepticism regarding claims that reproductive freedom lies in the unregulated market, free of the hand of government restraint. Proposed government action also requires scepticism, but where societal interests are strong and clearly furthered by policy, governmental efforts to change or influence the context in which

AR decisions are made may be warranted and may be done in a manner that supports, rather than undermines, individual autonomy.

B. Deconstructing the Opposition of Markets and Government Regulation

A central motif of political and legal discourse in the US identifies markets with individual freedom and government regulation with restriction of individual freedom. Within this rhetorical frame, markets and governments are treated as polar opposites. Markets allow individuals to exercise complete freedom to make choices most likely to benefit them. All government action necessarily intrudes on that personal freedom (Sunstein & Thaler, 2003).

This characterisation is problematic for many reasons. First, the purported opposition between government regulation and free markets is substantially overstated. As the legal realists demonstrated, well-functioning markets only exist by virtue of governmental and other forms of regulation. In well-ordered societies, market transactions take place against a dense backdrop of governmental regulation (Dunoff, 1998). For example, despite the absence of specific regulation of US fertility clinics, doctors who staff those clinics must pass and continue to meet state licensing requirements, carry medical malpractice insurance, and comply with tort and other civil and criminal law (Kindregan & McBrien, 2006). These background regulations provide consumers with reassurances of quality that allow them to make choices with greater confidence of quality. Lack of reassuring regulation, such as that seen in many US states regarding surrogacy, may lead wary consumers to remain outside the market.

Much contemporary governmental regulation is designed to enhance, rather than restrict, individual autonomy in market transactions. This is as true in the market for AR services as it is in markets for more conventional goods and services. For example, the US fertility clinic reporting requirement and HFEA league tables provide consumers with information to help patients make knowledgeable choices.

Just as the conventional understanding of governments and markets being in opposition to each other misconceives the role of government, it similarly misstates the role of markets in furthering human autonomy. Individuals with a very rare form of infertility may find that the market has failed to invest in unprofitable research. Similarly, the economics of fertility practices prevent clinics from serving lower income clients, meaning that the market provides little opportunity for many individuals to realise their autonomous choices regarding AR (Jain, 2006).

At the same time, government interventions into markets may open up choice. Requirements by some US states that health insurers fully fund fertility treatment or improved provision of fertility treatment by the NHS in the UK enhance the autonomy of lower income individuals. Neither markets nor governments are as far apart in their impact on autonomy as the myth would have us believe.

IV. GOVERNMENTAL INTERESTS IN ASSISTED REPRODUCTION

A. Identifying the Governmental Interests

Government has a range of interests in AR. As Johnson and Petersen (this volume) point out, it is essential for governments to clearly identify and justify these interests. One set of interests involves protecting the autonomy of all those involved: potential parents, donors, surrogates and resulting children. Assisted reproduction inevitably involves several different people whose autonomy interests may not always coincide. Conflicts may arise between potential parents—one may wish to withdraw consent to go forward with embryo implantation, or they may disagree about what to do with frozen embryos. Consent issues involving gamete donors or surrogates may also create conflicts with potential parents. Children born through donated gametes may desire to know their genetic origins, while donors may wish to remain anonymous. Legislators may act preventively to define and enforce one or more of these autonomy interests or allow courts to resolve conflicting autonomy claims with little legislative guidance. In either case, governments must resolve these conflicts. Governments' role in protecting autonomy interests may be especially strong for the children of AR, who cannot protect their own interests.

Governments also have a strong interest in protecting the health and welfare of their populations. AR can pose a number of health and welfare risks to mothers, surrogates, egg donors, and children (Jain *et al*, 2002). Treatments to stimulate ovulation or synchronise ovulation cycles carry health risks. Surrogates experience all the health risks associated with pregnancy and childbirth. Certain practices, such as the implantation of multiple embryos, create serious risks to the life and well-being of mothers and children (Practice Committee of the ASRM, 2006a). While adults involved in AR can make informed choices regarding these risks, children conceived through IVF cannot make such choices, and the government's *parens patriae* role may justify intervention. Governments aware of human cognitive limitations may also wish to ensure that clinics convey risks in a manner that patients can fully appreciate.

Governments also have a range of economic interests involved in AR. Countries with declining populations may have an economic interest in encouraging the use of AR to increase their populations. They may also have safety and economic interests in avoiding the cost of expensive treatments to alleviate suffering caused by risky procedures (Jain *et al*, 2002).

This may be particularly true in the context of risks of medical problems or disability for children born through AR, since government is likely to bear at least some of the expense of treatment and education for children with disabilities.

Finally, governments may have value interests at stake in the use of AR—value interests that are often conflicting. Governments may respond to religions that are deeply opposed to all or some forms of AR, or they may value the individual's role in defining their own ethical norms for use of AR. Gamete donation and surrogacy create complicated interlocking relationships among people that may be a cause of celebration or concern. AR can assist alternative family structures—single women or men or same-sex couples—to raise children, challenging traditional notions of family. Traditional family values may conflict with other social values such as individual autonomy, non-discrimination and diversity.

AR involves many highly contested interests, and this chapter does not undertake to examine and weigh each of the issues to identify when governments should intervene. Rather, it identifies three possible governmental goals, and suggests some strategies to employ our more complicated understanding of autonomy to reach those goals without unduly constraining the autonomy of those involved in AR. These governmental goals are: increasing access to reproductive technologies, reducing risky multiple gestations, and providing identifying information to children born through gamete donation.

B. Strategies to Achieve Governmental Interests

In each of these areas—access, multiple gestations, and children's identity rights—governments could choose from a variety of approaches. As largely characterises the US approach, governments could remain relatively passive, allowing market actors—acting individually or through professional associations—to determine the contours of the marketplace and the rights of individuals within the market (Johnson & Petersen, this volume). This passivity, however, allows restrictions on access to AR based on finances and other discriminatory criteria, the use of risky procedures such as implantation of multiple embryos, and leaves children's identity rights to contractual agreements to which children are not parties. At the other end of the spectrum, governments could ban certain practices. Some prohibitions, such as a prohibition on the use of AR by gay or lesbian couples, undermine the autonomy of prospective parents. One could argue that these prohibitions on procreative choice in AR should only be employed where there is substantial evidence of a likelihood of serious harm (Ryan, 2001; Storrow, 2007), and there is no alternative way to prevent the harm.

These two extremes do not, however, exhaust possible government actions. Governments can focus on ways to address the various conditions that affect individual decision-making about AR to shift individual attitudes and decisions in favour of governmental goals or to remove material limitations that prevent prospective parents from achieving their family goals.

Governments can do this through financial or other incentives or disincentives for certain behaviours. Governments could also seek to change the decisional, relational and broader contexts in which decisions are taken. They can adopt strategies that address internal characteristics such as bounded rationality and inaccurate forecasting that reduce prospective parents' ability to make decisions that reflect insight into the long-term issues of child-rearing rather than fear of childlessness.

V. GOVERNMENT INTERESTS AND STRATEGIES: ACCESS, MULTIPLE GESTATIONS AND IDENTITY

A. Access to Assisted Reproduction

One important goal that governments could adopt is improved access to AR. The most potent limitation is financial (Johnson & Petersen, this volume). Few Americans have full insurance coverage for fertility treatment; many have no coverage at all. A minority of US states require at least partial coverage, but most insurers limit coverage to diagnosis or surgical procedures (Kindregan & McBrien, 2006; Henne & Bunndorf, 2007). Most US states do not provide fertility treatments to women receiving public medical assistance, even though lower income individuals have higher rates of infertility, and many fertility clinics refuse to treat patients with public medical assistance (Heitman, 1995, Chavkin, 2001). NHS provision of fertility treatments has been patchy at best, leading 75% of UK fertility patients to turn to private providers of services (Blyth *et al*, 2003).

AR costs are enormous. Average estimates for one cycle of IVF are close to $10,000 in the US and £4,000 in the UK, out of reach for most US and UK residents. The financial costs have a disproportionate impact in the US on African American and Hispanic American households, which on average have lower annual incomes (Jain, 2006). British families without the resources for private care may find themselves on long NHS waiting lists, excluded from assistance, or limited to less expensive treatment options (Herring, 2006). Because of the expense associated with AR, many try less expensive and less effective treatments first, lengthening the period of emotional, physical and financial strain, while others have no treatment options available (Mundy, 2007). In large part due to financial constraints, the utilisation rate for ARTs in the US is one half the utilisation rate in Europe (Gleicher *et al*, 2006, Table 1). The UK rate is two thirds the continental

European rate, and only one half the rate of countries like Sweden and Belgium (Andersen *et al*, 2006).

The private market in the US and the government-run NHS in the UK have both failed to address the fertility treatment needs of middle and lower income persons. Dissatisfaction with the limited provision of AR by the NHS has led to political pressures and promises for improvement in the UK (Herring, 2006). In the US, where AR is much more firmly planted in the private market, it is often viewed as a luxury item for those with the financial ability to purchase it (Heitman, 1995). Prospects for dramatic improvements in insurance coverage for AR in the US are unlikely, and most of the population will continue to be excluded from many of the most promising treatments for infertility.

US and UK providers have both excluded individuals from AR services on grounds other than lack of financial resources. Few states in the US protect patients from discrimination on the basis of sexual orientation, marital status or age, and clinics are free to use their own criteria for 'clinical gate-keeping', serving only those 'customers' they choose, based on the private beliefs of those working in the clinics (Storrow, 2007). US fertility clinics are less likely to accept gay men than lesbian women as patients, although a few clinics market themselves to the gay population (Greenfeld, 2007). The Uniform Parentage Act of 2000, a model statute dealing with parent-age issues involving AR, excludes unmarried couples and single parents from access to 'gestational agreements' that would form the basis of legally enforceable surrogacy arrangements. This exclusion has a particularly strong impact on gay couples. The California Supreme Court is poised to decide a groundbreaking case determining whether lesbians are protected from discrimination by fertility clinics, although whatever precedent results will govern only clinics in California (*North Coast Women's Law Medical Group v Superior Court of San Diego County*, 2006).

Until recently many UK clinics discriminated on the basis of sexual orientation and marital status, relying on a provision of the HFE Act that required clinics to consider the resulting child's welfare, including the child's need for a father, before providing services to a woman (HFE Act 1990, section 13(5)). This requirement, as interpreted by the HFEA, led to widely varying practices and the frequent exclusion of lesbian couples and single mothers (HFEA, 2003). After extensive study of clinic screening practices, the HFEA issued revised guidelines that limited the welfare principle to an 'avoidance of harm' approach, which expects clinics to provide services unless there is evidence that the child is likely to be subject to serious physical or psychological harm. This screening must be conducted in a non-discriminatory fashion (HFEA, 2007a). Access to surrogacy is limited by the HFE Act (1990), which permits only married couples to have access to parental orders, which provide for a smooth transition from the surrogate to the commissioning couple. Others—including gay, lesbian and unmarried couples and single parents—must pursue the time-consuming and onerous adoption process, requiring approval by an adoption agency, even where the parents' own gametes have been used and the surrogate mother is content to hand over the child (Herring, 2006).

Lack of family financial resources and discriminatory policies by US private and UK NHS and private clinics have excluded many from AR options. Both market and regulatory approaches have resulted in material limitations on autonomy regarding assisted reproductive technologies.

Governments are well situated to address the material limitations on autonomy. The NHS has already recognised that it has failed to meet the fertility treatment needs of UK residents and claims to be increasing the allocation of resources to this field and reducing regional differences in access (Herring, 2006). The NHS has not yet committed itself, however, to full access to the forms of treatment recommended by British professional groups (Herring, 2006).

The financial access picture is more complicated in the US. All US states could follow the lead of a few, recategorise fertility treatment from a luxury item to necessary medical treatment, and require all health insurers to provide a full range of AR services. The federal government could mandate the inclusion of AR services in publicly funded medical assistance programmes. Even with these changes, however, the US is unlikely to reach all who want fertility treatment until it addresses its inexcusable lack of health insurance for more than 40 million Americans (Warren, 2004).

While it may take longer to change the broader context of societal views of non-traditional family structures, governments can act to ensure that all providers adopt non-discriminatory policies and establish a mechanism by which those refused treatment are able to challenge or question this refusal. However, it may be too great an intrusion on the autonomy of those donating gametes to require that they be willing to donate to all prospective parents. In that case, a matching programme may be more effective, if it includes efforts to recruit a wide variety of donors, and includes portrayals of both traditional and non-traditional families who are successfully raising children born through donation to address biases in accord with the availability heuristic.

B. Multiple Gestations

Multiple gestations create the greatest health risks associated with AR. US statistics for 2004 reveal that rates for multiple births from fresh, non-donor eggs were 29.9% twins and 2.6% triplets or greater (United States Department of Health and Human Services Centers for Disease Control and Prevention [CDC], 2006, fig 10). In the UK, the 2004 statistics are somewhat better but still demonstrate high rates of multiple births: 22.4% are twins, and fewer than 1% are triplets or higher (HFEA, 2007b, table 14a). These statistics do not capture the extent to which multiple pregnancies resulted in miscarriages or the selective reduction of fetuses (CDC, 2006).

Multiple gestations raise serious individual and social issues, including myriad health, welfare and economic concerns (Johnson & Petersen, this volume). They pose risks to both the mother and her children. Mothers of multiples face greater risks of harmful conditions such as pre-eclampsia, pre-term labour and delivery, and gestational diabetes (Practice Committee of the ASRM, 2006a). Multiple gestations increase risks of death and disability (Schieve *et al*, 2004). The death rate for singleton births is 0.43%, for twins 1.55%, and for triplets 2.1% (Practice Committee of the ASRM, 2006a). Disability rates for children who are multiples are higher, as is the incidence of maternal depression and anxiety (Blyth *et al*, 2003). Because of these health risks, the costs associated with multiple pregnancy, delivery, neonatal hospitalisations, and childhood services are dramatically higher (Mundy, 2007).

Multiple gestations result from different reproductive medicine practices. One practice involves the use of hormones to increase the production of mature eggs. This treatment raises the risk of multiple pregnancies, as the number of eggs fertilised cannot be controlled except by egg extraction and IVF. Those without money for IVF are more apt to use this type of treatment (Mundy, 2007). The second practice that results in higher rates of multiple pregnancies is IVF itself. Although IVF provides control through the number of embryos implanted, multiple embryos are often implanted. In the US in 2004, only 8% of embryo transfers involved one embryo, 39% involved two embryos and 52% involved three or more (Wright *et al*, 2007, table 6).

The high rates of multiple gestations with IVF are caused by several factors—including some factors that arguably limit the autonomy of prospective parents. Many patients prefer multiple gestations (Ryan *et al*, 2004; McCullough, 2007). They may fear that their partner does not have the emotional energy to continue with treatment and believe they need a successful pregnancy immediately. They may lack relevant information that fits within the 'availability heuristic' regarding the health risks associated with multiple children, or engage in inaccurate forecasting of the experience of raising multiples.

Fertility doctors may suffer many of the same cognitive and emotional limitations, since they see only their patients' frustration at not being pregnant or their initial happiness upon discovering they are pregnant. They are isolated from the trauma of selective reduction, the stress of multiple pregnancies, and neonatal care of premature multiples. Their reputation depends on rates of pregnancy and birth, creating incentives to downplay the risks of multiple gestations to themselves and their patients (McCullough, 2007).

Finally, material limitations due to lack of health insurance coverage in the US and inadequate NHS provision of fertility treatment in the UK make it prohibitively expensive for patients to make multiple tries at pregnancy, leading them to implant more embryos in each try in the hope of achieving pregnancy (Jones, 2003; Practice Committee of the ASRM, 2006a).

In the UK, the HFEA restricts the number of embryos that clinics are permitted to implant in one cycle to two embryos for women under the age of 40 and three embryos for older women (HFEA, 2007a). This limitation has been upheld by the judiciary (Herring, 2006). At the time of writing, the HFEA has announced its intention to work with professional bodies to increase the proportion of single embryo transfers in patients with a good prognosis, with the aim of reducing the proportion of multiple births from over 20% to 10% or less within the next three years (Braude, 2006).

US physicians face no legal restrictions on the number of embryos transferred. ASRM guidelines recommend transferring no more than two embryos for women under 35 who have a 'good prognosis' and up to five for others, depending on age and other factors. The guidelines urge consideration of single embryo transfer for women under 35 (Practice Committee of the ASRM, 2006a). These guidelines are unlikely to reduce the twins birth rate.

Governments could employ several different strategies to address the problem of multiple gestations. Sweden, which provides funding for fertility treatment, effectively mandated a single embryo transfer requirement except in cases in which the prognosis is poor (Braude, 2006). As a result, Sweden has reduced its twins rate following IVF to 5% with little effect on its success rate (Nygren, 2007). Belgium has succeeded in lowering its multiple birth rates with little effect on its pregnancy rate by limiting reimbursement for the first IVF cycle to single embryo transfers for women under 36 years old (Braude, 2006). A US IVF clinic significantly reduced twins rates while maintaining its overall pregnancy rate with a mandatory single embryo transfer policy for patients with a good prognosis, accompanied by an educational campaign (Ryan *et al*, 2007).

Because of the severe financial pressures facing IVF consumers in the US and UK, one strategy to reduce multiple pregnancies would be to eliminate the material limitations that lead to multiple embryo implantation. This could be accomplished through financial incentives that provide full funding through public resources or health insurers for several attempts at implantation of one embryo (or, when medically indicated, two). US health insurers and the NHS, if they consider the exorbitant costs of neonatal care for multiples that they often bear, have a strong financial incentive to provide initial funding for single embryo transfers in most cases.

Internal characteristics that lead to the decision to implant multiple embryos could also be addressed. Clinic reporting of success rates could exclude non-singleton births, or require inclusion of selective reductions, health problems of mothers, and prematurity and other negative outcomes for children associated with multiple gestations. The risks of multiple gestations can be made more vivid to prospective parents and fertility doctors by personalising those risks. Prospective parents and fertility doctors can visit neonatal units, meet with parents of multiples, or consult with obstetricians or neonatologists prior to implantation. Governments could shift the starting point by making single implantation the norm and requiring justification for any greater number. If these less intrusive measures fail, then governments could consider broader regulatory measures.

C. Children's Access to their Genetic Identity

A substantial number of parents do not tell their children that they are born as a result of gamete donation (Murray & Golombok, 2003; Lycett *et al*, 2005; Waldman, 2006). While research reveals that families who used donated gametes to achieve pregnancy function well, evidence suggests that keeping the donation secret may create greater tension within the family, and some adult children report feelings of betrayal if they later find out the truth of their conception. Even where one parent wishes to tell, that parent may feel constrained by the fear of the non-genetically related parent that the information will undermine their parent–child relationship (Lycett *et al*, 2005). More research is needed to determine whether secrecy leads to psychological harm for offspring or their families (Golombok, this volume).

Children's interests in knowing their genetic identity places the autonomy interests of children in sharp conflict with their parents' autonomy rights to determine what information to share with their children, as well as donors' interests in anonymity. Knowledge of genetic identity may also involve the health and welfare of the resulting children. Those who argue in favour of the right to know the identity of one's genetic parents point to the UN Convention on the Rights of the Child (not ratified in the US), Article 7, which states that children have the right to be registered immediately after birth, to have a name, to acquire a nationality, and to know and be cared for by their parents. They also include Article 8 of the UN Convention, which requires respect for the right of the child to preserve his or her identity. They have also argued that this knowledge falls within the European Convention on Human Rights Article 8 right to a private life, as well as Article 8 of the UK Human Rights Act 1998 (Jackson, 2006). The UN Committee on the Rights of the Child has never applied the Convention to provide for the right to know egg or sperm donors. Those who argue against recognition of such a right emphasise the parents' right to private family life and argue that knowledge of one's social and legal parent, not one's gamete donor, is the basic human right protected by the Conventions.

However, some European countries, including quite recently the UK, have identified the right to know one's origins as a human right. They argue that genetic identity includes knowledge of susceptibility to certain diseases, understanding where certain traits come from, and preventing half-siblings from meeting and marrying without knowledge of their genetic relationship. In response to this view, the UK ended gamete donor anonymity in 2005, and all resulting children will have access to all identifying information once they reach the age of 18. All donors must agree to disclosure of identifying information in order to be eligible to donate (HFEA (Disclosure of Donor Information) Regulations 2004). The law does not, however, require parents to inform children of the circumstances of their conception, so many may not know to seek out the registry information (Jackson, 2006).

In the US, access to information about egg and sperm donors remains firmly within the hands of the market (Waldman, 2006). Almost all gamete donations are anonymous, although prospective parents 'shopping' over the internet for donors will find detailed information available. Prospective parents may, however, seek out egg and sperm donors who are willing to make their identity known to any children born from their gametes, and prospective parents often pay an extra charge for this openness. Whether such information is available is a matter of contract between the donors and the prospective parents. Prospective parents are greatly influenced in their approach by the norms of the clinics and intermediaries providing connections to gamete donors (Mundy, 2007).

No US state currently requires that donor identification be disclosed to children. Some resulting children who have been informed of the circumstances of their conception have, however, employed the internet to locate half-siblings, identifying their donor by clinic and number (Mundy, 2007). Thus, children's access to this information is dependent on parental purchase of the right to the information at the outset, a clinic's willingness to contact an anonymous donor to see if he or she wishes to be contacted by the child, or internet serendipity. The US approach privileges the autonomy interests of the parents, and leaves the resulting children without any right to knowledge of their origins.

Since even the UK approach does not ensure that children will have access to donor information, both countries could consider a range of approaches to achieve greater openness through actions designed to alter the broader social and cultural context. The recent and dramatic shift from secrecy to disclosure in the context of adoption may serve as a model for achieving the same shift in AR, a shift that is already beginning. Educational programmes and publicity campaigns can reduce the fears of stigma and harm to the parent–child relationship. Encouraging openness about donor identity requires assisting parents with this process throughout their children's maturation. Ongoing supportive services to families created through gamete donation can assist parents who wish to tell their children, but do not know how or when to do so. Providing parents with the individual experiences of children born through donation can assist parents at the time of fertility treatment to make more accurate forecasts of whether they would want to have access to identifying information, and whether they should plan to inform their children. Clinics may assist the relational context by working individually with the parent who will not have a genetic connection to the child, to discuss how to feel secure in their parenting role where children are informed of the fact of donation.

VI. CONCLUSION

Autonomy in reproduction is a complicated concept. Individuals' choices are strongly influenced by the context for their decision-making, internal cognitive characteristics and material limitations. A market-based context for reproductive decision-making may give the illusion of full autonomy, but markets necessarily shape decisions and options, and may exclude some from any choices at all. Government intervention can work to advance important societal goals without unduly interfering with autonomy interests by using strategies to shift the decisional context, eliminate material limitations and overcome cognitive limitations. Judicious use of such strategies can help harmonise societal and individual goals in assisted reproduction.

BIBLIOGRAPHY

Andersen AN, Gianaroli L, Felberbaum R, deMouzon J & Nygren KG (2006) 'Assisted reproductive technology in Europe, 2002. Results generated from European registers by ESHRE'. *Human Reproduction* 21, 1680–97.

Berger PL & Luckmann T (1966) *The Social Construction of Reality: A Treatise in the Sociology of Knowledge*, Anchor Books, New York.

Blyth E, Martin N, Potter C (2003) 'Assisted human reproduction: Contemporary policy and practice in the UK'. In *Assisted Human Reproduction: Psychological and Ethical Dilemmas* (Eds, Singer D & Hunter M) Whurr Publishers Ltd, London, pp 1–27.

Braude P (2006) 'One child at a time: Reducing multiple births after IVF, Report of the Expert Group on Multiple Births after IVF'. Retrieved 11 February 2008 from the Human Fertilisation and Embryology Authority website, http://www.hfea.gov.uk/en/483.html#expert-group.

Chavkin D (2001) 'Medicaid and viagra: Restoring potency to an old program?' *Health Matrix* 11, 189–262.

Clement G (1998) *Care, Autonomy, and Justice: Feminism and the Ethic of Care*, Westview Press, Boulder, CO.

Dunoff JL (1998) 'Rethinking international trade'. *University of Pennsylvania Journal of International Economic Law* **19**, 347–88.

Dworkin G (1988) *The Theory and Practice of Autonomy*, Cambridge University Press, Cambridge.

Gleicher N, Weghofer A, Barad D (2006) 'A formal comparison of the practice of assistive reproductive technologies between Europe and the USA'. *Human Reproduction* **21**, 1945–50.

Greenfeld DA (2007) 'Gay male couples and assisted reproduction? Should we assist?' *Fertility and Sterility* **88**, 18–20.

Gurmankin AD, Baron J, Hershey JC, Ubel PA (2002) 'The role of physicians' recommendations in medical treatment decisions'. *Medical Decision Making* **22**, 262–71.

Heitman E (1995) 'Infertility as a public health problem: Why assisted reproductive technologies are not the answer'. *Stanford Law & Policy Review* **6**, 89–98.

Henne M & Bundorf M (2007) 'Insurance mandates and trends in infertility treatments'. *Fertility and Sterility* **89**, 66–73.

Herring J (2006) *Medical Law and Ethics*, Oxford University Press, Oxford.

HFEA (Human Fertilisation and Embryology Authority) (2003) *Code of Practice*, 6th edition.

—— (2007a) *Code of Practice*, 7th edition.

—— (2007b) 'A long-term analysis of the HFEA register data 1991–2006'. Retrieved 11 February 2008 from the HFEA website: http://www.hfea.gov.uk/en/1540.html.

Jackson E (2006) *Medical Law: Text, Cases and Materials*, Oxford University Press, Oxford.

Jain T (2006) 'Socioeconomic and racial disparities among infertility patients seeking care'. *Fertility and Sterility* **85**, 876–81.

Jain T, Harlow BL, Hornstein M (2002) 'Insurance coverage and outcomes of in vitro fertilization'. *New England Journal of Medicine* **347**, 661–6.

Johnson K (2007) 'Proposed Colorado measure on rights for human eggs'. *The New York Times Online Edition*, 18 November.

Jolls C, Sunstein CR, Thaler R (1998) 'A behavioral approach to law and economics'. *Stanford Law Review* **50**, 1471–550.

Jones HW (2003) 'Multiple births: How are we doing?' *Fertility and Sterility* **79**, 17–21.

Kindregan CP & McBrien M (2006) *Assisted Reproductive Technology: A Lawyer's Guide to Emerging Law and Science*, American Bar Association, Chicago.

Lycett E, Daniels K, Curson R, Golombok S (2005) 'School-aged children of donor insemination: A study of parents' disclosure patterns'. *Human Reproduction* **20**, 810–19.

McCullough M (2007) 'A push for single births'. *The Philadelphia Inquirer*, 20 November, pp A1, A10.

Mundy L (2007) *Everything Conceivable: How Assisted Reproduction is Changing Men, Women, and the World*, Alfred A. Knopf, New York.

Murray C & Golombok S (2003) 'To tell or not to tell: The decision-making process of egg-donation parents'. *Human Fertilisation* **6**, 89–95.

Nygren K (2007) 'Single embryo transfer: The role of natural cycle/minimal stimulation IVF in the future'. *Reproductive BioMedicine Online* **14**, 626–7.

Practice Committee of the American Society for Reproductive Medicine (ASRM) (2006a) 'Multiple pregnancy associated with infertility therapy'. *Fertility and Sterility*, **86, Suppl 4**, S106–S110.

Practice Committee of the ASRM (2006b) 'Revised guidelines for human embryology and andrology laboratories'. *Fertility and Sterility*, **86, Suppl 4**, S57–S72.

Ryan GL, Zhang SH, Dokras A, Syrop CH, VanVoorhis, BJ (2004) 'The desire of infertile patients for multiple births'. *Fertility and Sterility*, **81**, 500–4.

Ryan GL, Sparks AET, Sipe CS, Syrop CH, Dokras A, Van Voorhis BJ (2007) 'A mandatory single blastocyst transfer policy with educational campaign in a United States IVF program reduces multiple gestation rates without sacrificing pregnancy rates'. *Fertility and Sterility* **88**, 354–60.

Ryan MA (2001) *Ethics and Economics of Assisted Reproduction: The Cost of Longing*, Georgetown University Press, Washington, DC.

Schieve LA, Rasmussen SA, Buck GA, Schendel DE, Reynolds MA, Wright VC (2004) 'Are children born after assisted reproductive technology at increased risk for adverse health outcomes?'. *The American College of Obstetricians and Gynecologists* **103**, 1154–63.

Spar DL (2006) *The Baby Business: How Money, Science and Politics Drive the Commerce of Conception*, Harvard Business School Press, Boston, MA.

Storrow RF (2005) 'Quests for conception: fertility tourists, globalization and feminist legal theory'. *Hastings Law Review* **57**, 295–330.

—— (2007) 'The bioethics of prospective parenthood: In pursuit of the proper standard for gatekeeping in infertility clinics'. *Cardozo Law Review* **28**, 2283–320.

Sunstein CR (2004) 'Moral heuristics and moral framing'. *Minnesota Law Review* **88**, 1556–97.

Sunstein CR & Thaler RA (2003) 'Libertarian paternalism is not an oxymoron'. *University of Chicago Law Review* **70**, 1159–202.

United States Department of Health and Human Services, Centers for Disease Control and Prevention (2004) 'Assisted reproductive technology success rates: National summary and fertility clinic reports'. Retrieved 11 February 2008, from the Centers for Disease Control and Prevention website, http://www.cdc.gov/art/ART2004/index.htm.

Waldman E (2006) 'What do we tell the children?'. *Capital University Law Review* **35**, 517–61.

Warren E (2004) 'The new economics of the American family'. *American Bankruptcy Institute Law Review* **12**, 1–41.

Wright VC, Cheng J, Jeng C, Chen M, Macaluso M (2007) 'Assisted reproductive technology surveillance—United States, 2004'. *Morbidity and Mortality Weekly Report* **56**, SS-6, 1–22.

Legislation

European Convention for the Protection of Human Rights and Fundamental Freedoms, as amended by Protocol No 11, 4 November 1950, 213 UNTS 221.

Fertility Clinic Success Rate and Certificate Act 1992 (US).

Human Fertilisation and Embryology Authority (Disclosure of Donor Information) Regulations 2004, SI 2004/1511 (UK).

Human Rights Act 1998 (UK).

National Commissioners of Uniform State Laws, Uniform Parentage Act (2000, amended 2002) (US).

United Nations Convention on the Rights of the Child, Nov. 20, 1989, 1577 UNTS 3.

Cases

Eisenstadt v Baird, 405 US 438 (1972).

JF v DB, 897 A.2d 1261 (Pa Superior Court, 2006).

North Coast Women's Law Medical Group v. Superior Court of San Diego County, 40 Cal Rep 3d 636 (Cal Ct App 2006), *petition for review granted and opinion superseded* 139 P.3d 1 (Cal 2006).

10

Instruments for ART Regulation

What are the Most Appropriate Mechanisms for Achieving Smart Regulation?

MARTIN H JOHNSON AND KERRY PETERSEN

I. INTRODUCTION

T HE TERM 'ASSISTED reproductive technology' (ART) covers a range
of medical and related research procedures involving human gametes
and embryos. From its origins in the 1970s (Edwards *et al*, 1969;
Steptoe & Edwards, 1978), ART has been considered a candidate for special
regulatory control, over and above that imposed generally on medicine and
science. In some jurisdictions, highly prescriptive legislative controls operate (for example Italy and Germany: Robertson, 2004a), whilst in others a
free market and/or professional self-regulation have largely dominated (for
example Italy pre-2004, and the US: Adamson, 2002; Robertson, 2004a,
2004b; Spar, 2006). The UK and Australia, on which this chapter is largely
based, have both adopted hybrid regulatory structures with differing mixes of
statutory and non-statutory instruments at both general medico-scientific and
specifically reproductive levels (detailed in Figure 1 below). Regardless of the
form of regulation, all regulatory regimes intrude to a greater or lesser extent
on the reproductive autonomy of the patient and the professional autonomy
of the doctor and scientist. Thus, the reproductive choices of patients are
constrained, the physician's responsibility is divided between the patient and
the state, and the scientist is prevented, deterred or delayed from undertaking
potentially useful or creative research. Given the liberal-democratic presumption that individuals have the right to determine and choose their own ends
through their autonomous informed choices (Gavaghan, 2007), the justification for these intrusions on autonomy would seem to require a demonstration
of proportionate actual or potential harm, or at least offence, to the public
interest (Feinberg, 1984, 1985). Such a justification is particularly important, given the strong illiberal traditions in both the UK and Australia that
have restricted sexual and reproductive autonomy, often imposed through
religiously inspired moralities (Brooks-Gordon *et al*, 2004).

Figure 1: Schematic summary of the ART regulatory matrices in (a) the UK, and (b) the State of Victoria, to illustrate the different classes of regulatory possibility.

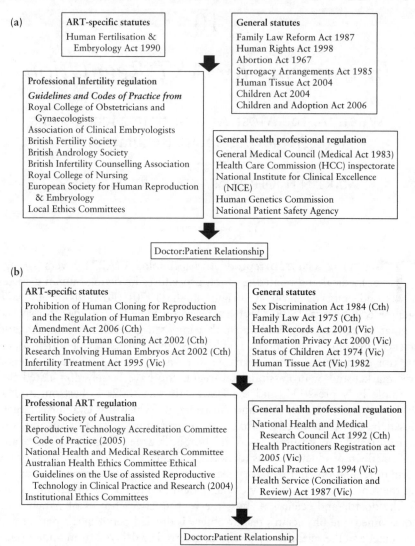

In each case, the right-hand boxes represent general regulatory elements that are not specific to ART, but with some examples chosen of particular relevance for ART. The left-hand boxes are those regulatory elements specific to ART. The regulatory structure is also tiered. The upper boxes contain examples of what we have called 'formal regulation': statutes that create offences and apply criminal sanctions. The lower boxes contain examples of what we call 'informal regulation', which includes by professional societies, which publish codes of practice. These have no legal force but *in Australia* compliance is required for clinics to be accredited (adapted from Johnson & Petersen, 2008).

Why then the call for regulation? In general, regulation is called for in situations in which some aspect of society is perceived as 'going wrong' in a sufficiently serious way (and for which private legal remedies seem insufficient) as to warrant intrusion in the 'public interest', a much abused expression used to capture this wider social concern. In a recent paper, we enquired into the possible nature of the various public interests that explicitly or implicitly might explain how the special regulation of ART is justified within a liberal democratic framework. We queried whether these public interests are robust enough to support the highly intrusive special regulation currently experienced in the UK (through the Human Fertilisation and Embryology Authority [HFEA]) and in the Australian State of Victoria (through the Infertility Treatment Authority [ITA]). We found that regulatory objectives were often unclear, when discernible many seemed outdated or distorted by minority values, and most could no longer justify a tier of regulation aimed specifically at ART in addition to the general regulation applicable to all of medicine and science (Johnson & Petersen, 2008; see Table 1 for a summary). A notable exception to this conclusion was the socio-political public interest of 'trust building' to address general concerns about the uncritical and uncontrolled application of scientific discovery to everyday life and to the process of reproduction in particular. Having a regulatory structure that gave space, time and a framework for sensible discussion and decision-making was advanced as the key historical and contemporary objective of regulation. However, whether there is hard social science evidence to support this conclusion is questionable (Joint Committee, 2007a, sections 14–23), even though opinions have been expressed supporting this view (Joint Committee, 2007b, pp 44–5, 112–14; see also Szoke, 2004).

Clear and justifiable objectives for state intervention are important, since without them it is difficult to see how appropriate regulatory control instruments could be and have been selected. Likewise, empirical research-based evidence on the impact of regulation (effectiveness and costs) is difficult to obtain in the absence of measurable objectives and, not surprisingly, is in meagre supply (Joint Committee, 2007a, section 92). We proposed a five-step approach to both the development and review of regulatory policy, somewhat akin to the 'quality control' procedures applied to clinical practice (Figure 2 below), which requires the identification and justification of explicit regulatory goals and objectives, the selection of regulatory instruments appropriate to the objectives, and the monitoring of the cost-effectiveness of their use in relation to objectives as part of continuing regulatory review. This

Table 1: A 12-cell matrix for identifying ART issues according to the type of potential public interest invoked and the type of regulatory model applicable (adapted from Johnson and Petersen, 2008)

Area of public interest	'Pure' market regulation*	'Values-influenced' market regulation*	'Values-based' regulation**
Health	Safety and well-being (eg medical competence, morbidity reduction) Quality assurance Approving use of new technologies Provision of guidance	Avoiding disability (eg in what cases is PGD allowed?) Avoiding consanguinity (by limiting offspring/donor, and through access to record-keeping)	Protecting the 'genetic solidarity' of future generations
Financial	Costs (eg consequential health costs) Pricing structures Ensuring accurate consumer information Commercial activities	Resource allocation and prioritisation Price fixing	
Ethico-legal	Supporting autonomy of competent individuals (patients, donors, surrogates, health professionals)	Protecting non-competent individuals (children— actual and potential)	Respecting the embryo Protecting human dignity
Socio-political		Protection from public backlash against the market	Public education Building public trust Risk management

* Market regulatory models adopt a 'patient/donor/surrogate as consumer' and 'doctor/scientist as provider' approach to regulatory issues. 'Pure' market approaches eschew cultural influences, whilst 'values-influenced' approaches admit the inability of markets to be free from cultural values and either try to be explicit about the intrusion of values on the market or use values-based influences explicitly to achieve specific policy outcomes through market manipulations. These regulatory models are in essence based on the economics, ethics and law of individuality.

** 'Values-based' regulation views individuals not as consumers/providers but as citizens sharing common cultural values and thus an agreed common social ethical and legal framework. It thus identifies and claims public interests that extend beyond simply those of the parties involved in ART (patients, donors, surrogates, doctors, scientists, etc) and indeed may infringe on the autonomy of those individuals.

Figure 2: Schematic view of the 5-step model for smart regulation (adapted from Johnson & Petersen, 2008).

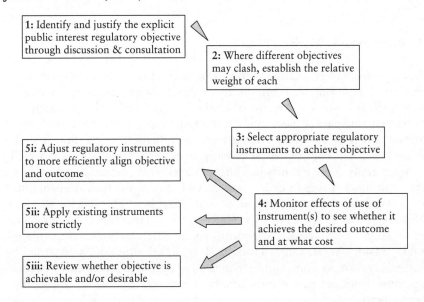

approach accords with the definition of 'regulation' given by Black (2002) as:

> The sustained and focused attempt to alter the behaviour of others according to defined standards or purposes with the intention of producing a broadly identified outcome or outcomes which may involve mechanisms of standard setting, information gathering and behaviour modification.

In this chapter, we develop this model further by examining the range of regulatory instruments available and the pros and cons of each. We then use three selected public interest objectives to illustrate how different instruments might be selected and might operate.

II. MODELS FOR SMART REGULATION

Regulation is smartest when it chooses a mix of regulatory instruments that maximises the achievement of regulatory objectives at minimum cost. The regulatory instruments available for use may be divided broadly into four categories, each with distinctive characteristics, effectiveness and cost (Gunnigham & Grabosky, 1998; White & Hollingsworth, 1999; Brownsword, 2005). First, we consider the general characteristics of each instrumental category. Then we relate their appropriateness for use in regard to selected ART regulatory objectives.

A. Regulating by Market Forces

One approach to regulation is to rely on market forces—whether in a free market like the US (see Glennon, this volume) or in a regulated market in which there is some oversight of charges and/or services. This approach is implicit in market-based public interest theory (column 1 in Table 1 above), but can also form part of values-influenced regulation (column 2 in Table 1). The approach already operates de facto internationally through reproductive tourism. Thus, patients from restrictive jurisdictions travel to other places in order to seek ART treatments that are prohibited or unavailable in their home state, and may even do so with the legal blessing of the home state (*R v HFEA*, 1997). Health professionals may move to clinics or research laboratories in different jurisdictions for the same reason (Anon, 2001; Horsey, 2007). This situation is regarded by some observers as unjust and inequitable, because it places extra burdens on those from restrictive jurisdictions. However, it could be argued that reproductive tourism is simply part of our pluralistic world in which people have freedom of movement and the right to exercise reproductive choice, and so avoids moral conflict and contributes to peaceful co-existence (Pennings, 2004). Questions may arise about the safety of services in different jurisdictions, or about the legal status of any child born in the home jurisdiction as a result of treatment overseas. For example, where women receive multiple embryo transfers overseas, and then return to the UK or Australia, it is there that the public health and financial burdens are borne. Similarly, although in most Australian jurisdictions and in the UK the birth mother is the legal mother and her consenting male partner is the legal father, there is currently only a proposed provision for legal co-parenting by lesbian couples in the UK (HFE Bill, 2008, clause 13(5)) or for legal recognition for non-birth mothers in Victoria (VLRC, 2007, pp 126–31), and no provision (actual or planned) for co-parenting by gay male couples in either jurisdiction (Anon, 2003). So whilst reproductive tourism may act as a compromise, it can bring its own problems with it. Thus, if severe restrictions are placed on reproductive choice, then solutions sought out with the jurisdiction may generate health, financial and legal problems.

However, even within a single jurisdiction, different clinics may offer different levels and types of service and make different charges for them, or even no charge at all in NHS units. Thus, in the US, 26% of ART clinics choose not to offer pre-implantation genetic diagnosis (PGD) for reasons that included market forces (Baruch *et al*, 2006). In the UK, the requirement under the HFE Act (1990) for clinics to 'take account of the child's need for a father' led some clinics to refuse IVF treatment to lesbian couples or single women, whereas others were willing to treat (Deech, 2007). Other clinics choose to restrict access by age or type or severity of infertility, influenced at least in part by market considerations of competitive league tables or cost to the public purse in NHS units. Costs and outcome rates (in terms of 'take-home-baby' rates) can vary widely and some of this information has been made comparatively widely available to patients in the UK through the HFEA's guide to clinics (HFEA, 2007–2008). A recent report from a parliamentary committee considering the UK government's draft Human Tissue and Embryos Bill (Joint Committee, 2007a, section 125) heard allegations of price-fixing and charging for unnecessary treatments such as immunotherapy or cost-ineffective services such as egg freezing, although no evidence was offered on this point. Notwithstanding, the Committee suggested (Joint Committee, 2007a, sections 126 and 127) that there should be greater regulatory supervision over market elements of service provision, an acknowledgement that market issues raised concerns. Indeed, in our previous paper, we identified market issues of service provision as constituting the largest single public interest element in ART, spanning health, financial and ethico-legal public interests (see left and middle columns in Table 1 above, and Johnson & Petersen, 2008). All of these three interests are essentially addressing the level of the competitive playing-field; are primarily of concern to the players in the market (providers and consumers); and arguably can be met through market regulatory principles and mechanisms, as already available for consumer protection generally in conjunction with standard-setting, quality assurance directives and monitoring bodies, such as are provided by the UK Healthcare Commission. However, like the parliamentary committee (Joint Committee, 2007a, section 127), we did not see that the regulation of these areas of ART required the cumbersome regulatory structures exemplified by the HFEA and the ITA, not least because none of the public interest issues raised was unique to ART, values-influenced market elements abounding elsewhere in medicine.

In conclusion, most markets do not operate without some sort of overview, which may take different forms. For example, consumer protection groups may monitor performance and bring consumer pressures to bear on providers. Professional bodies may publish codes of practice, conformation with which provides for best practice and also a measure of protection against consumer legal challenge. Simple ethical or self-interested self-control by most service providers occurs as a result of caution about the general legal rights of consumers to bring challenges through the courts. For example, in the US many high profile ART-related cases have been brought under general laws (see *Davis v Davis*, 1992; *AZ v BZ*, 2000;

JB v MB, 2001; *Litowitz v Litowitz*, 2002, for examples), a situation that does not occur in the UK and rarely occurs in Australia and is cited as one advantage for service providers of having a statutory regulatory body (English, 2006). Paradoxically, statutory bodies actually charged with regulating the market in ART medicine are rare or non-existent. Certainly, such a role does not feature in the statutory functions of either the HFEA or the ITA, even though the former has taken it upon itself to adopt that role in its HFEA *Guide to Infertility* (2007–2008), in which it claims to champion itself as 'Protecting the Patient', and in a series of subsidiary publications offers data on treatment outcomes.

B. Techno-regulation

A regulatory strategy engineered to guarantee compliance is often called techno-regulation (see Murray & Scott, 2002), for example, engineering seat belts that must be connected before a car will start. The techno-approach focuses entirely on engineering the desired behavioural outcome with little or no requirement for intellectual or moral agency, or in some cases even awareness, by the clients that they are being regulated. There is no choice available to them about whether or not to conform or rebel, other than to try and 'out-techno' the regulator. There may also be a corresponding reduction of the requirement for transparency or account-ability on the part of the regulator (Lessig, 1996), opening up possibilities for regulator abuse. Overall, techno-solutions are based fundamentally on absence of trust.

It is difficult to see how a techno-approach would handle most of the ART-related issues currently subject to regulation, especially those issues with a values-based component. However, the approach may have a limited role. For example, as part of a market regulatory control, one could envisage legally restricting ART clinic advertising to a Department of Health website that refused to accept advertisement placement unless in a prescribed format with contents (pricing format, outcome rates and so on) that were independently verified against a computerised database. If this were coupled with an agreement or requirement for health authorities, private health companies and, indeed, patients to commission treatments only through the choices offered on the website, effective compliance with information standards might be achieved.

C. Criminal Law Regulation

This approach to compliance relies on legal enforcement with criminal sanctions and is essentially hierarchical. It is the approach taken in most

European jurisdictions. In theory, a law on the statute book provides the strongest regulatory tool. However, it is never that simple. A recent study of ART clinics in New South Wales and Victoria found that health professionals were unclear about the nature and sources of restrictions on embryo research, even though several of the clinics were licensed to conduct this research (Petersen *et al*, 2005). Perhaps this is not surprising given the complexity and load of contemporary legislation in all areas of work, combined with the relative lack of staff stability that comes with a flexible job market. In addition to confusion, the use of criminal law may seem intimidating and heavy-handed to patients, doctors and scientists, resulting in undue caution and the stifling of creativity and inventiveness. It can also seem a blunt and over-powerful instrument, where the use of softer powers and milder penalties might encourage a better climate for regulation and opportunities for improvement of standards formatively. 'Is the objective of legislation to punish, to protect by promoting high standards of clinical practice, or a mixture of both?' becomes a crucial question to answer when developing regulatory policy.

The question is crucial because the legislative approach can take different forms. A rigid prescriptive statutory approach is designed to deter and, if needs be, punish. It is the approach of choice when there is a very clear and absolute objective that commands strong public support, for example, the ban on reproductive cloning in the UK and Australia (HRC Act, 2001; PHCR & RHERA Act, 2006) or the high status accorded to the in vitro human embryo in Italy (Benagiano & Gianaroli, 2004). This approach is usually values-driven by a deontological ethic. In contrast, a more flexible legislative approach that can be responsive to changing scientific, social or ethical (more usually utilitarian) understanding (Braithwaite *et al*, 2005) can be achieved by setting up a regulatory body with defined discretionary powers to administer the law, within the limits of an ethical and legal framework specified by Parliament, as is mostly the case in the UK. Thus, the HFEA is a statutory body responsible for administering the HFE Act (1990) on behalf of Parliament, to which it must report annually. As a statutory body it is open to challenge in the courts, where it has been challenged on several occasions (*R v HFEA*, 1997; *R v SSH & HFEA*, 2002; *R v SSH*, 2002, 2003; *Evans v UK* 2006, 2007). Should it find breaches of the HFE Act (1990), it may (but is not required to: HFE Act 1990, section 42) inform the Director of Public Prosecutions (DPP) who takes the final decision whether to prosecute. It is interesting to note that in the UK over a 16-year period only one publicly known case has been referred to the DPP and that resulted in the conviction of a scientist on eight counts of falsifying records and three counts of assault, but no convictions under the HFE Act itself (Anon, 2002). The HFEA has a limited range of softer powers (too limited in the view of some observers: Joint Committee,

2007a, paras 125–7; 2007b, p 33, para 8) with which to moderate and improve practice.

The state of Victoria in Australia has adopted a much less flexible legal approach, the prescriptive policy embedded in the IT Act 1995 through its guiding principles (IT Act, 1995, section 5(1), (2)) having the force of statute. Although, like the HFEA, the Infertility Treatment Authority (ITA) is principally a licensing body, it does not have the power to issue a Code of Practice susceptible to review and change in light of social and scientific developments. However, it does have the power to issue mandatory Licensing Conditions (ITA, 2006). Another difference is that there is no provision in the IT Act (1995) for the ITA to issue directions or for the Minister of Health to change the Act by a special regulation power. In contrast, the HFEA has the power to fine-tune licensing conditions (see HFE Act 1990, sections 23, 24) and the Secretary of State has the power to change certain provisions in the HFEA by regulation (HFE Act 1990, section 45(1), (4)). The ITA also *must* refer breaches to the minister (IT Act 1995, section 122(2)), but there have been no prosecutions to date.

In addition to their policing and quasi-punitive roles, both authorities are required to keep the legislation under review and advise the minister (IT Act 1995, section 122(1); HFE Act 1990, section 7), and the HFEA has a role in public education. This mixed role required of the HFEA and ITA can be uncomfortable territory for regulator and regulated (Johnson, 1998, 2000), and leads to charges of a conflict of interest (Joint Committee, 2007a, p 119).

D. Peer Regulation

This approach falls short of legislation, but nonetheless has a communal basis to it through encouraging norms of behaviour that promote voluntary behaviour changes (Ogus, 1995). For example, the state might encourage or support professional bodies to exert peer pressure to gain compliance for certain identified regulatory objectives (for example FSA/RTAC, 2008). Such a system operates in Australia in connection with research on human embryos, where professional codes of practice have, in effect if not in reality, the force of law (for example NHMRC, 2004; see Petersen & Johnson, 2007, for discussion). A state might also hold the threat of introduction of criminal legislation over the regulated as a powerful pressure for voluntary compliance—hence perhaps the generally more cavalier attitudes in the US where legislation seems remote, whilst in those Australian states such as Queensland which have never had specific ART statutes, the awareness of restrictive legislation in the state of Victoria may have provided a powerful pressure to moderate behaviour and have delayed the introduction of state legislation in the form of the ART Act (2007). In the UK, it was essentially this approach that operated from 1985 to 1991 through the Voluntary Licensing Authority (Gunning & English, 1993).

The main theoretical advantage of this approach is its capacity to engage those subject to regulation in the processes of understanding and formulating regulatory practice. Such an approach, it is argued, employs the technically and intellectually most competent at the lowest cost to the state in the most flexible and formative ways to achieve an optimised outcome at minimum regulatory load. This contrasts strongly with the more remote and hierarchical legislative regulatory approach, which can be under-informed, slow, inflexible and disempowering, and can lead to adversarial relationships with regulators and/or through the courts (Johnson, 2002; Taylor, 2007). Of course, critics of community solutions argue that particular sectional self-interests can dominate over all other interests (those of professionals over those of patients, for example). Such a criticism ignores the extent to which the medical profession as a whole has reviewed and revised its own professional standards (GMC, 2007; RCP, 2007), which now emphasise respect for patient autonomy. In so doing, the profession has demonstrated the nature and limits of its own professional autonomy. In parallel, the level of external regulatory supervision and inspection to which health professionals are now subjected has increased (Kings Fund, 2004; DoH, 2006a; HCC, 2007; NICE, 2007). High professional standards must incorporate transparency, accountability and a requirement for more inclusive membership and attitudes (Freckleton, 2006; Johnson & Petersen, 2007). One further way of allaying the concerns about peer regulation is to ensure that the peer-regulators are not too close to those they are regulating: for example, in the UK the Royal College of Obstetricians and Gynaecologists might be considered better placed to regulate ART in the UK than the British Fertility Society, given the broader interests of the former (see section on multiple births, p 180). Likewise, self-regulating bodies lack separation of powers, being responsible for standard-setting, performance monitoring and transgressor punishing, although the same can be said of statutory bodies with flexible powers such as the HFEA.

In short, the use of community bodies to achieve regulation can be effective if sufficient attention is paid to the conditions under which they operate. Thus, the state can commission and contract other bodies to undertake regulatory functions according to terms and conditions that can be similar to those set out for statutory regulators. By specifying features such as composition, procedure, review mechanisms, reporting requirements and limits of the regulatory domain, the state can seek to achieve as effectively disinterested a regulatory function as may be found in statutory regulators (Ogus, 1995), but perhaps more cheaply and effectively.

E. Some Comments on Models for Regulation

A clear and justified regulatory objective is the central plank of any justification for intrusion of public interest into autonomy. For that objective to be met, a regulatory regime should be put in place, and regulatory instruments selected for use within it, that is designed to: (i) achieve the specified objective and no more, ideally in a measurable form; (ii) be proportionate in its impact to the importance of the objective, ideally being minimally intrusive on autonomy (see for example Joint Committee, 2007a, section 56), and (iii) be as economic as possible in its use of resources (time, money) and thus its burden of cost. In the next section, we apply these three criteria in examining how instruments might be matched to three sample objectives concerning ART.

III. THREE CASE STUDIES

A. Multi-parity

There is general, but not universal, professional agreement that multi-parity is to be avoided if possible because of the increased risk of accompanying maternal and infant morbidity (Elster, 2000; Kissin *et al*, 2005; El-Toukhy *et al*, 2006). So, given that multi-parity poses significant public health and financial burdens, the reduction of multiple births is an identified public interest (Johnson & Petersen, 2007). What, then, is the smartest regulatory tool to use? The model of devolved statutory power used in the UK does not seem to have been particularly effective given the increase in twinning rates still observed (El-Toukhy *et al*, 2006). It seems likely that the prescriptive statutory model current in Italy, which permits the fertilisation of only three oocytes and mandates the uterine transfer of all three possible embryos (Banagiano & Gianaroli, 2004; Article 14 of Law 40/2004), is likely to increase multi-parity (Banagiano, 2005). Neither has the free market mechanism, operating in the US, prevented multi-parity, as rates there are even higher than in the UK (PCASRM, 2006; see Glennon, this volume). It is Scandinavia that has set the standard here, rates of multi-parity falling dramatically (Karlstrom & Bergh, 2007). Why this might be so is an issue we will return to below.

   In looking for an effective regulatory strategy, the smart regulator will look at the pressures that generate multi-parity and tailor regulatory tools to address these subversive elements. Multi-parity is not always seen as bad, especially by patients but also by some ART doctors (Moreton, 2007), and so preventing it is not seen as being in the individual patient interest, thereby providing a classic example of conflict between the public interest and autonomy. Thus, the expense of private treatment and the long waiting lists and restrictive access conditions for state-funded ART treatment, can, when coupled with the rapid decline in female fertility after the age of 35 years, induce an imperative in both patients and some doctors to complete ART families as quickly as possible. Birth of twins or triplets can seem (and is in some cases) a way of achieving this outcome. The fact that in other cases it can result in considerable maternal and infant morbidity and even mortality, can be under-emphasised by the ART doctors, because it is obstetricians, paediatricians, psychiatrists and social workers, not ART clinicians, who generally have to pick up the pieces and deal with the morbidity and its costs. In addition, publication of clinic outcome data in terms of total births without differentiating multiple from singleton births may encourage clinics to replace more embryos to maximise performance. So, with this in mind, what sort of regulatory mechanism might most effectively reduce multi-parity?

One possibility would be to adopt a market approach and to make ART clinics responsible for all obstetric and paediatric costs associated with multi-parity (Deech, 2002; Johnson, 2002) and, indeed, for consequential costs of other treatments such as ovarian hyperstimulation syndrome, and so on. Attractive as it may seem to impose the financial burden on the clinics rather than patients, there are at least three major problems with this market approach. First, given the private medical status of most ART clinics, the increased costs will simply be passed on to consumers. Whilst in principle inter-clinic competition should prevent this getting out of control, in practice other unavoidable market constraints such as only a single geographically convenient clinic and elements of market price/practice fixing might conspire to prevent this occurring. Secondly, some clinics (especially those that are publicly funded) may simply become over-conservative in their clinical management, thereby reducing pregnancy rates or increasing the numbers of treatment cycles needed to obtain a pregnancy. Both of these consequences have financial, psychological and physical costs for the patients. This is an example of how pricing mechanisms can have unintended knock-on effects depending on the unpredictable responses of the regulated, for whom costs are only one part of the picture. Thirdly, this regulatory approach is potentially discriminatory and unfair, as the clinics treating the wealthy and those from overseas, whose deliveries are not in the country of ART treatment, might be less penalised.

However, not all market strategies need have these defects. For example, imagine all clinics reaching a market agreement in which the cost of each IVF/ICSI (intra-cytoplasmic sperm injection) cycle of treatment included a single elective fresh embryo transfer, plus cryostorage of surplus embryos and subsequent frozen embryo transfers, should the fresh transfer fail. Such an approach would spread costs across patients taking the average cost up slightly for all, reduce the financial pressure for multiple embryo transfer, and remove league table pressure on clinics to get a pregnancy on the first (fresh) embryo transfer. A consequential reduction in multi-parity should follow (Karlstrom & Bergh, 2007). So, is such a system feasible? The most economic way to set up such a system would be a professional agreement to cost treatments this way, an agreement embedded in a Code of Practice that exposed any non-compliant clinician to expensive litigation, and thus would be easy to police and so cheap on the public purse. Of course, it could be argued that the lowest call on that purse might be achieved by allowing free cycles of treatment as long as they were restricted to single embryo transfers. The costs of treatment to the NHS or insurer might well be compensated for by the reduction in pregnancy, neonatal and lifelong support costs, indeed the National Institute for Health and Clinical Excellence (NICE, 2004) has argued for three free cycles of treatment in the UK.

A techno-solution involving required advertising via a regulated website, along the lines suggested earlier, might also work, but is likely to be more difficult and costly to police. Statutory regulation could also work, but could be cumbersome and non-responsive to clinical developments. A combination of intelligent market and professional regulation could thus offer a useful strategy. Indeed, in the UK the Department of Health or a statutory body such as the HFEA could take the lead in requesting the Royal College of Obstetricians and Gynaecologists (RCOG) to undertake this task in the public interest, perhaps with the ever-present implication of imposed regulation were effective self-regulation not forthcoming.

Interestingly, there is evidence from Victoria, Australia, that a system of (national) professional self-regulation (FSA/RTAC, 2005, Part 2, sections 4.5, 4.6) with oversight by the state regulatory body, the ITA, has brought multi-parity rates down to negligible levels (ITA, 1999, Table 6; ITA, 2007, Table 3). However, over the same period the cost of ART treatment to the patient has been reduced substantially, as health insurance picks up 80% of the costs, so the market pressure for multiple transfers has also reduced—a lesson for the UK?

B. Human Embryo Use In Vitro

The regulatory issue here is whether and how to constrain the use of human embryos in vitro. Given that societies vary considerably in the status accorded to the human early embryo, there is considerable variation in what can and cannot be done to and with embryos.

When an embryo is given essentially full human status from fertilisation, the full panoply of legal protection will and does apply, as in Italy (Banagiano & Gianaroli, 2004). In the UK, a similar motivation drove the Unborn Child (Protection) Bill of 1984, a Private Member's Bill introduced into Parliament by Enoch Powell. Although this Bill commanded overwhelming parliamentary support, it was not passed for technical reasons. The public interest in this special status of the human embryo is values-based and, being founded on such fundamental ethical, social and moral beliefs, is almost invariably therefore embedded in statutory legislation, in the same way as murder, with the absolute prohibition being tempered by legal qualifications (for example defence of provocation), or socially determined circumstance (for example diminished responsibility). Such a statutory approach may conflict with and indeed override the interests of other involved individuals (such as doctors and aspirant parents) and thereby may compromise the professionalism of clinicians and the reproductive autonomy of patients. For example, infertility treatment may be compromised directly by constraints on the number of embryos that can be produced when all those that are viable must be placed back in the woman, or by the banning of embryo cryopreservation or of the use of PGD for genetic disease prevention (German Embryo Protection Act, 1990; Benagiano, 2005). Indirect adverse consequences may also result when research on human embryos is prohibited. For example, a widely accepted utilitarian argument made in the UK in the 1980s was that a ban on research simply transferred the burden to women and any children born, who became the experimental objects instead of the embryos themselves: they were placed at risk in order to protect all those embryos that would otherwise have been used in experiments to develop better treatments (Braude *et al*, 1986).

Most societies do not take such an extreme position as that outlined above, some taking the view that the human embryo has, in and of itself, some special status beyond that of mere tissue. Others change over time as the public become more accepting. In Australia, for example, strict laws introduced in 2002 were reviewed and made more flexible in 2006 as a result of recommendations made by the Lockhart Committee (2005) (Chalmers, 2002; RIHE Act 2002; PHC Act 2003; PHCR & RHERA Act 2006 *(Cth)*; Cooper, 2006). In the UK, the Government Bill that led to the HFE Act (1990) adopted from the outset a less stridently embryocentric tone, based on the Warnock Committee's report (Warnock, 1984), which accorded to the human embryo 'special moral status'—less absolute than Powell and his supporters had wanted. This gradualist or developmental view of the status of the human embryo (Johnson, 2001) combines an acknowledgement of its potential with the reality of research and treatment issues by prioritising the interests of developed over undeveloped human entities. There seem to be two implicit key objectives at work in how the UK regulatory regime was framed (Johnson & Petersen, 2008). First, given that a small, but significant, section of the population sees the embryo as more or less the equivalent of a human being, there is an ethical public interest implicit in giving it some protection. This may not satisfy critics of embryo research, but does acknowledge their viewpoint. Secondly, there is a much wider public socio-political interest in allaying general fears about the possible abuses of science. These fears are less about research on embryos per se (especially when for purposes of prevention or treatment of disease) and more about the manipulation of the embryo in vitro for socially repellent consequential purposes, particularly acute when reproductive uses of the embryo to produce children are involved (Johnson, 2006a; Johnson & Petersen, 2008). Given these identifiable key public interest objectives, what is the best way to select the most cost-effective regulatory tools?

In the US, where the ethical strand of public interest is particularly strong, the approach has not been to place tight controls over the use of human embryos in vitro, but to ban public funding in whole or in part of such work. This is essentially a quasi-market approach that uses financial muscle to exert ethical, and thereby political, leverage. The result is a muddle, denying protection to embryos, exposing patients to risk, but allowing pockets of clinical and research creativity to flourish (Johnson, 2006b). In many European jurisdictions, use of the criminal law to specify what can and cannot be done is widespread, and provides a blunt instrument. The situation in the UK since the 1990 Act, whilst continuing to invoke legislative regulatory models, appears to be evolving in an interesting way. Thus, two important clarifications of regulatory objective seem to have emerged through regulator rulings, court judgments on them, and government legislative actions and proposals.

The first clarification is that the distinction between a 'research embryo' and a 'reproductive embryo', which was implicit in the HFE Act (1990), has now become more clearly established (Johnson, 2006a). This process began in earnest with the HFE ruling that reproductive cloning was banned in the 1990 Act, by interpreting it purposively, but that research on cloning was legally possible, by a literal interpretation of the Act (see Johnson, 2006a). This decision was upheld in the courts (*R v SSH*, 2003) and endorsed by Parliament (HRC Act 2001; HFERP Regulations 2001). More recently, in the government's proposed revisions to the HFE Act (HTE Bill 2007; HFE Bill 2008), the notion of the 'permitted embryo' was introduced as being an embryo fit to be placed in a woman, in essence a reproductive embryo. By implication, if not statutory specification, all other (non-permitted?) embryos are research embryos. The government also proposed a third category of embryo called the 'interspecies embryo', made of certain mixtures of animal and human material. That this latter proposal was muddled reflected, we suspect, the fact that the government was concerned at how far it could go to stretch further the now almost incredible ethical public interest argument about the special status of the embryo, whilst also being mindful of the other socio-political public interest of allaying public fears (Joint Committee, 2007a, paras 142–78). Indeed, the strongest implicit message from the HTE Bill is that the special status of the human embryo no longer provides a cogent enough public ethical interest to justify such an elaborate and intrusive regulatory structure in the UK. That a recent report on the HTE Bill from a select committee recommended going much further with research on interspecies embryos than the government, and that this proposal did not elicit significant public opposition, is pertinent to the second major clarification, which is that the public seems to have developed a general confidence that the UK has in place a sensible system for containing abusive use of human embryos in vitro (Joint Committee, 2007a, paras 14–27; HFE Bill, 2008). The HFEA is seen to provide a space and time to discuss new developments reflectively and ensure proper consideration of the issues (HFEA, 2007).

Given these shifts in the UK since 1990, it is important to ask afresh the question: is the regulatory regime put in place in 1990 really achieving what was wanted then and what is needed now, and does it do so in the smartest way possible? The government, in its HTE Bill (2007), thought that the framework was broadly right and proposed tinkering with legislative changes to catch up with court judgments, law changes in other areas (such as the Civil Partnership Act, 2004), and HFEA rulings. Given that, in our view (Johnson & Petersen, 2008), the sole continuing justifiable public interest for the present cumbersome regulatory system is the socio-political one of allaying fears, the continued existence of the HFEA as a confidence-inspiring body does seem crucial. It is paradoxical therefore that the government, whilst accepting the basic framework for regulating embryo use, then proposed changing the name of the regulatory body to the Regulatory Authority for Tissues and Embryos (RATE), a curiously unjustified proposal roundly and widely condemned (Joint Committee, 2007a, ch 5), and on which the government has now wisely backed down (HFE Bill, 2008).

We argue, in the interests of cost-effective smart regulation, that the exact opposite should have been proposed, namely to retain the HFEA (with its widely regarded brand value), but reduce the scope of its intervention into the autonomy of health workers and patients to accord with the primary socio-political public interest to allay public concern about abusive uses of ART. Thus, IVF, and many related ART procedures, are now regarded by most health professionals and the public as routine clinical work, which is therefore appropriately covered by general medical regulatory supervision such as is undertaken by the Healthcare Commission, and by working under Codes of Practice developed by professional bodies such as the RCOG and NICE (2004) according to guidance provided by the Department of Health. The real areas of public concern are (1) the development of novel technologies involving human embryos, and (2) their application clinically. Limiting the HFEA's statutory remit to the regulation of these two areas, and then giving it the authority to release the technologies for use as 'permitted' technologies not subject to further special supervision, would free the medical consultation from the additional layer of specialised HFEA bureaucracy and costs currently imposed on it. It would shrink massively the HFEA's workload, and make it what the public interest justifies: a body that examines novelty and its application and provides a space for discussion of the scientific, medical, social and ethical issues surrounding novel developments. The cost savings to the professions, the patients and the government should be considerable without losing public confidence. Here is a clear example of how identifying objectives and matching regulatory tools to the objective can prove cost-effective.

C. Access to Treatment

The issue here is: should access to ART treatments be unfettered, and if not, why not (what is the public interest?), and how should access be regulated. Currently in the UK access to IVF and related procedures is mostly restricted not by regulation but by price (Brown, 2006; Ledger, 2006). There is no obvious regulatory objective here, other than perhaps to discourage ART treatment altogether—especially for the economically deprived. However, as the state neither interferes with nor supports the exercise of this freedom, by failing to ensure subsidised treatment, the only ethico-legal issue might be that of social justice in relation to access to healthcare resources, an area from which the courts shy away and for which the common law provides no remedy. In policy terms, it may be useful to consider the adverse consequences of the operation of pricing mechanisms, such as increased multi-parity, increasing morbidity and added stress-impairing treatment outcomes. Unrestricted free or cheap access (as is now occurring in Australia through Medicare provision of up to 80% of costs) might actually reduce financial claims on the public purse and so be more cost-effective.

More explicit regulation is observed in those jurisdictions in which access to treatment is restricted on grounds of marital status, sexuality or age. Sometimes, explicit values-based objectives drive the imposition of such restrictions, based on sectional moral viewpoints such as the sanctity of marriage. However, denial of treatment on grounds of marital status or sexuality conflicts with other legislation on human rights and with the provisions of the Adoption and Children Act (2002) and the Civil Partnership Act (2004) in the UK, thus potentially bringing clinicians into conflict with the law (see for example in Australia *McBain v Victoria*, 2002). Indeed, the Victorian Law Reform Commission (VLRC, 2007) has recently published a report stating that the assessment of the best interest of children should not be based on parents' sexuality and marital status. In the UK and Australia, therefore, a refusal to treat on grounds of being unmarried or lesbian is discriminatory and unlawful.

Access restrictions are more likely to be justified explicitly in terms of child welfare, whatever the underlying motivation may actually be. Thus, section 13(5) of the HFE Act (1990) prevents a woman from receiving treatment from a UK fertility clinic

> unless account has been taken of the welfare of any child who may be born as a result of the treatment (including the need of that child for a father) and of any other child who may be affected by the birth.

There are two strands here. First, it is clear from a reading of the parliamentary debates leading up to the Act (and its 2008 revision) that the 'need for a father' clause is a compromise between legislators who did not want to place moral restrictions on those seeking fertility treatment and those opposed to lesbians and single women accessing treatment on the grounds that otherwise marriage and/or fathers are devalued. Objections that fatherless children suffer (Deech, 2007) do not rest on convincing evidence from IVF-conceived families but from other sorts of family altogether (Blyth, 2007), so it is unclear exactly on what justifiable evidence base such a 'taking into account' could be made sufficient to withstand challenge under other laws (see above), hence presumably the UK government's commitment to the removal of this clause (DoH, 2006b; HFE Bill, 2008).

The second strand, however, deserves more serious consideration as a potentially legitimate public interest, namely the welfare of any child that may be born and of any other child who may be affected by the birth. The well-established public interest duty to protect children under the ancient common law doctrine *parens patriae* (*Wellesley v Duke of Beaufort*, 1827) has been used to justify ethically the inclusion of mandatory 'child welfare' provisions in ART statutes (Coady, 2002). Such an extension of this duty to non-existent persons in the public interest raises difficult ethico-legal issues (McLean, 2006; Johnson & Petersen, 2008), hence presumably use of the term 'take account of' rather than 'make paramount' as applies to existing children (Children Act, 2004; but see below in the context of the State of Victoria). However, accepting for the moment that such a public interest does exist, how best to regulate for it? In practice, the statutory requirement in HFE Act (1990) to 'take account of the welfare' has proved very difficult for clinics to implement with any consistency and so has become an almost meaningless source of vexation (Patel & Johnson, 1998; HFEA, 2005). Recently, the HFEA has used the flexibility given to it under the HFE Act (1990) to revise its guidance in the Code of Practice (HFEA, 2007) to a risk-based assessment. Thus, section G.3.3.2 sets the criterion for refusal to treat as the potential child being at risk of: 'serious physical or psychological harm or neglect', and section G.3.4.5 says

In circumstances in which further information has been collected, treatment should be refused if the centre concludes that either the child to be born or any existing child of the family is likely to experience serious physical, psychological or medical harm or where the treatment centre is unable to obtain sufficient further information to conclude that there is no significant risk.

This clause sets the threshold for refusal quite high and at a level that clinics should find practically feasible to determine in most cases. Incidentally, such a threshold suggests that the simple absence of a father or presence of a lesbian mother could not constitute such a serious risk. Additionally, the current Code of Practice at section G.3.2.2 reads: 'In particular, patients should not be unfairly discriminated against on grounds of gender, race, disability, sexual orientation, religious belief or age', which seems to provide as clear a statement as possible that access restriction should not be made on morally selective values-based criteria alone, but on risk to potential offspring. Given that such a risk-based position could equally well be achieved by professional guidelines (indeed probably already is), one must ask, having now got to this position, why statutory regulation is needed any longer and if the matter could not be left to professional guidance entirely, against a background of anti-discrimination law?

In Australia, the Victorian Law Reform Commission (VLRC, 2007, pp 52, 54) has reached a similar conclusion to that reached by the HFEA about risk assessment. The VLRC recommends abolishing the requirement that women must be married or in relationships with men to be eligible for ART treatment because these rules are discriminatory and are not based on identified risks to children. The commission further recommends that clinics play a more active role in screening people seeking treatment and proposes an elaborate review system rather than a reduced, less formal one. Thus, the VLRC recommends (like the UK) that the best interests of children to be born as a result of ART should be based on objective and verifiable risk factors, and retains the present provision stating that the welfare and interests of children should be the *paramount* consideration (a higher priority than in the UK, thereby perhaps explaining the divergence of pathways at this point). The VLRC then details prescriptively a set of mechanisms for implementing the risk assessment, rather than leaving it to the discretion of people seeking treatment and their clinicians. Curiously, it justifies this approach by recognising that doctors and counsellors

> need a mechanism for determining whether or not to treat the person or a couple which is transparent, procedurally fair and allows each case to be treated on its merits. (VLRC, 2007, p 63)

To this end, all licensed clinics would be required to establish a clinical ethics committee and the committees would be required to develop procedural guidelines and processes in line with the guiding principles of the IT Act (1995). The presumptions of risk include cases where a person seeking treatment has a history of sexual offences and/or violence, or has had a child protection order made against them. The mechanism proposed would require all people seeking treatment to make a statutory declaration in respect of these matters, giving rise to a presumption against treatment. Finally, an independent review panel, operating in accordance with proper procedural processes, would be established to hear cases where patients have been refused treatment—with a further right to review by the Supreme Court on points of law.

It seems to us that this complex system advocated by the VLRC is designed more to protect the rights of patients and to protect doctors from litigation than to protect the welfare of a child, although given that a child does not yet exist perhaps this is understandable! What these examples show is that there are different instruments available to regulate to similar ends. Whether either set of UK or Victorian proposals will find expression in law remains to be seen.

IV. CONCLUSIONS

Our model for analysing regulatory impact (Figure 2) requires clear identification of regulatory objectives. In reality, although sometimes these objectives are clear (for example multi-parity avoidance), mostly they are not explicit or well justified (for example embryo use, access to treatment, best interests of children to be born of ART). So the first imperative is to set clear and justifiable regulatory objectives. Only then can an intelligent approach to the selection of proportionate and cost-effective regulatory instruments occur. We have used the three case studies here to illustrate how this sequence might operate and also how opaque some of the paths linking legislation to evaluation actually are. Without such an analytic process, it is difficult to see how the impact of regulation can be measured (is it effective? At what cost?), and how regulatory instruments can be better adapted to regulatory purpose. Indeed, our analysis has led us to question seriously whether the regulatory mechanisms currently in place are suited to contemporary purposes.

We are *not* advocating a market in ART services free from regulation. We *are* advocating that regulation be set at a level and mediated through instruments appropriate to the regulatory objective. Such regulation need not be statutory, but could take the varied forms described here, within the modern context of medical and scientific practice, with the changing nature of and limits to professional autonomy.

ENDNOTE

UK

Human Fertilisation and Embryology Act 2008 (as amended) UK. This Act was assented to on 13 November 2008 and can be downloaded at http://www.dh.gov.uk/en/Publicationsandstatistics/Legislation/Actsandbills/ DH_080211.

Victoria

The Assisted Reproductive Treatment Act 2008 (Vic) (Art Act, 2008) was assented to on 11 December 2008. It can be downloaded at: http://www.legislation.vic.gov.au/. This Act repeals the Infertility Treatment Act 1995 (Vic) (IT Act, 1995) but will not be implemented until the middle of 2009. The ART Act 2008 is far less prescriptive than its predecessor. Some provisions of the IT Act, 1995 have been retained, but the following changes are relevant to this chapter. The new regulator, the Victorian Assisted Reproductive Treatment Authority (VARTA), has a similar role to the ITA with some changed functions, eg, a new public education and community consultation role (Part 10). The guiding principles have a broader application (s 5). A woman without a male partner will be eligible for treatment (s 10), however, all applicants (and partners if any) seeking reproductive treatment will have to agree to police checks and child protection order checks. A new 'presumption against treatment' is being introduced in cases where the checks reveal that the woman or her partner have a proven history of sexual/violence offences or a child protection order has been made removing a child from the care of the woman or her partner. As well, a newly created Patient Review Panel will be authorised to consider an application for treatment in the above cases, and also where a person is ineligible for treatment or where a registered ART provider or doctor has refused treatment because of concerns about the well-being of a child born as a result of ART (ss 10(1)(b), 11, 12, 14, 15, 85 (b, d, e)). Non-birth mothers may be listed on a child's birth certificate as well as the birth mother (Part 14). The surrogate mother will be presumed to be the mother of the child unless or until a substitute parentage order is made in favour of the commissioning parents. A substitute parentage order will name both (if there are two) commissioning parents as the child's legal parents, unless a person named as a commissioning parent can show that he or she did not consent to the surrogacy arrangement (Part 14).

BIBLIOGRAPHY

Adamson D (2002) 'Regulation of assisted reproductive technologies in the United States'. *Fertility & Sterility* 78, 932–42.

Anon (2001) 'US brain drain', *BioNews*, www.bionews.org.uk/new.lasso?storyid=965.

—— (2002) 'Fielding found guilty'. *BioNews*, www.BioNews.org.uk/new.lasso?storyid=1473.

—— (2003) 'Gay dads want fourth child'. *BioNews*, www.bionews.org.uk/new.lasso?storyid=1816.

Baruch S, Kaufman D, Hudson KL (2006) 'Genetic testing of embryos: practices and perspective of US IVF clinics'. *Fertility & Sterility*, doi:10.1016/j.fertnstert.2006.09.003.

Benagiano G (2005) 'The Four Referendums attempting to modify the restrictive Italian IVF legislation failed to reach the required quorum'. *Reproductive BioMedicine* 11, 279–81 Editorial.

Benagiano G & Gianaroli L (2004) 'The new Italian IVF legislation'. *Reproductive BioMedicine* 9, 117–25.

Black J (2002) 'Critical reflections on regulation'. Discussion paper at www.lse.ac.uk/collections/CARR/pdf/Disspaper4.pdf.

Blyth E (2007) 'Infertility treatment and the welfare of the child'. *BioNews*, www.bionews.org.uk/commentary.lasso?storyid=3549.

Braithwaite J, Healy J, Dwan K (2005) *The Governance of Health Safety and Quality*, Commonwealth of Australia.

Braude PR, Bolton VN, Johnson MH (1986) 'The use of human pre-embryos for infertility research' in *Human Embryo Research Yes or No?*, CIBA Foundation, Tavistock Publications, London and New York, pp 63–82.

Brooks-Gordon B, Gelsthorpe L, Johnson MH, Bainham A (eds) (2004) *Sexuality Repositioned: Diversity and the Law*, Hart Publishing, Oxford.

Brown C (2006) 'IVF: The continuing agony of treatment by postcode or bank balance'. *BioNews*, http://www.BioNews.org.uk/commentary.lasso?storyid=2988.

Brownsword R (2005) 'Code, control, and choice: Why east is east and west is west'. *Legal Studies* 25, 1–21.

Chalmers D (2006) 'The regulation of cloning and stem cell research' in *Disputes and Dilemmas in Health Law* (Eds, Freckelton I & Petersen K), The Federation Press, NSW, pp 237–56.

Coady M (2002) 'Families and future children: the role of rights and interests in determining ethical policy for regulating families'. *Journal of Law and Medicine* 9, 449–56.

Cooper D (2006) 'The Lockhart Review: Where now for Australia?'. *Journal of Law and Medicine* 14, 27–44.

Deech R (2002) 'Multiple birth costs should be met by clinics'. *BioNews*, www.bionews.org.uk/new.lasso?storyid=1218.

—— (2007) 'Welfare and the need for a father'. *Bionews*, 13 August, www.bionews.org.uk/commentary.lasso?storyid=3537.

DoH (Department of Health) (2006a) 'Good doctors, safer patients: Proposals to strengthen the system to assure and improve the performance of doctors and to protect the safety of patients', www.dh.gov.uk/prod_consum_dh/idcplg?IdcService=GET_FILE&dID=28496&Rendition=Web.

—— (2006b) *Review of the Human Fertilisation and Embryology Act: Proposals for revised legislation (including establishment of the Regulatory Authority for Tissue and Embryos)*, Cm 6989, Department of Health/HMSO, Norwich.

Edwards RG, Bavister BD, Steptoe PC (1969) 'Early stages of fertilization *in vitro* of human oocytes matured *in vitro*'. *Nature* 221, 632–5.

Elster N (2000) 'Less is more: the risks of multiple births. The Institute of Science, Law and Technology Working Group on Reproductive Technology'. *Fertility & Sterility* 74, 617–23.

El-Toukhy T, Khalaf Y, Braude P (2006) 'IVF results: Optimize not maximize'. *American Journal of Obstetrics and Gynecology* 194, 322–31.

English V (2006) 'Autonomy versus protection—who benefits from the regulation of IVF?'. *Human Reproduction* 21, 3044–49.

FSA (Fertility Society of Australia)/RTAC (Reproductive Technology Accreditation Committee (2005) *Code of Practice for Assisted Reproductive Technology Units*, RTAC, Melbourne, Australia.

—— (2008) *Code of Practice for Assisted Reproductive Technology Units*, RTAC, Melbourne, Australia.

Feinberg J (1984) *Harm to Others*, Oxford University Press, Oxford.

—— (1985) *Offence to Others*, Oxford University Press, Oxford.

Freckelton J (Ed) (2006) *Regulating Health Practitioners*, Federation Press, NSW, Australia.

GMC (General Medical Council) (2007) *Good Medical Practice*, www.gmc-uk.org/guidance/good_medical_practice/index.asp.

Gavaghan C (2007) *Defending the Genetic Supermarket: Law and Ethics of Selecting the Next Generation*, Routledge-Cavendish, London.

Gunning J & English V (1993) *Human In Vitro Fertilization: A Case Study in the Regulation of Medical Innovation*, Aldershot, Dartmouth.

Gunningham N & Grabosky P (1998) *Smart Regulation: Designing Environmental Policy*, Clarendon Press, Oxford.

HCC (Healthcare Commission) (2007), http://2007ratings.healthcarecommission.org.uk/homepage.cfm.

HFEA (Human Fertilisation and Embryology Authority) (2005) *Tomorrow's Children. Report of the policy review of welfare of the child assessments in licensed assisted conception clinics*, HFEA, London.

—— (2007a) HFEA statement on its decision regarding hybrid embryos, http://www.hfea.gov.uk/en/1581.html.

—— (2007b) *Code of Practice*, 7th edn, HFEA, London.

—— (2007–2008) *Guide to Infertility*, HFEA, London.

Horsey K (2007) 'Alan Trounson to head California Stem Cell Institute', *BioNews*, www.bionews.org.uk/new.lasso?storyid=3575.

ITA (Infertility Treatment Authority) (1999) *Annual Report*, ITA, Melbourne, Australia.

—— (2006) *Infertility Treatment Authority Conditions for Licences: Applications for Licences By Hospitals and Day Procedure Centres*, ITA, Melbourne, Australia.

—— (2007) *Annual Report*, ITA, Melbourne, Australia.

Johnson M (1998) 'Should the use of assisted reproduction techniques be deregulated? The UK experience: options for change'. *Human Reproduction* 13, 1769–76.

Johnson MH (2000) 'The regulation of human embryo research in the UK: what are the implications for therapeutic research?' in *Assisted Conception: Research, Ethics and Law* (Ed, Gunning, J) Ashgate Publishing, Dartford, pp 117–26.

—— (2001) 'The Developmental Basis of Identity'. *Studies in History and Philosophy of Biological and Biomedical Sciences* 32, 601–17.

—— (2002) 'The Art of Regulation and the Regulation of ART: The impact of regulation on research and clinical practice'. *Journal of Law and Medicine* 9, 399–413.

—— (2006a) 'Escaping the tyranny of the embryo?'. *Human Reproduction* 21, 2756–65.

—— (2006b) 'Regulating the Science and Therapeutic Application of Human Embryo Research: Managing the Tension Between Biomedical Creativity and Public Concern' in *Freedom and Responsibility in Reproductive Choice* (Eds, Pedain AL & Spencer JR), Hart Publishing, Oxford, pp 91–106.

Johnson MH & Petersen K (2008) 'Public Interest or Public Meddling? Towards an objective framework for the regulation of Assisted Reproductive Technologies'. *Human Reproduction* 23, 716–28.

Joint Committee (2007a) *Human Tissue and Embryos (Draft) Bill, Volume I: Report*, Joint Committee of the Houses of Lords and Commons, The Stationery Office, Norwich.

—— (2007b) *Human Tissue and Embryos (Draft) Bill, Volume II: Evidence*, Joint Committee of the Houses of Lords and Commons, The Stationery Office, Norwich.

Karlstrom PO & Bergh C (2007) 'Reducing the number of embryos transferred in Sweden—impact on delivery and multiple birth rates'. *Human Reproduction* 22, 2202–7.

Kings Fund (2004) 'On Being a Doctor—Redefining medical professionalism for better patient care', www.kingsfund.org.uk/summaries.

Kissin DM, Schieve LA, Reynolds MA (2005) 'Multiple-birth risk associated with IVF and extended embryo culture: USA 2001'. *Human Reproduction* 20, 2215–23.

Ledger WL (2006) 'Infertility treatment in the UK: Implementing the NICE guidelines'. *BioNews*, http://www.BioNews.org.uk/commentary.lasso?storyid=2887.

Lessig L (1996) 'The Zones of Cyberspace'. *Stanford Law Review* 48, 1403.

Lockhart Committee (Legislative Review Committee) (2005) *Legislative Review of Australia's Prohibition of Human Cloning Act 2002 and Research Involving Human Embryos Act 2002*, Issues Paper, August, Commonwealth of Australia, Canberra.

McLean S (2006) *Modern Dilemmas: Choosing Children*, Capercaillie Books, Edinburgh, Scotland.

Moreton C (2007) 'Jane Denton: This nurse would rather my family did not exist', news.independent.co.uk/people/profiles/article2725647.ece.

Murray A & Scott C (2002) 'Controlling the new media: hybrid responses to new forms of power'. *Modern Law Review* 65, 491–516.

NHMRC (National Health and Medical Research Council) (2004) *Ethical Guidelines on the Use of Assisted Reproductive Technology in Clinical Practice and Research, Commonwealth of Australia*, NHMRC, Canberra, Australia.

NICE (National Institute for Health and Clinical Excellence) (2004) *Fertility Assessment and Treatment for People with Fertility Problems*, NICE Clinical Guidance 11, RCOG Press, London.

—— (2007), www.nice.org.uk.

Ogus AI (1995) 'Rethinking Self-Regulation'. *Oxford Journal of Legal Studies* 15, 97–108.

PCASRM (Practice Committee of the American Society for Reproductive Medicine) (2006) 'Multiple pregnancy associated with infertility therapy'. *Fertility & Sterility* 86, Suppl 4 S106–S110.

Patel J & Johnson MH (1998) 'A survey of the effectiveness of the assessment of the welfare of the child in UK IVF units'. *Human Reproduction* 13, 766–70.

Pennings G (2004) 'Legal harmonisation and reproductive tourism in Europe'. *Human Reproduction* 19, 2689–94.

Petersen K, Baker HWG, Pitts M, Thorpe R (2005) 'Assisted Reproductive Technologies: professional and legal restrictions in Australian clinics'. *Journal of Law and Medicine* 12, 373–85.

Petersen K & Johnson MH (2007) 'SmARTest regulation? Comparing the regulatory structures for ARTs in the UK and Australia'. *Reproductive BioMedicine* 15, 236–44.

RCP (Royal College of Physicians) (2007) 'Setting Clinical Standards', www.rcplondon. ac.uk/standards.asp.
Robertson JA (2004a) 'Protecting embryos and burdening women: assisted repro-duction in Italy'. *Human Reproduction* **19**, 1693–6.
—— (2004b) 'Reproductive technology in Germany and the United States: an essay in comparative law and bioethics'. *Columbia Journal of Transnational Law* **43**, 189–203.
Spar DL (2006) *The Baby Business*, Harvard Business School Press, Boston, MA.
Steptoe PC & Edwards RG (1978) 'Birth after the reimplantation of a human embryo'. *Lancet* **2**, 366.
Szoke H (2004) 'Social Regulation, Reproductive Technology and the Public Interest'. Doctoral dissertation, University of Melbourne.
Taylor A (2007) 'Top IVF doctor cleared'. *BioNews*, http://www.bionews.org.uk/ new.lasso?storyid=3633.
VLRC (Victorian Law Reform Commission) (2007) *Victorian Law Reform Commission Final Report: Assisted Reproductive Technology and Adoption*, VLRC, Melbourne.
Warnock M (1984) *Report of the Committee of Enquiry into Human Fertilisation and Embryology*. Cm 9314, HMSO, London.
White F & Hollingsworth K (1999) *Audit, Accountability and Government*, Clarendon Press, Oxford.

Legislation

Adoption and Children Act 2002, c 38 (UK).
Assisted Reproduction Technologies (ART) Bill 2007 (New South Wales, Australia).
Children Act 2004, c 21 (UK).
Civil Partnership Act 2004, c 33 (UK).
German Embryo Protection Act (1990), in *Human Reproduction* (1991) **6**, 605–6.
Human Fertilisation and Embryology Act 1990 (UK).
Human Fertilisation and Embryology Bill 2008 (UK). Note that this Bill is now an Act, having been given the Royal Assent on 13th November 2008 and can be downloaded at http://www.dh.gov.uk/en/Publicationsandstatistics/Legislation/ Actsandbills/DH_080211.
Human Fertilisation and Embryology (Research Purposes) Regulations 2001, SI 2001/188 (UK).
Human Reproductive Cloning Act 2001, c 23 (UK).
Human Tissue and Embryos (Draft) Bill 2007, Department of Health, Cm 7087.
Infertility Treatment Act 1995 (Victoria, Australia).
Law 40/2004, Article 14 'Norms on the matter of medically assisted procreation' (Repubblica Italiana).
Prohibition of Human Cloning Act 2003 (Cth, Australia).
Prohibition of Human Cloning for Reproduction and the Regulation of Human Embryo Research Amendment Act 2006 (Cth, Australia).
Research Involving Human Embryos Act 2002 (Cth, Australia).

Cases

AZ v BZ 2000, 431 Mass 150; 725 NE 2d 1051 (US).

Davis v Davis 842 S.W. 2d W2d 588; Tenn 1992 (US).

Evans v The United Kingdom [2006] 1 FCR 585; [2006] *Family Law* 357; [2006] 156 NLJ 456 (ECHR).

Evans v the United Kingdom (2007) Application no 6339/05, Grand Chamber of the European Court.

JB v MB 2001 WL 909294 (US).

Litowitz v Litowitz 2002 48P. 3d 261, 271 (US).

McBain v Victoria (2002) 99 FCR 116 (Australia).

R v Human Fertilisation and Embryology Authority, ex parte Blood [1997] 2 All ER 687, [1997] 2 WLR 806 (UK).

R (Quintavalle) v Secretary of State for Health [2002] QB 628, CA (UK).

R (Quintavalle) v Secretary of State for Health [2003] 2 AC 687, HL (UK).

R (on the application of Rose and another) v Secretary of State for Health and the Human Fertilisation and Embryology Authority [2002] EWHC 1593 (UK).

Wellesley v Duke of Beaufort (1827) 2 Russ 1 (UK).

11

Which Children can we Choose?

Boundaries of Reproductive Autonomy

MARTIN RICHARDS

I. INTRODUCTION

FROM THE LATE nineteenth century, eugenicists aspired to build a good society through breeding better babies. In that era, when an ideology of reproductive responsibility dominated, they preached a doctrine of reproductive selectivity through education, persuasion and sometimes legislation.[1] Their anxiety was that medical care and welfare provisions had blunted the cleansing effects of natural selection on the population, leading to degeneration and the accumulation of deleterious mutations. They were disturbed by the higher birth rate of the lower orders while that of their own kind was falling. So they aimed to increase the reproduction of the 'fit' and curb that of the 'unfit'.

By the mid-twentieth century, there had been an ideological shift from the focus on reproductive responsibility to a promotion of reproductive autonomy and individual choice (Paul, 2002). And from that time on we have seen many new reproductive and genetic technologies and practices—reliable and easy contraception, prenatal screening and diagnosis, accessible safe abortion, IVF, genetic testing and embryo selection—which have separated sex and reproduction and have brought new reproductive possibilities and choices. It has become possible to terminate a pregnancy when the fetus has a serious abnormality, or to choose the sex of a child. In this new reproductive world, interest in eugenics has faded but there has been an, at least implicit, policy of avoiding births of abnormal children (whether or not the condition might be heritable) through providing new

---

[1] In Britain, there was only a single piece of eugenic legislation, the Mental Deficiency Act (1913). This allowed the incarceration of people who could be described as 'idiots, imbeciles, feeble minded persons or moral defectives'.

reproductive choices. However, the growing possibilities of enhancements, or choices of the characteristics or kinds of children we might have, have been resisted.

While many would agree with Emily Jackson that we should 'strive to carve out maximum possible respect for the reproductive autonomy of individual men and women and see this as a goal to be actively pursued' (2001, p 318), there is also acceptance that there are at least some justifiable limits to reproductive autonomy. Restrictions might be justified with reference to John Stuart Mill's (1859) principle of harm:

> The only purpose for which power can rightfully be exercised over any member of a civilised community against his will is to prevent harm to others. His own good either physical or moral is not a sufficient warrant ... [nor] because it will make him happier, because in the opinions of others, to do so would be wise or even right. (p 35)

Mill was, of course, a great champion of individual freedoms, but mindful of reproductive responsibilities he thought that the reproduction of certain social groups should be curbed., although, unlike most eugenicists, he was not a hereditarian, and his reasons were not to do with the transmission of a poor genetic endowment. Rather, he was concerned with the social and economic costs of some reproduction to society and the reduced well-being and life chances of children whose parents might be unable to offer adequate care and education. He supported access to birth control, thought that sexual restraint was desirable in some circumstances and that legislation forbidding marriage of those who lacked the means to support children was justified. As Paul and Day (2008) comment, 'Mill believed that reproduction was quintessentially social, with consequences in the first place for the child-to-be'.

In this chapter I will chart the limits of some aspects of reproductive autonomy. Of course, for a social activity such as reproduction, one can argue that, as all actions take place in and are indeed part of a social world, so they are all shaped by it. But my concern here is where we try to constrain the activities of others, most obviously by legislation, but also by social pressures and practices which may reduce decisional autonomy, or by regulating the provision or access to services which could offer possibilities and reproductive choices. What are the potential harms that are envisaged that may lead to restrictions of reproductive autonomy? I will focus on children and the kinds or characteristics of the children we might have. This is, of course, territory which has been extensively considered by moral philosophers (for example Harris, 1998; Glover, 2006) but I will consider where and why we have sought to draw limits for reproductive autonomy.

The mid-twentieth-century shift to a focus on the pursuit of reproductive autonomy and individual choice also coincided with—and was not unrelated to—the decline of eugenic thinking. Historically, eugenics has meant rather different things to different people, making it difficult to provide a simple characterisation of eugenic thought or practice. And some terrible things have been done in the name of eugenics (see, for example, Kevles, 1985; Paul, 1995), not least the denial of some peoples' reproductive autonomy for the supposed good of society as a whole. As Buchanan *et al* (2000) in their 'ethical autopsy' of eugenics say, 'apart from the Nazis' crimes, the involuntary sterilisation of tens of thousands of Americans and Europeans [was] the worst stain on the record of eugenic movements' (p 50). Even though eugenic involuntary sterilisation was not generally practised in the UK, such violations of reproductive freedoms have left a long shadow which still colours our discussions of reproductive matters. At times this may make it very difficult even to discuss reproductive matters outside a frame of individual autonomy and choice. Considerations of the social responsibilities of reproduction are generally avoided in discussions of public policy. At times, the claim that something is eugenic has seemed to cut off further discussion. My aim in this discussion is to step out of that shadow, not least by acknowledging that history directly.

Reproduction is essentially uncertain in its outcome. We can decide (within some constraints that I am not going to discuss) with whom and when we may try to have children. But, at least until very recently, there was no way to determine any of the characteristics of the children we might have. Of course, children bear some resemblances to their parents, through inheritance and the social processes of development and upbringing, but beyond that, it depends on the changes and chances of the processes of human reproduction and development—a girl or a boy, dark or fair, a calm or reactive temperament, healthy or malformed, or whatever. Birth control and some assisted reproductive technologies have made possible a separation of sexual intercourse and conception. But until recently the only possible way to influence the characteristics of children born was through the choice of a partner or, at least, a co-progenitor. But, that aside (although more will be said later), by and large it was a matter of luck which kinds of children were born. But no longer.

Today, we are able, at least in principle, to avoid at least a few of the uncertainties in the outcomes of reproduction. There are techniques that allow us to make choices which will influence the kinds of children we are able to have. These are based on selection—of fetuses that may, or may not, continue to develop to birth, or of the embryos that are implanted in IVF procedures or of the gametes that may meet at conception. In principle, these provide a broadening of reproductive choices, but such new choices are constrained, and I will discuss the limits of reproductive autonomy in these areas.

II. SEX SELECTION

While there is a very long history of the use of practices which were believed to influence whether a boy or girl would be born, it is unlikely that any of these were effective. However, we now have techniques which can be used to determine the sex of a child. These are (i) fetal sexing and selective abortion, (ii) embryo selection and IVF and (iii) sperm sorting with artificial insemination. Globally, the first is the most widely used and is, for example, the means by which wide distortions of the sex ratio at birth have been produced in parts of India (despite legislation intended to prevent it). Clearly, it is first necessary to identify the sex of the fetus. This is usually done by ultrasound scans, but amniocentesis, chorionic villus sampling (CVS) and the analysis of fetal DNA in the mother's blood can all be used. There are companies advertising on the internet that offer this latter kind of testing and provide home kits for collection of samples which are then sent off for laboratory analysis.[2]

The second approach, embryo selection, involves inducing ovulation and collecting eggs which are then fertilised *in vitro*. A cell is removed from each embryo and is tested to reveal the sex. Embryos of the desired sex are then implanted in the would-be mother. Clearly, intensive and complex techniques are involved here and there is further limitation in that, as with any IVF treatment, the pregnancy rate after implantation is low (25% or less).

The third method, sperm sorting, uses techniques that have been widely employed in agriculture for some time. This depends on the fact that males produce two kinds of sperm—those bearing an X or a Y chromosome. An egg fertilised with the first produces a female embryo, and with the latter, a male. So sperm is sorted into these two kinds and the appropriate one used in artificial insemination. Although straightforward in principle, it turns out to be rather more difficult to sort human sperm than, for instance, that of cattle. The technique is offered commercially, but it produces a baby of the required sex with less than 100% accuracy. This may be why uptake has been relatively modest, although techniques of this kind have been available in the US and elsewhere for more than a decade. A clinic operating in London in the 1990s saw 800 couples in its first 18 months.[3] Treatment was offered only to couples who already had a child ('gender balancing'), and couples had to undertake to carry the pregnancy to term whatever the sex of the resulting fetus. The majority of its clients were British couples of Indian or Pakistani origin who desired a son (Liu & Rose, 1995).

---

[2] This technique (as well as amniocentesis and CVS) may be used together with samples from potential fathers as paternity tests. Pregnancy paternity testing coupled with possible termination offers a means of selecting a fetus with a particular father (see HGC, 2006).

[3] This used a technique that was probably less accurate than some available today.

But what are couples' preferences? British evidence from a survey of 2,359 pregnant women is provided by Statham *et al* (1993). Fifty-eight per cent said they had no preference, while 5% preferred a boy and 6% a girl, 12% would quite like a boy and 19% would quite like a girl. The authors concluded that while their study did not address sex selection, their results would suggest that if techniques of sex selection were to be freely available, this would be unlikely to affect the overall sex ratio. A widespread preference for a 'pigeon pair'—one of each—is also evidenced by birth statistics which show that couples having two children of the same sex are more likely to go on to have a third. Within this broad picture there are a few communities with strong preferences for sons or daughters. And there have been claims that there are a few ethnic minority communities in Britain that show an 'excess' of males suggesting that sex selection may be used but there is a lack of compelling evidence.

Polls indicate that most people do not think would-be parents should be able to employ any technique that would ensure the birth of a child of a particular sex. In one survey, for instance, 75% of a sample of some 1,000 respondents (weighted to profile the UK population) agreed that 'genetic techniques should not be made available to parents so that they can have a baby of the sex they choose' (HGC, 2001). Asked to explain such views, many say that sex selection is 'unnatural' or 'playing God'. There is a broad consensus that people should be content with whatever they get and that sex selection is an inappropriate kind of intervention. Some describe sex selection as 'eugenic'. If what is meant by that term is modifying the pattern of human heredity, clearly sex selection will not change anything except perhaps the sex ratio. But it seems that 'eugenic' now has a much broader meaning, often simply a critical descriptor of any procedure which might be used to determine the kinds of children we might have.

Should parents be able to choose the sex of their children? Or is this an issue where it would be justifiable to limit parental reproductive autonomy? Are there harms that might follow the exercise of parental choice? Sex selection is lawful and available in the UK, but only if it is being used to avoid the birth of children with sex-linked diseases.[4] Indeed, in common with most of the other cases I will consider, procedures are available and may be used to avoid having certain kinds of children, but the use of procedures to make a positive selection for the kinds of children

---

[4] Sex- or X-linked genetic diseases are forms of genetic disease where the gene mutation responsible is carried on the X chromosome. Most predominantly affect boys because they inherit a single X chromosome. Women have two X chromosomes and, as it is very unlikely that there will be a mutation in both copies of the gene, they generally will not develop the disease. We should note that where fetal diagnosis is not possible for an X-linked condition, all male fetuses may be aborted whether or not they have the X-linked condition to avoid the birth of an affected child.

we might have is not permitted. At present, UK law does not mention sex selection. But it is banned under HFEA guidelines for non-'medical' reasons in relation to embryo selection and for sperm sorting, insofar as these come under the HFEA remit. This remit, however, does not cover the use of fresh sperm outside licensed clinics, so using sperm-sorting techniques could be permissible, although it currently does not seem to be available in the UK. However, under the Human Tissue and Embryos (draft) Bill this aspect of HFEA guidance would become black-letter law.[5] However, this legal change would not remove another possibility for couples; that of using a technique to establish the sex of a fetus and then seeking a termination of pregnancy under the 'social' grounds of the Abortion Act (1967). In addition, people may go abroad to countries where some or all the possible sex selection techniques are available.

Sex selection does not harm children, so the limiting autonomy cannot be justified by Mill's ethics unless it causes more general social harm. And, as well as its unpopularity with the public, a number of other grounds for banning sex selection have been put forward. Some object to the use of termination of pregnancy or embryo selection for reasons other than avoiding births of abnormal babies. Others object to both of these for any reason. But these are not arguments about sex selection itself, simply certain procedures, and do not relate to the use of sperm sorting. Similarly, the 'playing God' or 'eugenic' arguments are general ones about any exercise of choice about kinds of children—and some would like to extend these to include selecting out embryos and fetuses with major abnormalities. A further general argument is that sex selection involves a diversion of (scarce and expensive) medical resources for non-medical purposes.

But there are two more specific kinds of objection. The first is an argument about future worlds—a world where there could be an imbalance in the sex ratio because of the wide use of sex selection favouring one particular sex. Some parts of the Indian sub-continent already show signs of moving towards such a world. It is not difficult to imagine some of the social problems that may arise in such a society. Indeed, we have direct evidence from a number of historical examples of sex-unbalanced societies—for example, the past colonial immigration societies of Australia and New Zealand with their great lack of women, or post-Great War Britain with its missing generation of men. But at least in contemporary Britain, if we were to go on current preferences of couples, and if more of these were converted into sex selection choices, it seems unlikely that there would be a change in the overall sex ratio of the society. However, there might be a few sex-unbalanced communities.

---

[5] Practices designed to secure that any resulting child will be of one sex rather than the other will not be licensable (except when avoiding sex-linked disease) and 'sperm-sorting kits' will not be able to be sold, supplied or advertised.

The other arguments concern sex stereotypes and sexual discrimination: that in making a choice, parents would be placing a value on the sex of their children and that their worth is then based on their sex. It is also suggested that selected children might act in a more sex-stereotyped way—to fill their chosen gender role. Some of these arguments seem to be based on assumptions that most sex selection will involve choices of males, which might well not be the case in Britain. To avoid any bias of sex ratios, some suggest the use of sex selection should be limited to 'family balancing'—as was the practice in the London clinic which operated in the 1990s.

On the other side, arguments focus on the extension of reproductive autonomy that the availability of these techniques would permit (for example Savulescu, 1999; Rhodes, 2001), although some would qualify this by limiting it to family balancing and excluding all those who do not already have children. But, in practice, it would seem that the majority rules and, as I have mentioned, limitations of autonomy in regard to most sex selection, apart from its use to prevent births of abnormal children, will soon have a statutory prohibition in Britain, so adding to the limits to reproductive autonomy.

III. ENHANCING AND SELECTING EMBRYOS

Those who disapprove of the use of techniques like sex selection often refer to these as producing 'designer babies'. The term misleads because these babies are not made according to pre-selected plans, rather the parents choose between fetuses, embryos or kinds of sperm. 'Design' would be more accurately applied to a situation where a baby is engineered to have particular characteristics. Doing that is beyond current technology and understanding and, indeed, seems an unlikely future possibility, at least for the kinds of characteristics that are usually discussed in this context. But what some 'slippery slope' critics fear is that we may move beyond choosing on the basis of sex, to designing in such characteristics as high intelligence, particular personality type or physical attractiveness. To do this, there would need to be some genetic or other bio-markers which would characterise the more attractive, more intelligent or the desired personality type which could be used to select from the available embryos in a pre-implantation genetic diagnosis process—or to select out less desirable fetuses. But unfortunately for those who might wish to exercise such choices, there are no such markers available on which to base these sorts of choices. Differences in these characteristics depend on the outcome of very complex developmental systems involving interactions of many genes and all sorts of other elements in a system operating in variable environments. Even if we fully understood such developmental systems, it seems unlikely that there would be any one marker, or even a small set of markers, which would allow us to distinguish the required eventual adult characteristic in an embryo or fetus. We can do this to separate male and female embryos because they differ in the presence or absence of a particular chromosome—the Y chromosome—and it can be done in those rare cases where a particular gene variant has an overwhelming effect in the developmental system so that it more or less predictably produces a genetic condition such as Huntington's disease or cystic fibrosis. But variations in IQ test performance or physical attractiveness do not arise in this way. So it seems that, even if we were to accept a slippery slope argument here, there is not much prospect of a slope to slide down.

Another approach to enhancement would be to intervene in some way in the development of an embryo or fetus to 'bias' the developmental system towards producing the desired phenotypic characteristic. In theory, this could be some form of genetic engineering[6] or a biochemical or physiological intervention. Post-birth, this is already a possibility for certain characteristics. For example, growth can be enhanced in children with growth hormone. This may be done medically for children with certain growth-limiting abnormalities, and can also be used for 'normal' children to make them taller for social or cosmetic reasons. However, enhancement of embryos and fetuses by such means is considerably more complicated even for a characteristic such as height for which the biology is relatively well understood.

We might note that critics often do not explain why they think selecting for high IQ, personality type, attractiveness, and so on, would be such a dangerous idea—or at least arguments do not usually get much beyond saying that this would be eugenics, playing God or because the techniques are likely to be very expensive; society could divide into the successful 'GenRich' and an underclass of 'naturals' who could not afford enhancements (Silver, 1998). Sandel (2007) has argued that enhancements would represent a triumph of wilfulness over giftedness, of dominion over reverence and of moulding over beholding:

> a Gattaca-like world in which parents become accustomed to specifying the sex and genetic traits of their children would be a world inhospitable to the unbidden, a gated community writ large. The awareness that our talents and abilities are not wholly our own doing restrains our tendency towards hubris. (Sandel, 2007, p 9)

Sandel sees no reason not to use techniques to repair damaged bodies, to replace defective genes or select out the abnormal. However, it is difficult to see why these do not involve the same 'kind of hyperagency—a Promethean aspiration to remake nature' (p 5) that he objects to in sex selection, enhancements and any kind of selection.

---

[6] We should note that the (draft) Human Tissue and Embryos Bill (2008) will ban the use of eggs, sperm or embryos if the nuclear or mitochondrial DNA has been altered.

Enhancement of these kinds of characteristics involving intervening in developmental systems is not the only way to change the frequency of individuals with desired characteristics in the population: there is also selective breeding. And what is more, we do not even have to understand developmental biology to breed selectively, although it could help in that it may indicate how effective selection is likely to be. Since the dawn of farming we have been selectively breeding plants and animals—genetically modifying populations—to produce the domestic breeds and more productive agricultural plants and animals. All that is required is that, over generations, you breed from those which have the best of the desired (heritable) characteristics and do not breed from those that do not. And at least since classical Greece there have been discussions about using such techniques for human selective breeding. But, of course, it would take a great deal of control and organising to set up such a system in a human population, and there have to be decisions about what the desirable characteristics should be. But there are a few examples of practice. For instance, a nineteenth-century bible communist utopian community in upstate New York selectively bred 58 children by choosing potential parents on the basis of health, spirituality and intelligence over the one generation of the community's existence (Richards, 2004). Francis Galton, who is often seen as the father of eugenics, imagined a utopia in which only young men and women who graduated from the eugenic college could reproduce. Fantasy is one thing—and in fact Galton never published his utopian vision, 'Kantsaywhere' (Gillham, 2001)–but in reality most eugenicists[7] ruled out selective breeding. Major Leonard Darwin (son of Charles and President of the Eugenic Education Society) spoke for most when at the Second International Conference of Eugenics in New York in 1923 he said:

> [O]ur experiences in the stock yard enable us to better understand the laws of natural inheritance, yet our reliance on these laws carries with it no implication whatsoever that our methods of animal breeding ought to be introduced into human society. (Darwin, 1923, p 9)

Other eugenicists proposed schemes based on artificial insemination, hoping that if sperm from 'superior' men was on offer, married couples would forgo their own biological paternity in favour of a eugenic choice (Brewer, 1935; Muller, 1936; see Richards, 2008). But there was little sign of demand, although, as a kind of afterthought to the eugenic era, a sperm bank (the Repository for Germinal Choice) offering sperm from selected donors

---

[7] But not all; Alfred Dachert, a multi-millionaire manufacturer who grew rich in World War I, set up *Les Jardins Ungemach*, a 'eugenical' garden suburb of Strasburg in 1921. Prospective tenants were selected on eugenic grounds and required to contemplate having at least four children (Dachert, 1931; Goethe, 1946).

was set up in California in 1980 and some 215 babies were born to users over the 20 years of its operation (Plotz, 2005; Richards, 2008). However, this attracted infertile couples seeking safe sperm rather than eugenically inspired altruists. Today there are many commercial sperm banks in the US which provide sperm for infertile couples, single women and lesbian couples. Couples can choose donors on the basis of a wide range of characteristics from photographs, detailed descriptions and personal statements. Interestingly, most couples seem much more interested in finding a 'match' for the infertile would-be parent so the child will fit with the family, rather than selecting particular desirable characteristics (Richards, 2002). Some object to this marketing of sperm. And Sandel (2007) suggests that anyone troubled by the eugenic aspects of the Repository for Germinal Choice should also be equally troubled by commercial sperm banks. 'What', he asks, 'is the moral difference between designing children according to an explicit eugenic purpose and designing children according to the dictates of the market?' (p 8)

In Britain, most artificial insemination by donor (AID) takes place in clinics licensed by the Human Fertilisation and Embryology Authority (HFEA). Clinics may assist in providing a match between donor and social father but the Human Fertilisation and Embryology Act (1990) and HFEA guidelines severely limit the information that would-be parents have about donors and this effectively excludes the possibility of any enhancement. In this it may be rather different from the earlier pre-regulation practice. In her description of pre-war practice Wilmot (in press 2009) mentions that some doctors not only attempted some matching, but also might give a 'step up' in intelligence for 'eugenic' reasons.

The availability of artificial insemination by donor (AID) extends reproductive choice for infertile couples as well as those without male partners. Under a recent change, donor anonymity has ended in UK clinics so that those born after donation can, when they reach the age of 18, enquire of the HFEA and will be told the name of the donor involved. However, most couples with donor-conceived children do not tell their children of the manner of their conception (see, for example, Richards, 2002). Others believe that it is desirable for children to know (see Golombok, this volume). Among a number of advantages, this might avoid the possibility of related children forming inappropriate relationships in ignorance. A case of separated and adopted twins who later met and married in ignorance of their relationship was recently reported.[8] Annotation of birth certificates has been proposed as a way of ensuring more donor-conceived people learn of their status, and a practical scheme for this which preserves privacy has been proposed

---

[8] Although in this case the twins were conceived without the help of ARTs. They were adopted at birth and brought up separately without knowing of the existence of each other.

(Blyth, 2007). However, the government seems to prefer educational measures rather than legislation as a way of encouraging more parents to tell their children of their origins. Preserving the autonomy of parents who do not wish to tell their children is thus maintained in the face of arguments about the desirability of children knowing that they are donor conceived.

In recent years the use of AID has declined (HGC, 2006). This reflects the point that couples only use AID if they are unable to conceive children with their own gametes. There is a very strong preference to have 'your own' children. Intra-cytoplastic injection (ICSI) is a technique which can be used to extract sperm from the testes and inject it directly to an egg. Its use means that some infertile men who would otherwise have been unable to have their own children can now do so, and avoid the use of a donor.

A similar conflict between what parents choose and what some see to be in the best interests of children that may be born arises in the regulation of ARTs in respect of multiple births (see Johnson & Pedersen, this volume). This is a complex issue, but in essence: IVF accounts for 1%–2% of all UK births but almost 20% of twin births—and twin numbers are increasing. IVF twins are more likely to be stillborn or born prematurely. They have a higher risk of neonatal problems and may require intensive care. In the longer term they have a higher risk of poor educational achievement, health problems and reduced life chances. Multiple birth is also associated with health risks for the mother. However, both parents and clinics may favour practices and choices which make multiple births more likely: parents because they may be of an age that makes future successful IVF cycles unlikely or because they may not be able to afford further IVF cycles (almost 80% of fertility treatment is in the private commercial sector and availability in the NHS is very restricted). Clinics want good outcomes and good statistics to attract patients—and the way statistics are presented make multiple births appear as 'successful' outcomes of treatment. Practice elsewhere shows it is possible to reduce the numbers of multiple births. However, it is only very recently that the regulator has called for a new national strategy designed to reduce the number of multiple births (HFEA, 2007). There is a basic underlying issue here: should we curtail parents' freedom to choose particular fertility treatments, and the freedom of clinicians to advise these[9] in the interests of reducing the frequency of multiple births? We have good evidence that twins risk poorer health and life chances, and there seems to be widespread agreement that a lower twinning rate would be desirable. But we should note that reducing the twin rate would not directly protect any children from harm, it would simply mean that there would be fewer twin births and more singleton births.

---

[9] General issues of the regulation of ARTs, including professional autonomy, are discussed by Johnson and Pedersen, this volume.

Here I should acknowledge Parfit's (1984) non-identity problem. Children born as twins after IVF cannot be said to be harmed by current clinic policies and parental decisions. We may assume they are glad to be alive and to exist. Had policies been changed, or parents had made different choices, they would not have existed. A different (singleton) child might have been born in their place, so no child is worse off than they might have been. As Jonathan Glover (2006) comments,

> this seems the argument of an over-ingenious defence lawyer ... but the consequence is that, in these decisions affecting future generations, morality cannot be simply a matter of what we owe to people. Some serious harms are 'impersonal', with no-one being denied anything owing to them. (p 46)

So our basis for criticising clinic practices and parental choices or lack of desirable regulation must rest on comparisons of the relative well-being of different groups of people—the current IVF children, including many twin pairs, and another (future) generation with many fewer twins, from which we may conclude that, in general, people will be better off in such a future generation.

Before leaving the topic of choosing children we need to discuss three further cases.

A. Deafness and the Deaf

The Deaf[10] are a community of those who use sign language as their first or preferred form of communication. They see deafness as a difference, rather than a disability. Some in that community would prefer to have a deaf child rather than a hearing child as a member of their family and of their community. Most congenital deafness results from inherited conditions. Deaf people tend to find partners within the Deaf community, which may increase the chance that their children will be deaf like themselves. For some couples, if the particular inherited condition has been identified, prenatal diagnosis would be possible and if a fetus was found to have the inherited condition, the pregnancy could be terminated. However, most of the Deaf (unlike others outside the community) avoid such tests, and indeed, genetic counselling more generally (Middleton, 1995), as they are happy to have a deaf child or at least let nature take its course. In a widely reported US case, a Deaf lesbian couple used a sperm donor from the Deaf community and had two deaf children. One of the mothers was reported as saying 'It is

---

[10] The capital D is deliberate. It is the way in which many of those who are congenitally deaf describe their own community.

nice to have a deaf child who is the same as us. A hearing baby would be a blessing. A deaf child is a special blessing' (Anon, 2002). In Britain, under HFEA guidelines, someone who is deaf as a result of an inherited condition probably would not be accepted as a sperm or egg donor in a licensed clinic.[11] The Human Genetics Commission in its report on 'Making Babies' (HGC, 2006) notes that this exclusion might be seen as controversial for some, but it thought this restriction should be maintained. However, a Bill currently before Parliament goes a step further. The Human Fertilisation and Embryology Bill (clause 14(4)) amends the HFE Act (1990), section 13(9) so that:

> Persons or embryos that are known to have a gene, chromosome or mitochondrial abnormality involving a significant risk that a person with the abnormality will have or develop
>
> (a) a serious physical or mental disability
> (b) a serious illness, or
> (c) any other serious medical condition
>
> must not be preferred to those that are not known to have such an abnormality.

The Explanatory Note (109) for the Bill singles out deafness in relation to this clause.[12] So, under this clause, there could be no preference for deaf donors or selection for would-be deaf embryos in pre-implantation genetic diagnosis (PGD). This has caused a storm in the Deaf community with claims of a new eugenic programme or 'genocide' being launched against the community (see, for example, Grumpy Old Deafies, 2007). Their reproductive

---

[11] However, in advice to clinics, the HFEA (1994) has stated: 'matching of donors should be carried out sensitively in discussions between those seeking treatment and the centre. However, the Authority would not regard it as good clinical practice if a licensed centre allowed a woman's preference for a child of different ethnic origin from herself, for social reasons, to determine the choice of an egg donor. Similarly, a woman seeking donor insemination should not be allowed to choose for social reasons a sperm donor of a different ethnic group from her partner'. In the Deaf community this has been interpreted as a guidance that would mean that a Deaf couple should have a Deaf donor.

[12] Following a meeting of concerned representatives of the Deaf community and others with Department of Health officials the 'D[epartment of] H[ealth] team promised to find out if Explanatory Note could be revised, thus not singling out deafness in relation to Clause 14(4)' (Webb, 2008). This letter also states that the policy is that 'embryo testing should only be permitted where the intention is to *avoid* a serious medical condition, serious illness or disability' and that the Bill 'directly mirrors the HFEA policy on licensing PGD ... The HFEA have previously licensed PGD to avoid an inherited form of deafness and therefore, based on that, we took the position that the embryo testing provisions in the Bill may also include deafness ... It is not appropriate, if it were possible, to use the technology to select for positive attributes such as athleticism, intelligence or hair colour .... if deafness is considered by an individual couple to be a positive attribute, it would also not be appropriate to use that technology to select for this attribute' (Webb, 2008, pp 2–3). But what the letter does not say is that the HFEA has permitted the selection of embryos on the basis of a positive attribute—a particular HLA characteristic to produce a saviour sibling.

autonomy is being limited by those in the hearing community who see deafness not as a difference, but as an abnormality.

Suppose, as a principle, we decided that potential parents should aim for a child that they can have with the greatest chance of a good life (Savulescu, 1999). But we need to be very precise here: this would not be saying that parents should aspire to have the best possible of all possible children—that is not realistic—just the best for them in their situation. If such a principle were accepted, and we also believed that being born deaf rather than hearing in the Deaf community gave the best chance of a good life, there would be no reason for objecting to the choice of a deaf sperm donor (or choosing a deaf embryo). A child would not have been harmed. The argument then is whether or not being deaf does give the best chance of a good life to a child born into the Deaf community. On that point those inside and outside the Deaf community may well differ. But, here, it is important to distinguish between a reproductive choice, or a choice of partner, that might lead to the birth of a deaf child, and an action taken to deafen an existing child. For the latter, a hypothetical scenario in which a child would be harmed is one in which a pregnant mother took a 'deafness pill' which destroyed the hearing of her fetus. In this case the child has been denied the possibility of hearing—and in the future might well blame the parents for the action they had taken. But choosing a deaf embryo or donor does not harm any child, although it would, of course, increase the number of deaf children in the population.

B. Transmission of Serious Genetic Disorder

A wider related issue concerns couples who know that they are at risk of having a child with a serious genetic disorder. In this situation a couple may decide not to have children, may adopt or may go ahead and try for a child but use prenatal diagnosis and seek a termination of pregnancy if the fetus is found to have the genetic disorder. Or they may simply decide to have a child: a child that may or may not have the genetic disorder that runs in the family. If this is a dominantly inherited genetic condition such as Huntington's disease, a couple would have a 50:50 chance of having an affected child. With Huntington's disease the debilitating and eventually fatal neurological symptoms do not usually become apparent until middle age (as is the case for most other dominantly inherited genetic conditions). Any child born with the condition is in exactly the same (genetic) situation as the parent who carries the gene mutation associated with the disease, and from whom a child may inherit it. Anon (1996) provides an autobiographical account of someone who had children in this situation where there was a risk of Huntington's disease, as some parents choose to do. Relatively little use of prenatal diagnosis is made by couples where one carries the gene mutation associated with Huntington's disease. One reason for this is that many believe that effective treatment for the disease will be available in the future.

Some people believe that couples should be prevented from having children in this situation. In one survey (HGC, 2001) a third of the respondents agreed with the statement that 'couples who are at risk of having a child with a serious genetic disorder should be discouraged from having children of their own', and 43% disagreed. In a number of countries (although not the UK) there have been eugenic laws for the involuntary sterilisation of various categories of the 'unfit', which in some cases have included those at risk of having children with genetic conditions such as Huntington's disease. In Nazi Germany several hundred people were killed because they came from families that carried the disease (Harper, 1992).

New developments have made direct testing for most genetic conditions possible. In fact, Huntington's disease was the first for which such predictive testing became available. This means that instead of someone knowing that they are at risk of carrying the gene mutation because a parent or grandparent has the disease, the test can show whether or not they have inherited the gene mutation, or whether a fetus carries it. Many of those from families with Huntington's disease will go to a genetic clinic where they can learn of their risk of passing on the disease to children and receive information about the disease, and where they can discuss their reproductive options. A small minority opt for the predictive genetic test to establish whether or not they have the gene mutation associated with the development of the disease. Making decisions about testing is complex but for many avoiding testing maintains the hope that they may not have the gene mutation (Wexler, 1984).

C. Saviour Siblings

There is a final choice I will discuss which some justify in terms of the well-being of children already born. This is the situation where a 'saviour sibling' is created. It is the rarest, but probably the most widely discussed and most controversial use of PGD. This is a strategy that may be used if there is a child with a life-threatening disease which may be cured by a stem cell or bone marrow implant, but where there is no matching donor in the family. Without a tissue match the transplant is likely to be rejected. But embryos can be created through IVF procedures, and one that would be a tissue match can be selected (if it is available). The HFEA has licensed this.[13] Opinions are divided between those who see this as justifiable creation and

---

[13] Tissue typing of embryos for the creation of saviour siblings is specified in law for the first time in the (draft) Human Tissue and Embryos Bill as something that can be licensed by the HFEA on a case-by-case basis, but not on a general condition-bycondition basis as is the case for genetic abnormalities.

selection of a child to (potentially) cure another in the family and others who feel that children should only be conceived for their own sake and never as the means of providing benefits for others. Some foresee a possibility of troubled relationships in the family, whether or not the treatment from the saviour sibling is successful. This issue is the theme of a best-selling novel in which things did become very difficult for a saviour sister (Picoult, 2004). Of course, there are many other circumstances in which children are conceived for a wide variety of reasons, or inadvertently. Some object to all PGD because it involves the creation of embryos some of which are subsequently destroyed, but the use of PGD to make saviour siblings has proved to be particularly controversial. The licensing of PGD to create saviour siblings runs counter to the general policy of restriction of this technique to situations where the intention is to select out embryos that may have serious medical conditions or abnormality—as instanced in clause 14(4) of the HFE Bill. The intention in the saviour sibling situation is to create a (normal) fetus with a specific genetic characteristic to provide the means of treatment of an existing sibling. Thus, no selecting out of abnormality is involved. Such use of PGD is discussed further below.

IV. CHOOSING NOT TO HAVE CERTAIN CHILDREN

Thus far, I have considered situations where parents may want children with particular characteristics. I now turn to the much more common case where an embryo or fetus is rejected because of its characteristics, considering (a) prenatal diagnosis (PND) and termination of pregnancy if a fetus has a serious disorder, and (b) pre-implantation genetic diagnosis (PGD), which may be used to select out embryos with a serious genetic condition in an IVF procedure. There is a third procedure which takes place in most IVF, where an embryologist screens and selects embryos from those available for implantation on the basis of their apparent viability and normality. However, given that parents are not usually involved in making these selective decisions, I will not discuss this third situation further. But we should note that it is a sanctioned selection of embryos with particular characteristics. And the procedure is of significance to anyone who holds that embryos have the moral status of a person, as those embryos judged to be less viable are discarded.

A. Prenatal Diagnosis and Termination of Pregnancy

Screening for Down's syndrome and other chromosomal abnormalities, and ultrasound scans for visible fetal structural abnormalities are offered to all pregnant women in Britain. In addition, couples known to carry particular genetic conditions, or at risk of these, may choose to have fetal diagnostic tests. Each year some 2,000 terminations of pregnancy are carried out under section 1(1)(d) of the Abortion Act (1967), which permits abortion without gestational age limit where 'there is a substantial risk that if the child were born it would suffer from such physical or mental abnormalities as to be seriously handicapped'.

PND provides a reproductive choice. It can be used to avoid the birth of a child at risk of serious abnormality or genetic disease, and the social, psychological and financial costs which may be associated with bringing up a child with abnormality. At the societal level, it has been suggested that it costs less to provide screening, diagnosis and termination than the medical and social care, special education and support for some children born with serious abnormality.

But mothers can opt out of screening and diagnostic procedures and, if there is a diagnosis of a serious fetal problem, it is their choice whether or not to have a termination of pregnancy. However, there may be questions of how autonomous the decisions about these procedures are (see HGC, 2006). Social pressure may encourage engagement with screening and it can prove difficult for mothers to avoid this and subsequent diagnostic procedures. Those who choose to opt out may be advised to change their minds. And it has been suggested that the ways in which screening is organised and presented carries an implicit message that screening is good and the good mother-to-be who is concerned for the well-being of her child will want to take part. Similarly, for the small minority for whom there is a diagnosis of serious fetal abnormality, there may be presumptions among professionals that a termination of pregnancy is the sensible course of action.[14]

While most do not see a moral equivalence of fetus and person, some do and so would reject termination of pregnancy for themselves. Others go a step further and want all abortion banned or its use further restricted. But we should note that, among those pregnant women who would not themselves consider termination of pregnancy, some may choose to proceed with prenatal fetal diagnosis because they wish to know the result and prepare for the delivery. So we should not assume there is an inevitable progression from screening and diagnosis to termination of pregnancy. However, it is the case that the great majority of those who are given a diagnosis of a serious fetal disorder will choose to end the pregnancy.

The disability lobby and others insist that selective abortion implies that a disabled child is less valued in society, and that the existence of screening programmes, fetal diagnosis and termination of pregnancy for medical indications implies that the lives of those already living with disability are not worth living and promotes the stigmatisation of people with disability

---

[14] The legal situation is not the same across the whole of the UK. In Northern Ireland mothers who have received a diagnosis of a serious fetal abnormality may find it difficult to obtain a termination of pregnancy.

(see HGC, 2006). There is a further related argument that prenatal screening programmes, in the absence of treatment for abnormalities, are disease prevention through selection, rather than through the development and use of cures. And these programmes may reduce interest in both the development of treatments and appropriate services for those with serious congenital or genetic conditions. Insofar as these arguments imply that discrimination against those with impairments, services for them and developments of treatments are all adversely effected by the existence of screening, diagnosis and termination of pregnancy, it seems difficult to sustain the idea that services or development of treatments have got worse over the past 50 years or so that these procedures have been in use. While much may remain to be done, there have been significant improvements. In terms of the value to be placed on the lives of all people—impaired or otherwise—a distinction may be drawn between screening for a condition and the devaluation of the lives of those with that condition. Here, once again, the arguments may rest, in part at least, on the view of the moral equivalence of person and a fetus. This contrast has the sharpest relief in families who carry serious genetic disorders. In such families, couples may use fetal diagnosis and termination to avoid births of children with the disorder, but this does not mean that they regard the lives of existing affected family members as being worthless or to be devalued. So, more generally, decisions to use prenatal diagnosis and termination or PGD do not necessarily imply that a child with a disability has a life not worth living, or indeed, that disabled and able-bodied people are not of equal moral worth, and equally worthy of respect.

A more general argument is made by some disability activists, that we should change society, not people, so that impairments do not become disabilities. Clearly, it is important that we continue to move in this direction. However, even if much more radical changes were achieved, some impairments would continue to result in disability.

Finally, there is the claim that these procedures are eugenic. As earlier, we must be precise about what is meant by 'eugenic' in this context. Some past eugenic programmes violated reproductive freedoms (see Buchanan *et al*, 2000). However, even if we accept that there may be some limitation of decisional autonomy with respect to prenatal screening, diagnosis and termination of pregnancy, broadly speaking these create, rather than violate, reproductive freedoms as they allow parents to avoid the birth of some abnormal or impaired children. And we should note that from the 1930s, the so-called 'reform eugenics' which predominated in the British movement espoused voluntaristic policies (Kevles, 1985). And it was in the context of these reform eugenic aspirations that techniques and procedures for prenatal screening and diagnosis were developed in the post-war decades (Kevles, 1985; Paul, 1998). We may also note that the Abortion Act (1967) included what Kevles indicates was sometimes referred to as the 'eugenic clause', which permits abortion where there is a substantial risk that the child would be seriously handicapped. Many of those involved in these developments saw prenatal screening and diagnosis as desirable because these would reduce the 'burden' of births of impaired individuals for society as well as offering new reproductive choices to parents. As with genetic counselling, there was a wide belief that if people were provided with appropriate choices, they would generally act in ways that would benefit society in general. So, for instance, the prominent clinical geneticist Lionel Penrose (1969) thought that most people would act reasonably so that 'the result of skilful [genetic] counselling, over a long period of years, will undoubtedly be to diminish, very slightly but progressively, the amount of severe hereditary diseases in the population'.

The Eugenic Society followed these developments of prenatal screening and diagnosis with interest. In 1978, celebrating its seventy-fifth birthday, it devoted its Annual Symposium to 'Developments in Human Reproduction and their Eugenic, Ethical Implications' (Carter, 1983). At this symposium practitioners and researchers described new techniques in contraception, prenatal diagnosis, genetic counselling and testing, and assisted reproduction. These developments were welcomed for the choices they offered to couples as well as for the benefits they brought for society. So if the claims that prenatal screening, fetal diagnosis and the possible termination of pregnancy are eugenic in that beyond offering new reproductive choices to parents, there is an intended benefit for future society through a reduction of the number of births of children with serious impairments, the claims may be taken as accurate and they are part of reform eugenics (or what some describe as 'liberal eugenics'). Reform eugenicists (along with many others) believed that reducing the number of individuals in society afflicted by serious impairment or genetic disease was a desirable goal. But what has changed since the 1970s is the discourse. Today, following the ideological shift from reproductive responsibilities to promotion of reproductive autonomy and individual choice, and the increasing emphasis placed on the latter, prenatal testing is predominately discussed as a choice offered to parents. Discussion is focused on the morality of such choices, rather than reproductive responsibilities for future society. While we may celebrate the eradication of infectious diseases such as smallpox, the potential reduction of genetic disease or serious congenital impairment is not usually considered in the context of prenatal screening and diagnosis.

But, in conclusion, it should be pointed out that screening, fetal diagnosis and termination of pregnancy are hardly an ideal way of providing the choice not to have a child with a serious disorder. Ending a wanted pregnancy can never be an easy situation. Better and less painful and distressing reproductive choices and procedures are needed. These might include preventative measures to reduce the incidence of fetuses with serious impairments. But given that most fetal abnormalities result from developmental errors occurring at or soon after conception, this may prove very difficult.

B. Pre-implantation Genetic Diagnosis

PGD, which involves using IVF techniques, was developed in the UK in the 1990s (see Franklin & Roberts, 2006). A number of embryos are created in the laboratory using the couple's eggs and sperm, or perhaps donor gametes. The embryos develop for two or three days before one or more cells are removed from each for genetic analysis. Tests indicate the presence or absence of the relevant genetic condition that runs in the family. Then one or two of the viable embryos without the inherited condition (if these are available) are placed in the woman. As with other IVF procedures, there is about a one in five chance of a successful pregnancy. This is a complex, difficult, expensive and sometimes stressful process, with a rather low chance of producing a baby and, not surprisingly, few embark on it—probably around 200 babies have been born in the UK since the technique was developed. It also has a very small but significant error rate, and it is usual practice to offer prenatal diagnosis to couples using PGD to check that the procedure has successfully avoided the implantation of an affected embryo.[15] The process for so-called saviour siblings is just the same, except that the embryonic cells go through human leukocyte antigen (HLA) tissue typing to select any that may be a tissue match. PGD is licensed by the HFEA for a limited number of serious genetic conditions, HLA tissue typing, or for sex selection in the cases of X-linked genetic diseases.

Some of the arguments about PND parallel those for PGD, but of course embryo selection is involved, not termination of pregnancy. Some couples who would not have a termination of pregnancy find PGD acceptable. But demand is not high, and it is only available in a limited number of centres. And, unlike PND, couples may have to pay the cost of PGD (around £6,000) although practice varies across the NHS. It is also available in some commercial clinics.

Some see PGD as less morally acceptable than PND because it involves the destruction of a larger number of embryos. Others take the opposite view because PGD avoids the destruction of a fetus. Because it is an expensive procedure with a very limited success rate involving very few parents, it has been suggested that it is not an appropriate use of NHS resources (HGC, 2006).

Some judgements about whether or not the use of PND or PGD is appropriate partly depend on the 'seriousness' of the condition involved. The phrase in the Abortion Act (1967) is, 'if a child were born it would suffer from such physical or mental abnormalities as to be seriously handicapped'.

---

[15] There is a case currently before the courts in Australia in which a couple claim that an embryo was negligently implanted because geneticists had misread the genetic test and had selected an affected fetus. They are claiming damages to cover a lifetime of medical expenses for the impaired child and the cost of having a further child without the genetic disorder they would not have otherwise had, as well as compensation for distress and pain (Roberts, 2008).

There is no such legal requirement for PGD, following a distinction in the moral status of the embryo and the fetus that is widely drawn (and as is implied in the Human Fertilisation and Embryology Act (1990) by the 14-day limit for embryo research). PGD is only licensed for a limited number of specific conditions. The Human Tissue and Embryos (draft) Bill will allow licensing for embryo testing for gene, chromosome or mitochondrial abnormality when the HFEA is satisfied that there is significant risk that a person with the abnormality will have, or develop, a serious physical or mental disability, a serious illness or other serious medical condition.

The distinction between fetus and embryo has allowed the licensing of PGD for some of the inherited cancer syndromes[16] which are not generally held to constitute 'seriously handicapped' in terms of the Abortion Act (1967). This distinction could have a further implication. When PND is being used in cases where parents wish to avoid having a child with a recessively inherited genetic disease (the most common genetic conditions, such as cystic fibrosis), only affected fetuses are aborted, not those which are carriers. Carriers are not themselves affected by the disease, but if they have children with another carrier they have a one in four chance of having an affected child (and a one in four chance of a normal non-carrier child and a one in two chance of a carrier child). In PGD, it has been recommended (HFEA, 2006) that where there are both carrier and unaffected embryos of equal quality, parents should be able to request which they prefer to be implanted. Cases where this is possible would be the only situation (without using donor gametes or embryo) in which parents could be sure of avoiding having a carrier child. As being a carrier does not constitute a serious handicap, termination on medical grounds would not be justified.

V. CONCLUSION

Having surveyed the territory, what does the map look like? The most striking difference is between the possibility to make choices not to have children with abnormality or disability and the extension of reproductive autonomy in that realm, and the restriction of autonomy in relation to positive choices of children with particular characteristics. In the first situation there has been a wide development of techniques and practices which are now generally[17] available for prenatal screening and diagnosis, termination of pregnancy and embryo selection. But this is in sharp distinction

---

[16] These will include the inherited breast cancer syndrome. Here, like Huntington's disease, the cancer is unlikely to develop until middle age, although, unlike Huntington's disease, it is not inevitable that it will develop at all in those who carry relevant gene mutations and it is a potentially curable disease.

[17] On mainland Britain; as pointed out earlier, the situation is rather different in Northern Ireland.

to an increasing restriction being placed on use of technologies to make choices about the kinds of children we might like to have. Thus, there is the possibility of using sex selection if there is a chance that a fetus or embryo of one sex may have an impairment, but its use is denied where a couple may simply wish to have a child of one or other sex. The distinction is marked by two descriptors. A pregnancy may be terminated, or sex selection may be used for *medical* reasons—that is, to avoid the birth of a child who may be impaired, but the possibility of *designer babies*, those with characteristics that parents may prefer and have chosen, is not permitted (with the exception of PGD saviour siblings). With the 'medical' situation aside, we resist the idea that we might reduce the uncertainties of reproduction and we prefer it to remain as an apparently natural sphere beyond the reach of direct human actions and choices. Indeed, we can see long historical struggles over the boundaries of 'natural' reproduction, as in the case of contraception. It has taken almost a century to bring what was once called 'artificial birth control' into the realm of everyday taken-for-granted social practice. And we no longer call it 'artificial' or indeed 'control'; it is contraception. A similar historical process may be seen as 'artificial' insemination has become 'donor' insemination as the procedure has moved from eugenic proposal and fringe medical activity to a mainstream and regulated procedure for the alleviation of infertility (Department of Health and Social Security, 1984).

Ethicists talk of a distinction between treatment and enhancement, stretching these categories so that pregnancy screening, diagnosis and abortion are 'treatment',[18] while sex selection is an 'enhancement'. Some (for example Buchanan *et al*, 2000) point out three potential complications of enhancements that do not arise when treating a disease or abnormality. First, there may be problems for society if enhancements are widely used. So, for example, sex selection to avoid (rare) sex-linked disorders will not significantly unbalance the sex ratio but widespread choosing of one sex would. Secondly, enhancements may be self-defeating if everyone used them—let's say increasing the height of their children (and would be unfair if only the rich could afford to do so). And enhancements are likely to be expensive and, as they are not 'treatment', we cannot necessarily expect them to be available on the NHS. Thirdly, eliminating disease and impairment is generally seen to be to the advantage of the society as a whole but whether some enhancements are benefits will depend on values individuals hold, and parents' values may not coincide with those of their children. To these three complications, some would add the 'playing God' or remaking nature arguments, laudable to strive to eliminate disease and impairment, but to think we can choose better babies is arrogance or worse. But of these

---

[18] And, in effect, the use of PGD to create a saviour sibling falls under the treatment or medical descriptor.

four, only the 'playing God' argument could be used to justify banning sex selection for family balancing. And history might suggest that in due time 'artificial' sex selection may become prudent gender choice.

Some eugenic programmes set the needs or benefits (real or imagined) for the population at large above the reproductive autonomy of some individuals. Indeed, many wrongs were done in the name of eugenics. However, eugenic name calling does not make reproduction any less quintessentially social—today, as it was at the time of John Stuart Mill. Indeed, it does no violence to our history or present practice if we describe prenatal screening diagnosis and termination of pregnancy and PGD as reforms or liberal eugenics. And we may be certain that social and political processes will continue to set limits for our reproductive autonomy.

ACKNOWLEDGEMENTS

I hold an Emeritus Fellowship from Leverhulme Trust. I am most grateful for their support and to Jill Brown for her continuing secretarial labours.

There is the usual long cast of musicians who have assisted my work. The Be Good Tanyas, Kitty Wells, Blue Highway, Alison Krauss and, Bob Dylan (*Modern Times*) deserve special thanks. Pandora provided their unique personal radio stations based on the fruits of the music genome project until they were closed down in the UK by copyright restrictions. Another night when music died.

BIBLIOGRAPHY

Anon (1996) 'Living with the threat of Huntington's disease' in *The Troubled Helix* (Eds, Marteau T & Richards M) Cambridge University Press, Cambridge, pp 23–6.

—— (2002) *The Guardian*, 8 April.

Blyth E (2007) 'Donor conception: what to do about birth certificates?' *BioNews* 438, 1–2.

Brewer H (1935) 'Eutelegenesis'. *Eugenics Review* 37, 121–6.

Buchanan A, Brock DW, Daniels N, Wickler D (2000) *From Chance to Choice: Genetics and Justice*, Cambridge University Press, Cambridge.

Carter CO (1983) 'Eugenic implications of new techniques' in *Developments in Human Reproduction and their Eugenic Ethical Implications* (Ed, Carter CO) Academic Press, London, pp 205–11.

Dachert, A (1931) 'Positive eugenics in practice: an account of the first positive eugenic experiment'. *Eugenics Review* 23, 15–18.

Darwin L (1923) 'Aims and methods of eugenical societies' in *Second International Congress of Eugenics. Eugenics, Genetics and the Family, Vol 1* Williams and Watkins, Baltimore, MD, pp 5–19.

Department of Health and Social Security (1984) *Report of the Committee of Inquiry into Human Fertilisation and Embryology* (the Warnock Report), Cmnd 9314, HMSO, London.

Franklin S & Roberts C (2006) *Born and Made. An Ethnography of Preimplantation Genetic Diagnosis,* Princeton University Press, Princeton NJ.

Gillham, NW (2001) *A Life of Sir Francis Galton,* Oxford University Press, Oxford.

Glover J (2006) *Choosing Children. The Ethical Dilemmas of Genetic Intervention,* Oxford University Press, Oxford.

Goethe, CM (1946) *War Profits and Better Babies,* Keystone Press, Sacramento, CA.

Grumpy Old Deafies (2007), www.grumpyolddeafies.com/2007/11/parliament_deaf_embryo_select.html.

Harper PS (1992) 'Huntington's disease and the abuse of genetics'. *American Journal of Human Genetics* 50, 460–64.

Harris, J (1998) *Rights and Reproductive Choice,* Oxford University Press, Oxford.

HFEA (Human Fertilisation and Embryology Authority) (1994) *Letter to all Directors of Centres, CH (94) 02,* HFEA, London.

HFEA (2007) 'HFEA calls for national strategy to reduce the biggest risk of fertility treatment: multiple birth', www.hfea.gov.uk/en/1625.html.

HGC (Human Genetics Commission) (2001) *Public Attitudes to Human Genetic Information,* HGC, London.

HGC (2006) *Making Babies: Reproductive Decisions and Genetic Technologies,* HGC, London.

Jackson E (2001) *Regulating Reproduction,* Hart Publishing, Oxford.

Kevles DJ (1985) *In the Name of Eugenics,* Harvard University Press, Cambridge, MA.

Liu P & Rose GA (1995) 'Social aspects of 800 couples coming forward for gender selection of the children'. *Human Reproduction* 10, 968–71.

Middleton A (1995) *Attitudes of Deaf Adults and Hearing Parents of Deaf Children Towards Issues Surrounding Genetic Testing for Deafness,* PhD thesis, University of Leeds.

Mill JS (1859/1977) *On Liberty,* Routledge & Kegan Paul, London.

Muller HJ (1936) *Out of the Night,* Gollancz, London.

Parfit D (1984) *Reasons and Persons,* Oxford University Press, Oxford.

Paul DB (1995) *Controlling Human Heredity: 1865 to the present,* Humanity Books, New York.

Paul D (1998) 'Eugenic origins of medical genetics' in *The politics of heredity,* State University of New York Press, Albany, NY, pp 133–56.

Paul DB (2002) 'From reproductive responsibility to reproductive autonomy' in *Mutating Concepts. Evolving Disciplines in Genetics, Medicine and Society* (Eds, Parker LS & Ankeny RA) Klever Academic, Boston, MA.

Paul DB & Day B (2008) 'John Stuart Mill, innate differences and the regulation of reproduction'. *Studies in the History and Philosophy of Biology and Biomedical Sciences,* in press.

Penrose L (1969) 'Genetics and society'. Unpublished ms in Lionel S Penrose Papers(held in University College London library), file 103.

Picoult J (2004) *My Sister's Keeper*, Hodder, London.

Plotz D (2005) *The Genius Factory*, Simon and Schuster, London.

Rhodes R (2001) 'Ethical issues in selecting embryos'. *Annals NY Academy of Science* 943, 360–67.

Richards MPM (2002) 'Future bodies, some history and future prospects of human genetic selection' in *Body Lore and Laws* (Eds, Bainham A, Day Sclater S, Richards MPM) Hart Publishing, Oxford.

—— (2004) 'Perfecting people: selective breeding at the Oneida Community 1869–1879 and the eugenic movement'. *New Genetics and Society* 23, 49–71.

—— (2008) 'Artificial insemination and eugenics: celibate motherhood, eutelegenesis and germinal choice'. *Studies in History and Philosophy of Biology and Biomedical Sciences* 39, 211–21.

Roberts M (2008) 'Australian parents launch wrongful birth claim for negligent genetic testing'. *BioNews* 29 January.

Sandel M (2007) *The Case against Perfection: Ethics in the Age of Genetic Engineering*, Harvard University Press, Cambridge, MA.

Savulescu J (1999) 'Sex selection: the case for'. *Medical Journal of Australia* **171**, 373–5.

Silver L (1998) *Remaking Eden,* Weidenfeld and Nicholson, London.

Statham H, Green J, Snowdon C, France-Dawson M (1993) 'Choice of baby's sex'. *Lancet* 341, 364–5.

Webb T (2008) *Letter to Dr Middleton*, Department of Health, London.

Wexler N (1984) 'Huntington's disease and other late onset genetic disorders' in *Psychological Aspects of Genetic Counselling* (Eds, Emery AEH & Pullen IM) Academic Press, New York.

Wilmot SAH (2008) 'Doctors, artificial insemination and eugenics: the interweaving of reproductive medicine and agriculture in mid-twentieth century Britain'. *Medical History*, in press 2009.

Legislation

Abortion Act 1967

Human Fertilisation and Embryology Act 1990

Mental Deficiency Act 1913

12

Anonymity—or not—in the Donation of Gametes and Embryos

SUSAN GOLOMBOK

I. INTRODUCTION

ONE AREA OF family life in which the state has intervened in recent years relates to children born through assisted reproduction involving donated gametes (sperm, eggs or embryos). Children conceived by gamete donation through a licensed clinic and born after April 2005 will, on reaching the age of 18, be entitled to identifying information about their donor(s). The removal of donor anonymity has been, and continues to be, highly controversial. While some opponents argue for this legislation to be reversed, others believe that it has not gone far enough and propose that donor conception should be registered on a person's birth certificate to put pressure on parents to tell their child about his or her donor conception, with some believing that there should be a statutory duty on parents to do so (Department of Health, 2006). In this chapter, autonomy is discussed with respect to freedom to obtain, or withhold, information about the use of donated gametes and the identity of gamete donors from the perspective of each of the main parties involved: (i) the offspring, (ii) the parents and (iii) the donors.

It is first important to clarify the differences between gamete donation and adoption. Arguments in favour of the identification of donors have tended to draw on the experiences of adoptees. It is now generally accepted that adopted children benefit from information about their origins and their birth parents, and that children who are not given such information may become confused about their identity and at risk of psychological problems (Brodzinsky et al, 1998; Grotevant & McRoy, 1998). As donor insemination and egg donation are similar to adoption in that the child lacks a genetic link with one or other parent, and embryo donation is identical to adoption to the extent that the child is genetically unrelated to both parents, it has been suggested that lack of information about donation may be harmful for the donor-conceived child. However, gamete donation differs from adoption in ways that may protect children who do not have such information against psychological harm. First, donor insemination and egg donation children do have a genetic link with one parent and that parent's family. Secondly, parents of donor insemination, egg donation and embryo donation children have experienced the pregnancy and birth of their child. Moreover, the children were not relinquished by their genetic parents following their birth but, instead, were born to parents who went to great lengths to conceive them. Thus, unlike many adopted children, they did not experience a relationship with a genetic parent that was later broken; donor-conceived children are generally much-wanted children who do not have the history of rejection by birth parents that is associated with adoption. It cannot necessarily be assumed that the psychological consequences for children of being conceived by gamete or embryo donation will be the same as for adoption. In many ways donor insemination children have more in common with children resulting from extra-marital affairs. Or, in cases where the male partner is infertile, with children who have been conceived through the involvement of a male family member, as is acceptable practice in some cultures.

II. THE OFFSPRING

Although empirical data on the consequences for children of being conceived by gamete donation are sparse, a number of studies do exist. Due to the secrecy surrounding these procedures, most of this research focuses on families in which the children have not been told about their donor origins. These studies are informative about the outcomes of gamete donation for children who are unaware of their donor conception. Qualitative studies have also been conducted with children and adults who know that they were conceived by donor insemination. These studies provide information about the impact of such knowledge on the individuals concerned.

A. Families in which Children have not been told about their Genetic Origins

The first controlled, systematic study of the quality of parent–child relationships in donor conception families was the European Study of Assisted Reproduction Families. In the first phase of the investigation, conducted when the children were between four and eight years old, 111 donor insemination families were studied in comparison with matched groups of 115 adoptive families where the child had been adopted in infancy, and 120 families with a naturally conceived child (Golombok *et al*, 1995, 1996).

In-depth, standardised interviews were conducted with mothers and fathers separately by highly trained psychologists, and ratings of the quality of parent–child relationships were made according to strict coding criteria to produce reliable and valid assessments of constructs such as the mother's warmth towards her child, the mother's emotional involvement with her child, and the degree of the mother's and the father's day-to-day interaction with their child. The findings of this study indicated that the quality of parent–child relationships in families with a four-to eight-year-old child conceived by donor insemination was superior to that shown by natural conception families. The adoptive families fell between these two family types. Thus it was concluded that donor insemination children of preschool and early school age appear to experience positive relationships with their parents. Similar findings were reported in later studies of families with children in the same age range who had been conceived by egg donation (Golombok *et al*, 1999) and embryo donation (MacCallum & Golombok, 2007).

The donor insemination and egg donation families were followed up as the children reached adolescence. It is at adolescence that issues relating to identity become particularly salient to children and thus it is at adolescence that difficulties for donor conception families may be expected to arise. To the extent that the experiences of adopted children are relevant to children conceived by donor insemination, early adolescence is the time when adopted children begin to show a greater incidence of behavioural problems in comparison with their non-adopted counterparts, alongside a greater interest in their biological parents (Brodzinsky *et al*, 1998; Grotevant & McRoy, 1998). The focus of the follow-up study was on parental warmth and parental control, two aspects of parenting that are considered to be important for the psychological adjustment of the adolescent child. The findings showed that donor insemination families with an early adolescent child were characterised by high levels of warmth between parents and their children, accompanied by an appropriate level of discipline and control (Golombok *et al*, 2002a, 2002b), and comparable findings were obtained with the smaller sample of families with an egg donation child (Murray *et al*, 2006).

With respect to the well-being of the children themselves, the first uncontrolled studies found no evidence of emotional or behavioural problems in children conceived by donor insemination (Clayton & Kovacs, 1982; Leeton & Blackwell, 1982). Similarly, controlled studies that have used standardised measures have shown no evidence of psychological disorder in donor conception children. For example, donor insemination children aged between six and eight years old were studied in comparison with matched groups of adopted and naturally conceived children in Australia (Kovacs *et al*, 1983); four- to eight-year-old donor insemination and egg donation children were compared with adopted and naturally conceived children as part of the European Study of Assisted Reproduction Families (Golombok *et al*, 1995, 1996, 1999) and embryo donation children of between two and five years were compared with adopted and IVF children by MacCallum *et al* (2007). None of these investigations identified a higher incidence of psychological problems among donor-conceived children. In addition, when the families in the European study were followed up at age 12 (Golombok *et al*, 2002a, 2002b), and again at age 18 (Owen & Golombok, 2007), the children were found to be functioning well.

B. Families in which Children are Aware of their Genetic Origins

Little is known about children who are aware of their donor conception or about the impact of this knowledge on their relationship with their parents. Until families who have told their children about their donor origins have been compared with those who have not, it will not be possible to come to a full understanding of the consequences of secrecy versus disclosure on parenting or on the psychological well-being of children. However, the small but growing number of studies of the consequences of disclosure of donor insemination to children and adults are increasing understanding of this issue. In an investigation of parents in New Zealand who had told their children about their conception by donor insemination, 57% reported feeling pleased about having done so (Rumball & Adair, 1999). In Sweden, it was found that the small proportion of parents who had been open with their child did not regret their decision to tell (Lindblad *et al*, 2000), and in the UK, parents who had told their children described the experience as a positive one (Lycett *et al*, 2005). The children in these studies were reported to have responded with either curiosity or disinterest.

The first study to have asked children directly about their feelings regarding their donor conception was an investigation of children born to lesbian mothers who were being raised in the absence of a father in Belgium (Vanfraussen *et al*, 2001). Twenty-seven per cent of the representative sample of 41 children aged between 7 and 17 years who participated in the study reported that they would like to know the identity of their donor, 19% wished to have non-identifying information about his appearance and personality, and the remaining 54% preferred donor anonymity at that point in their lives. In the US, a study of donor offspring conceived through the Sperm Bank of California, where identifying information about the donor may be obtained at the age of 18, found that most of the offspring, the majority of whom were born to lesbian or single heterosexual women, intended to request the identity of their donor (Scheib *et al*, 2005). Most recently, a survey of donor offspring searching for their donor relations through the Donor Sibling Register, an internet site based in the US, has found not only that contact between offspring and donors is generally positive but also that offspring are finding, and developing positive relationships with, their donor siblings, that is, their half-siblings (Jadva *et al*, 2007). On average, five siblings were found by each person searching, with many finding more than ten, and one group of donor siblings numbered 55! To date, more than 4,000 matches between donor offspring and their donor relations have been made through this website, indicating that many donor offspring wish to have information about, and make contact with, their donor and donor siblings. The website has created a startling new phenomenon whereby family relationships based on genetic connections between children are being formed across multiple family units. Unlike children whose parents have separated, who may have a small number of half-siblings in another household (or sometimes in two or three other households), these new family constellations may comprise children with large numbers of half-siblings in large numbers of different households. Further distinctions between donor sibling families and step-families are that donor-conceived siblings are generally of a similar age, and may not find out about the existence of their donor siblings until adolescence or beyond.

Qualitative studies of donor-conceived adults who are aware of the nature of their conception shed some light on the longer-term effects, although it should be emphasised that the number of individuals interviewed on this topic remains very small. Snowden interviewed seven young adults who had been told in their late teens or twenties about their conception by donor insemination and found them to be accepting of this information and pleased that they had been very much wanted by their parents (Snowden *et al*, 1983). However, other investigators have reported more negative feelings following disclosure, including hostility, distance and mistrust. For example, Turner and Coyle (2000) reported on the responses of 16 adults to a questionnaire on the impact of disclosure about their conception by donor insemination. The authors concluded that the identity of these donor insemination adults, including their self-esteem, had been threatened by the disclosure. The respondents expressed feelings of loss and grief in relation to their lack of knowledge about their genetic origins, and a need to find out about their donor father and, if possible, to have some sort of relationship with him in order to achieve a sense of genetic continuity. Some had felt since childhood that something was amiss and attributed their poor relationship with their father to their donor origins.

The main difference between the young adults interviewed by Snowden and the adults who participated in the study by Turner and Coyle was that the former sample was recruited from a representative group of donor insemination offspring conceived through a specific clinic, whereas the latter comprised individuals who had joined a donor insemination support group. It is clear from the reports of support group members that some people become extremely distressed or angry on learning about their donor conception, and feel deceived by their parents. It is not known, however, how representative members of donor insemination support groups are of the entire population of donor insemination adults who know about their genetic origins. Although their experiences are highly informative and important, it cannot be assumed that the views of members of support groups reflect the views of donor insemination adults in general. It may be expected, for example, that those who join a support group are more likely to be concerned about their donor conception, and to have experienced a poor relationship with their parents. It is also conceivable that donor insemination adults may tend to attribute difficulties with their parents to their donor origins. However, many young people who are genetically related to their father also report a distant or hostile relationship with him. In the absence of empirical data on this issue, the question of whether or not this situation is more common among donor insemination families than among natural conception families remains a matter for speculation. Due to the lack of information about the representativeness of donor insemination adults recruited to studies through support groups, attempts to generalise from their experiences should be viewed with some caution.

C. Conclusions regarding Offspring

From the information that is currently available from investigations of families in which children have not been told about their genetic origins, it appears that the psychological well-being of children, and the quality of their relationships with their parents, is not compromised by secrecy. Nevertheless, this does not necessarily mean that it is better for children not to be told about their donor conception. First, few controlled, systematic studies exist of the psychological consequences for children of secrecy about their donor conception, and those that have been carried out have focused more on donor insemination than on egg or embryo donation. Secondly, a major problem with investigations of donor conception families is the low co-operation rate associated with the parents' desire to maintain secrecy about their child's conception: parents who are most concerned about secrecy are the most reluctant to participate in research. For this reason, the extent to which the families investigated are typical of donor conception families as a whole cannot be fully established. Thirdly, the children studied so far are young and have not yet developed a sophisticated understanding of their relationship with their parents. No systematic data are as yet available on the psychological consequences for children conceived by gamete donation beyond the adolescent years.

Family therapists have argued that secrecy can jeopardise communication between family members, cause tension and result in the distancing of some members of the family from others (Karpel, 1980; Bok, 1982; Papp, 1993). In relation to donor conception, it has been argued that keeping the circumstances of conception secret will separate those who know the secret (the parents) from those who do not (the child) (Clamar, 1989). Psychological research has shown that children can sense when they are not being told something because a taboo surrounds the discussion of certain topics (De Paulo, 1992). Parents often give themselves away by their tone of voice, facial expression, body posture, or by abruptly changing the subject. It is not known what proportion of children conceived by gamete donation become aware that a secret about their parentage is being kept from them, but it is likely that they will become suspicious if their parents always change the topic of conversation whenever the subject of whom they look like is raised. Evidence that some donor insemination children do sense that something is unusual in their family comes from the studies of adults who know about their genetic origins. In each of these studies, some individuals reported that they had suspected from childhood that something was not right.

Furthermore, up to 50% of gamete donation parents who opt to keep the donor conception secret from the child have told someone else about it. Thus there is a genuine risk that individuals conceived by gamete donation will find out about the nature of their conception through someone other than their parents. The greater use of genetic testing in medical diagnosis, and of paternity testing, also increases the risk that donor conception children and adults will discover that the person they know of as their father or their mother is not their genetic parent (Richards, 2007). It is recommended that adopted children are told about their adoption in an age-appropriate way during the pre-school years. Adoption research has shown that accidental disclosure about a child's origins is much more likely to be damaging to family relationships than purposeful and planned disclosure (Brodzinsky *et al*, 1998; Grotevant & McRoy, 1998). It seems probable, therefore, that a child who is told about his or her donor origins at an early age in the context of a loving family is less likely to experience psychological distress than a person who finds out by accident in adolescence or adulthood, or at a time of family trauma such as parental death or divorce. From the limited information available, it appears that an individual's reaction to discovering that he or she was conceived by gamete donation may depend on a number of factors, including the quality of the relationship with his or her parents, his or her age at the time of disclosure, and the manner in which the disclosure takes place.

It is important to distinguish between telling children about the nature of their conception and providing them with identifying information about their donor. By ameliorating the negative effects of secrecy on family relationships, openness with children about the circumstances of their birth may be all that is required. It has been argued that because adoptees often wish to know the identity of, and make contact with, their genetic parents, the same will be true of individuals conceived by gamete donation, and thus identifying information about the donor should be made available to those concerned. Evidence from the investigations of adults who are aware of their donor origins provides support for this view in that many of these adults reported a desire for identifying information about the donor. The same conclusion may be drawn from the study of donor offspring searching for donor relations through the Donor Sibling Registry. However, as discussed above, it is not known how typical these adults are of donor offspring in general. It should also be pointed out that not all adoptees wish to search for their genetic parents and that many adoptees request information about their genetic parents not because they are deeply distressed by the absence of this information but from a sense of curiosity and to allow themselves to develop a clearer sense of who they are and of their past (Howe & Feast, 2000). As donor insemination and egg donation fall between natural conception and adoption with respect to genetic relatedness to parents it may be expected that fewer adult donor offspring than adult adoptees would wish to know the identity of their donor, whereas adults conceived by embryo donation may resemble adult adoptees in this respect.

III. THE PARENTS

Donor conception parents have tended not to tell their children about the nature of their conception. In a review of the 12 studies of parents' disclosure of donor insemination published between 1980 and 1995, Brewaeys (1996) found that few parents (between 1% and 20%) intended to tell their child about her or his genetic origins, and in 8 of the 12 studies fewer than 10% of parents intended to tell. The most recent information on this issue comes from a study that is currently being conducted at the University of Cambridge Centre for Family Research. Of the 45 parents of donor insemination babies born between 1999 and 2001, 46% intended to tell their child about his or her donor conception, and of the 46 egg donation parents in the study, 56% intended to do so (Golombok *et al*, 2004). These figures suggest a marked rise in the proportion of donor insemination and egg donation parents who plan to be open with their child. However, only 5% of the donor insemination parents and 7% of the egg donation parents had actually done so by the age of three (Golombok *et al*, 2006). Previous research suggests that some parents who consider disclosure when their child is young change their mind as the child grows up. For example, although none of the 111 sets of donor insemination parents of four- to eight-year-olds in the first phase of the European Study of Assisted Reproduction Families had told their child about their donor conception, 12% intended to do so in the future and a further 13% were still considering this issue. When these parents were interviewed again when the child was aged 11–12 years old, only eight sets of parents (8.6%) had disclosed this information to their child. Even in Sweden, where legislation gives individuals the right to obtain information about the donor and his identity, a survey found that only 11% of parents had informed their child about the donor insemination (Lindblad *et al*, 2000). It should also be remembered that donor insemination parents who are most concerned about keeping the child's genetic origins secret are least likely to participate in research, and thus the figures relating to the proportion of donor insemination parents who intend to be open with their children represent an over-estimate. In spite of the greater encouragement of disclosure in recent years, and a trend towards greater openness by parents, it seems that many parents do not tell their children that they were conceived by donor insemination.

A number of studies have examined donor insemination parents' reasons for their decision not to tell their child. The predominant motive is parents' concern that disclosure would upset their child and would have an adverse effect on parent–child relationships. In particular, they fear that the child may feel less love for, or possibly reject, the father (Cook *et al*, 1995; Lycett *et al*, 2005). Other considerations that are taken into account in parents' decision not to tell include a desire to protect the father from the stigma of infertility, concern about a negative reaction from paternal grandparents who may not accept the child as their grandchild, uncertainty about the best time and method of telling the child, and lack of information to give the child about the donor. In addition, some parents, emphasising the greater importance of social than biological aspects of parenting believe that there is simply no need to tell. Such parents may be following the long-standing tradition of non-disclosure found in families with children conceived through extra-marital affairs. With respect to egg donation, the predominant reason for non-disclosure was again to protect the child (Golombok *et al*, 1999). Where the child is conceived through an egg-sharing arrangement, whereby a woman undergoing in vitro fertilisation (IVF) donates some of her eggs to another woman in return for free or reduced-cost treatment, the situation becomes even more complex. In some cases the woman who receives the eggs gives birth to a child, whereas the woman who donates the eggs does not.

For lesbian and single heterosexual women who become mothers through donor insemination the situation is somewhat different as these mothers need to explain to their children why they do not have a father. As a result, lesbian and single heterosexual mothers are generally open with their children about the circumstances of their birth. In a Belgian study of a representative sample of 30 lesbian families with children conceived by donor insemination, Brewaeys *et al* (1995) found that all of the mothers intended to tell their child about their donor conception, and 56% would have opted for an identifiable donor had that been possible. Comparable findings regarding the openness of lesbian mothers have been reported in the US (Leiblum *et al*, 1995; Jacob *et al*, 1999).

With respect to single heterosexual mothers, a study in the UK found that 93% planned to disclose the donor conception to their child (Murray & Golombok, 2005). Thus, the openness of lesbian and single heterosexual mothers to this issue is in striking contrast to that of heterosexual couples who prefer not to tell.

Conclusions regarding Parents

The majority of parents choose not to tell their children that they were conceived by donor conception. When we asked donor insemination mothers who were intending to tell whether they would have preferred their donor to be identifiable, only 22% said that they would (Golombok *et al*, 2002a). It seems that a genetic link with their children remains important to parents, as reflected in the decline in the use of donor insemination and a corresponding rise in the uptake of intracytoplasmic sperm injection (ICSI), a treatment for male infertility whereby conception is achieved by injecting a single sperm into an egg. However, one reason for parents' decision not to be open with their child is the absence of information about the donor. Some parents feel that to tell children about the donor, and then to be unable to answer their inevitable questions about who the donor is, would create too much confusion and uncertainty for them and it is for this reason that they decide not to tell. For these parents, donor identification may be considered as a benefit. Parents are also uncertain about when, what and how to tell children about their donor conception. If parents were to be offered advice and support on disclosure during their children's early years, they may find it easier to be open with their children, they may discover that their fears of being rejected by their child were unfounded and they may be more accepting of donor identification.

IV. THE DONORS

Before the removal of donor anonymity, it was commonly claimed that the number of men willing to donate semen would decline dramatically were information about the identity of the donor to be made available to donor offspring. Although this claim was largely based on the opinions of clinicians, evidence in support of this view came from studies of the motivations and attitudes of donors themselves. For example, in a survey commissioned by the Human Fertilisation and Embryology Authority involving 14 licensed clinics in the UK, almost two-thirds of donors stated that they would not donate semen if the law allowed their name to be given to their offspring on reaching the age of 18 (Cook & Golombok, 1995).

In contrast, studies conducted in Australia and New Zealand indicated a greater openness by donors to future contact with their offspring, most probably due to the greater encouragement of openness in these countries (Daniels & Haimes, 1997). In Australia, Daniels found that 68% of donors would not object to identifying information being given to offspring at the age of 18, and another study reported that 60% of donors would not mind meeting offspring at the age of 18. In New Zealand, it was found that 68% of donors were agreeable to their identity being made available to offspring on reaching maturity. It appears, therefore, that the ability to recruit donors who are willing to be identified to adult offspring depends, to some extent at least, upon prevailing cultural attitudes. In New Zealand, the importance to Maori culture of knowing one's genealogy has been influential in the development of policy designed to support openness, and in the State of Victoria in Australia donor offspring have a legal right to identifying information about their donor.

The individual characteristics of donors also seem to play a part in their attitudes towards openness. In a comparison between donors attending two clinics in the UK, one that tended to recruit older, married men with children of their own whose motivation to donate was primarily altruistic, and the other that tended to recruit unmarried students and young professionals who were primarily motivated by payment, a higher proportion of the former group (41%) than the latter (18%) reported that they would be willing to continue providing semen if the resulting offspring could eventually learn of their identity (Daniels *et al*, 1996). This suggested that the recruitment of older men who had completed their family and whose primary motivation was to help childless couples may result in a higher proportion of donors who are willing to be identified to their offspring. The attitudes presented by clinics also seem to be important. The Sperm Bank of California is successful in attracting donors who are amenable to the release of their identity to their offspring when they reach the age of 18 (Scheib *et al*, 2003).

The situation regarding the supply of sperm donors in the UK since the removal of donor anonymity in March 2005 is still evolving. As a result of this legislation, as predicted, there was a fall in donor numbers. However, there are signs of an upturn in response to new recruitment techniques (HFEA, 2007). The examination of changes in the pattern of sperm donor recruitment in Sweden following the introduction in 1985 of legislation giving donor-conceived adults the right to identifying information about their donor sheds some light on the likely consequences of the removal of donor anonymity for donor numbers in the UK. From an examination of the situation in Sweden, it was concluded that following the passing of the legislation there was a decline in the number of semen donors but that this situation later reversed (Lalos *et al*, 2007). Nevertheless, many doctors, as well as couples requesting donor insemination, were reported to be unhappy with the legislation, and some clinics closed down. In addition, there is evidence to suggest that a large proportion of Swedish couples who wish to have donor insemination travel abroad for treatment. In the UK it is still too early to know whether a sufficient number of identifiable semen donors will come forward to match demand. Egg donors have always been in short supply and it appears that the removal of donor anonymity has resulted in a decline in both altruistic and egg-sharing donors (HFEA, 2007). The number of couples who donate their excess embryos has also shown a downward trend (HFEA, 2007).

Conclusions regarding Donors

In the UK, there has been a marked decrease in the number of men willing to donate semen since the removal of donor anonymity, although there are indications of an increase in donor numbers in response to new recruitment strategies. Before the change in legislation, the majority of donors were young men who were largely motivated by payment. In an HFEA survey, the average age of donors was 24 years, and 70% reported that payment was an important consideration in their decision to donate (Cook & Golombok, 1995). There is evidence to suggest that a different type of donor, namely older men who have completed their own family and who are largely motivated by the desire to help a childless couple, may be more open to the provision of identifying information to their donor offspring. However, it is not yet known whether a sufficient number of such donors can successfully be recruited. Moreover, the poorer sperm quality of older men is likely to result in a higher proportion of potential donors failing the screening process. Reports from licensed clinics in the UK indicate that a greater number of donors are required, and that the decline in donor numbers has resulted in the demand for donated gametes exceeding the supply. Thus the change in legislation to remove donor anonymity has produced a greater proportion of infertile people who do not have access to donated gametes, and a consequent rise in reproductive tourism whereby people are travelling abroad to obtain the treatment they require.

V. GENERAL CONCLUSIONS

The advantages and disadvantages of the identification of donors differ according to the party concerned. With respect to the offspring, an advantage of donor identification is that those who so wish, providing they are aware of their donor conception, will be able to find out about, and possibly have contact with, their donor(s) and donor relations including donor siblings. The proportion of donor-conceived adults who are likely to request this information is currently unknown. Nevertheless, there is growing evidence that many donor offspring do wish to obtain identifying information about their donor(s). As the law currently stands, whether or not donor offspring will have access to this information is dependent on parents' decision to tell—or not to tell—their children about their donor conception. Under the present legislation parents are not required to do so, although there is growing support for the introduction of a mechanism such as birth certificate registration to give children easier access to this information.

From the perspective of parents, the majority of whom currently choose not to tell their children about their donor origins due to a fear of rejection, donor identification may be viewed as potentially threatening, and may discourage some parents who may otherwise have done so from disclosing this information to their children. However, for other parents, donor identification may encourage openness with their children thus allaying the potential difficulties associated with secrecy about this issue, and there does seem to be a trend in that direction.

Regarding the donors themselves, the recruitment of men and women who are willing to be identified to their offspring is currently presenting difficulties, and new strategies need to be employed. There are signs of an increase in sperm donor numbers alongside a change in social attitudes towards greater openness in donor conception. However, people who opt for donor conception as a route to parenthood, especially where donated eggs or embryos are involved, are currently facing problems due to an insufficient number of donors to meet demand.

The current legal situation is effectively a compromise between the view that parents should have the autonomy to withhold information about donor conception from their child and the opposite view that parents should have a statutory obligation to disclose. If the present legislation results in children being told about their donor conception because parents believe it right to do so—a situation that would be most beneficial for the child—parents will maintain their autonomy with respect to disclosure by ameliorating the need for further state intervention in this delicate area of family life.

BIBLIOGRAPHY

Bok S (1982) *Secrets*, Pantheon, New York.

Brewaeys A (1996) 'Donor insemination, the impact on family and child development'. *Journal of Psychosomatic Obstetrics and Gynecology* 14, 23–35.

Brodzinsky DM, Smith DW, Brodzinsky AB (1998) *Children's Adjustment to Adoption. Developmental and Clinical Issues*, Sage Publications, London.

Clamar A (1989) 'Psychological implications of the anonymous pregnancy' in *Gender in Transition: A New Frontier* (Ed, Offerman-Zuckerberg J) Plenum, New York and London, pp 111–21.

Clayton C & Kovacs G (1982) 'AID offspring: initial follow up study of 50 couples'. *Medical Journal of Australia* 1, 338–9.

Cook R & Golombok S (1995) 'A survey of sperm donation. Phase II: The view of donors'. *Human Reproduction* 10, 951–59.

Cook R, Golombok S, Bish A, Murray C (1995) 'Keeping secrets: a study of parental attitudes toward telling about donor insemination'. *American Journal of Orthopsychiatry* 65, 549–59.

Daniels K & Haimes E (1997) *International Social Science Perspectives on Donor Insemination*, Cambridge University Press, Cambridge.

Daniels K, Curson R, Lewis G (1996) 'Semen donor recruitment: a study of donors in two clinics'. *Human Reproduction* 11, 746–51.

De Paulo BM (1992) 'Nonverbal behaviour and self-presentation'. *Psychological Bulletin*, 111, 203–43.

Department of Health (2006) *Review of the Human Fertilisation and Embryology Act: Proposals for revised legislation (including establishment of the Regulatory Authority for Tissues and Embryos)*, Cm 6989, Department of Health, London.

Golombok S, Cook R, Bish A, Murray C (1995) 'Families created by the new reproductive technologies: quality of parenting and social and emotional development of the children'. *Child Development* 66, 285–98.

Golombok S, Brewaeys A, Cook R, Giavazzi MT, Guerra D *et al* (1996) 'The European study of assisted reproduction families'. *Human Reproduction* 11, 2324–31.

Golombok S, Murray C, Brinsden P, Abdalla H (1999) 'Social versus biological parenting: family functioning and the socioemotional development of children conceived by egg or sperm donation'. *Journal of Child Psychology and Psychiatry* 40, 519–27.

Golombok S, MacCallum F, Goodman E, Rutter M (2002a) 'Families with children conceived by donor insemination: a follow-up at age 12'. *Child Development* 73, 952–68.

Golombok S, Brewaeys A, Giavazzi M, Guerra D, MacCallum F *et al* (2002b) 'The European study of assisted reproduction families: the transition to adolescence'. *Human Reproduction* 17, 830–40.

Golombok S, Lycett E, MacCallum F, Jadva V, Murray, C *et al* (2004) 'Parenting infants conceived by gamete donation'. *Journal of Family Psychology* 18, 443–52.

Golombok S, Murray C, Jadva V, Lycett E, MacCallum F, Rust J (2006) 'Non-genetic and non-gestational parenthood: consequences for parent–child relationships and the psychological well being of mothers, fathers and children at age 3'. *Human Reproduction* 21, 1918–24.

Grotevant MD & McRoy RG (1998) *Openness in Adoption: Exploring Family Connections*, Sage, New York.

HFEA (Human Fertilisation and Embryology Authority) (2007) *A Long-term Analysis of the HFEA Register Data 1991–2006*, HFEA, London.

Howe D & Feast J (2000) *Adoption, Search and Reunion: The long-term experiences of adopted adults*, The Children's Society, London.

Jacob M, Klock S, Maier D (1999) 'Lesbian mothers as therapeutic donor insemination recipients: do they differ from other patients?' *Journal of Psychosomatic Obstetrics and Gynecology* 20, 203–15.

Jadva V, Freeman T, Golombok S (2007) 'Searching for donor siblings'. Paper presented at the 63rd Annual Meeting of the American Society for Reproductive Medicine, Washington, DC, October.

Karpel MA (1980) 'Family secrets: I. Conceptual and ethical issues in the relational context. II. Ethical and practical considerations in therapeutic management'. *Family Process* 19, 295–306.

Kovacs, G, Mushin, D, Kane H, Baker H (1983) 'A controlled study of the psychosocial development of children conceived following insemination with donor semen'. *Human Reproduction* 8, 788–90.

Lalos A, Gottleib C, Lalos O (2007) 'Legislated right for donor insemination children to know their genetic origin: a study of parental thinking'. *Human Reproduction* 22, 1759–68.

Leeton J & Blackwell J (1982) 'A preliminary psychosocial follow-up of parents and their children conceived by artificial insemination by donor (AID)'. *Clinical Reproduction and Fertility* 1, 307–10.

Leiblum S, Palmer M, Spector I (1995) 'Non-traditional mothers: Single heterosexual/ lesbian women and lesbian couples electing motherhood via donor insemination'. *Journal of Psychosomatic Obstetrics and Gynecology* 16, 11–20.

Lindblad F, Gottlieb C, Lalos O (2000) 'To tell or not to tell- what parents think about telling their children that they were born following donor insemination'. *Journal of Psychosomatic Obstetrics and Gynecology* 21, 193–203.

Lycett E, Daniels D, Curson R, Golombok S (2005) 'School-aged children of donor insemination: a study of parents' disclosure patterns'. *Human Reproduction* 20, 810–19.

MacCallum F & Golombok S (2007) 'Embryo donation families: mothers' decisions regarding disclosure of donor conception'. *Human Reproduction* 22, 2888–95.

MacCallum F, Golombok S, Brinsden P. (2007) 'Parenting and child development in families with a child conceived by embryo donation'. *Journal of Family Psychology* 21, 278–87.

Murray C & Golombok S (2005) 'Going it alone: solo mothers and their infants conceived by donor insemination'. *American Journal of Orthopsychiatry* 75, 242–53.

Murray C, MacCallum F, Golombok S (2006) 'Families created by egg donation: Follow-up at age 12'. *Fertility & Sterility* 85, 610–18.

Owen L & Golombok S (2007) 'Families created by assisted reproduction: parent-child relationships in late adolescence'. Submitted to *Journal of Adolescence*.

Papp P (1993) 'The worm in the bud: secrets between parents and children' in *Secrets in Families and Family Therapy* (Ed, Imber-Black E) Norton, New York, pp 66–85.

Richards M (2007) 'Genes, genealogies and paternity: making babies in the twenty-first century' in *Freedom and Responsibility in Reproductive Choice* (Eds, Spencer J & du-Bois Pedain A) Hart Publishing, Oxford.

Rumball A & Adair V (1999) Telling the story: parents' scripts for donor offspring. *Human Reproduction* 14, 1392–1399.

Scheib J, Riordan M, Rubin S (2003) 'Choosing identity-release sperm donors: the parents' perspective 13–18 years later'. *Human Reproduction* 18, 1115–127.

—— (2005) 'Adolescents with open-identity sperm donors: reports from 12–17 year olds'. *Human Reproduction* 20, 239–52.

Snowden R, Mitchell GD, Snowden EM (1983). *Artificial Reproduction: A Social Investigation*, George Allen & Unwin, London.

Turner A & Coyle A (2000) 'What does it mean to be a donor offspring? The identity experiences of adults conceived by donor insemination and the implications for counseling and therapy'. *Human Reproduction* 15, 2041–51.

Vanfraussen K, Ponjaert-Kristoffersen I, Brewaeys A (2001) 'An attempt to reconstruct children's donor concept: a comparison between children's and lesbian parents' attitudes towards donor anonymity'. *Human Reproduction* 16, 2091–25.

13

Autonomy and the UK's Law on Abortion

Current Problems and Future Prospects

LAURA RILEY AND ANN FUREDI

I. INTRODUCTION

SINCE THE ABORTION Act received Royal Assent on 27 October 1967, almost seven million women have benefited from safe, legal abortion in Britain (Department of Health, 2007a; ISD Scotland, 2007), and tens of millions of people have been able to enjoy sex knowing that an unwanted pregnancy need not result in unwilling motherhood. The Abortion Act (1967) has served society well by permitting basic access to care. However the legislation can only allow so much clinical interpretation, and 40 years on, the 1967 Act now holds providers back from offering women the most up-to-date medical treatment. The predominantly medically based grounds on which abortion under the Act is predicated were framed with little regard to the autonomy of women seeking abortion. The autonomy of doctors with a conscientious objection to abortion is not well served by the lack of clarity of the Act in this area. Autonomy could be better facilitated by increased statutory or regulatory protections for women. We will argue that amendments to the 1967 Act and other changes are needed to enable women's autonomous choices to be respected more fully.

II. THE UK'S ABORTION LAW

Estimates as to how many illegal abortions occurred in England and Wales before 1967 vary from 200,000 to 150,000 annually (Department of Health, 2005a). The treatment of clandestine abortion accounted for one-fifth of gynaecological admissions within the NHS in this period (Lane Committee, 1974). Maternal mortality from illegal abortion was acknowledged to be unacceptably high and introducing legal abortion was primarily seen as a solution to a persistent public health problem. David Steel's Abortion Bill reflected and codified the concerns of the pre-'feminist' period in the 1960s and was shaped by contemporary debates. Although this was a time of social reform and changing attitudes, the large-scale cohesion of the 'women's movement' and the establishment's awareness of their aims were still some years away. The 1967 Labour Government sought to promote a consensus that social problems could be solved through welfare policies, and abortion was framed as a means to help women unable to cope with pregnancy and motherhood, rather than as an expression of women's bodily or reproductive autonomy.

The Bill was also discussed as a means to minimise the numbers of 'unfit' mothers and 'unfit' children. Dr John Dunwoody, a Labour MP and general practitioner, expressed a common contemporary sentiment in arguing for legal abortion because:

> in many cases today when we have over-large families the mother is so broken down physically and emotionally ... it becomes quite impossible for her to fulfil her real function, her worthwhile function as a mother holding together the family unit, so that all too often the family breaks apart, and it is for this reason that we have so many problem families. (Sheldon, 1997)

Public awareness of the emerging effects of Thalidomide had also raised concern about the management of identified fetal abnormality, prompting the inclusion of a ground for abortion in the Abortion Act (1967) when 'there is a substantial risk that if the child were born, it would suffer from such physical or mental abnormalities as to be seriously handicapped', as well as new regulation for medicines.

Despite the far-reaching social changes of the last 40 years, UK abortion law has changed remarkably little since 1967, although accompanying regulation is updated regularly. Abortion providers must be approved by the Secretary of State for Health and must comply with the Abortion Act (1967) (as amended by the Human Fertilisation and Embryology Act, 1990), the Care Standards Act (2000) (as amended), and the Health and Social Care (Community Health and Standards) Act (2003). They must also meet several regulatory requirements. The Abortion Act (1967) still does not extend to Northern Ireland. In 1990, via section 37 of the Human Fertilisation and Embryology Act (1990), the Abortion Act was amended to introduce a time limit of 24 weeks' gestation for abortions performed under section 1(1)(a), the most commonly used legal ground, making abortion permissible if two doctors agree

> that the pregnancy has not exceeded its twenty-fourth week and that the continuance of the pregnancy would involve risk, greater than if the pregnancy were terminated, of injury to the physical or mental health of the pregnant woman.

In England and Wales in 2006, 97% of abortions were undertaken under this ground (Department of Health, 2007a).

However, no time limit is specified if

the termination is necessary to prevent grave permanent injury to the physical or mental health of the pregnant woman; or

... the continuance of the pregnancy would involve risk to the life of the pregnant woman, greater than if the pregnancy were terminated; or

... there is a substantial risk that if the child were born it would suffer from such physical or mental abnormalities as to be seriously handicapped.

Before this change, a 28-week limit had applied for all grounds in England and Wales, without stipulation of an upper time limit in Scotland.

III. AUTONOMY IN ABORTION CARE

BPAS (the British Pregnancy Advisory Service) is a UK charity providing not-for-profit sexual healthcare, 92% of which is under contract to the National Health Service (NHS). Around 55,000 women each year have abortion treatment with BPAS, and around 85,000 men and women discuss pregnancy and contraception with the charity. The facilitation of autonomous decision-making about fertility is a central function of BPAS.

Our discussion envisages autonomy as decision-making by a competent individual which may affect various aspects of their life and physical self, in some aspects potentially for an indefinite time. Autonomy is compromised unless offered in a healthcare environment respectful of self-determination, which offers practical support for autonomous decision-making. Facilitating this environment in abortion care requires (for example) accurate, appropriate and timely non-directive information from healthcare professionals to enable each individual to fully explore their options, with a commitment to appropriate confidentiality, and for a choice of appropriate treatment methods to be offered in order to maximise the acceptability and accessibility of each option.

Autonomy is supported by offering a higher level of appointment flexibility than is usual in other healthcare services, providing an indefinite number of counselling appointments, and permitting repeated cancellation and rebooking of scheduled treatment if women need more time to reach a decision. 'Autonomy advocacy' becomes effectively part of the role of the BPAS contracts team, who, when negotiating arrangements with NHS commissioners, may need to explain why it is unacceptable for a Primary Care Trust (PCT) not to fund consultations or treatment for women who have missed appointments, not to fund extra counselling appointments, or not to fund treatment because the individual has had an NHS-funded abortion, or because the number of weeks' gestation is lower or higher than the PCT has set for its eligibility criteria.

In our experience, women making autonomous abortion decisions tend to take into account far-reaching considerations far beyond the risks to life and health involved. Risks from abortion, especially in the first trimester, are lower than those from continued pregnancy and birth. Eighty-nine per cent of abortions in England and Wales were carried out at under 13 weeks' gestation (Department of Health, 2007a), and even around the UK's 24 weeks' gestation legal upper time limit for most abortions, abortion is not more risky than continuing the pregnancy and birth. Many BPAS clients say that their decision to continue, or to end, a pregnancy involved careful consideration of the interests and views of others. Women may discuss their decision with their partner, close family or friends over a period of time. At least 37% of women having an abortion in England and Wales in 2006 either were married or had a regular partner (Department of Health, 2007a).

In making a decision about a pregnancy, the pregnancy, or the fetus, may be considered by the woman in its current gestational state and/or hypothesised as a born child. American research by Jones *et al* (2008) finds women stating their sense of responsibility for their existing and future children and motivation to 'be good parents' as central factors in an abortion decision. In 2006, 47% of women having abortions in England and Wales were already mothers, and in the US mothers account for three-fifths of women having abortions. (Department of Health, 2007a; Jones *et al*, 2008). Similarly to some of the childless women involved in the US research, women without children often tell BPAS staff that part of their decision involves trying to reconcile their current situation with their imagined scenario of embarking on motherhood.

By their nature, decisions about an unintended pregnancy often involve weighing burdensome pragmatic issues. The woman's current or prospective economic, relationship and housing situation and family duties and relationships may fetter completely 'free' or instinctively felt decision-making. For some commentators, these factors impinge on true autonomy in decision-making, and negate the validity of women's choices, although this argument is usually only heard if the decision is for abortion. Those arguing from this position often feel that given more support and money, few (or no) women would or should choose abortion. In our experience, abortion decisions (or in this view, barriers to continuing with the pregnancy) are usually much more complex than that, although government and society could better support autonomy by tackling some of the practical factors that can prevent women making the choices they want.

Any decision about an unintended pregnancy may never feel entirely emotionally clear-cut, and sometimes women say they are deciding on their 'least worst' option. But a woman's decision made in the reality of her circumstances can still be autonomously arrived at, as long as she has the support needed to reach her decision herself. Pregnancy decisions are often complex and time-limited and each is made within the confines of each woman's situation at the particular time that she is faced with it.

Whether or not a woman has previously experienced pregnancy or abortion, her previous attitude to abortion is not always a pivotal decision-making factor. Women from religious backgrounds that oppose abortion are as likely to use contraception and abortion services as other populations. In the same way that many people who would not consider abortion as an option for themselves do not seek to restrict access to abortion for others, not all women choosing an abortion approve of abortion being accessible to others. A minority of clients are keen to tell staff that they do not approve of abortion being available but that it is right for their current situation, or that their own case is 'different' from that of the other abortion-seeking women coming to BPAS.

IV. CURRENT PROBLEMS

The importance of bodily autonomy and permitting competent individuals to consent to, or refuse, medical treatment has been particularly central to medical ethics since the 1940s, although this has been slow to be translated into practical or political support for women's choices around pregnancy and birth. In abortion care in the UK, autonomy is currently fettered in some areas by over-restrictive statute, and in others, autonomous decision-making is offered little support or protection by law or regulation.

A. The Abortion Exception

Access to abortion in the UK remains legally detached from a competent woman's decision-making, setting abortion apart from the process of informed consent used with other medical treatment. In the UK, access to abortion under the Abortion Act (1967) (as amended by the Human Fertilisation and Embryology Act 1990) additionally depends on the agreement of two doctors that the woman meets the medically based legal criteria for abortion, otherwise a crime is committed. The woman's request not to remain pregnant is not among these criteria.

This is anomalous, as the same competent pregnant woman could legitimately refuse medical treatment where such refusal would threaten the life of the fetus, up to and including during the birth process. The Court of Appeal found that competent women may refuse an emergency Caesarean section, even if the fetus might die. Lord Justice Judge said of this: 'The autonomy of each individual requires continuing protection, particularly when the motive for interfering is as readily understandable, and indeed to many would appear commendable.'

He continued that

> Pregnancy does not diminish a woman's entitlement whether or not to undergo medical treatment. Her right is not reduced or diminished, merely because her decision to exercise her right may appear morally repugnant. (*St George's Healthcare NHS Trust v S* [1998])

The General Medical Council (GMC)'s guidance for doctors states that patients have the 'right to decide whether or not to undergo any medical intervention even where a refusal may result in harm to themselves or in their own death', and it further specifies that 'this right applies equally to pregnant women as to other patients, and includes the right to refuse treatment where the treatment is intended to benefit the unborn child' (GMC, 1998, para 1).

The Department of Health's *Good Practice in Consent Implementation Guide: Consent to Examination or Treatment* states that:

> Competent adult patients are entitled to refuse treatment, even when it would clearly benefit their health. The only exception to this rule is where the treatment is for a mental disorder and the patient is detained under the Mental Health Act 1983. A competent pregnant woman may refuse any treatment, even if this would be detrimental to the fetus. (Department of Health, 2001)

We feel that the 'abortion exception' to the usual principles of autonomy is unsustainable. The law should be amended to allow competent adults (and young people as per *Gillick* [1985] and *R (Axon)* [2006]) to consent to abortion on the basis of informed consent as with other medical care. The two doctors' signatures required by the 1967 Act are a solely legal exercise, offering no clinical benefit. In England and Wales since the implementation of statutory instruments in 2002, doctors need not have examined or even met the woman, only to have read her medical notes.[1]

The two doctors' confirmatory signatures brought in by the Abortion Act (1967) provide them with a defence to what remains a criminal act. The Abortion Act (1967) came into effect on 27 April 1968 in England, Scotland and Wales, permitting treatment on the basis of a medically based defence to a criminal act, although in fact its interpretation by doctors has allowed (usually) relatively straightforward care for women. The literal sense of the most frequently used ground in the Act, available up to 24 weeks' gestation, has become redundant, that is that

---

[1] Abortion (Amendment) (England) Regulations 2002, SI 2002/887; Abortion (Amendment) (Wales) Regulation 2002, SI 2002/289 (W 275).

the continuance of the pregnancy would involve risk, greater than if the pregnancy were terminated, of *injury to the physical or mental health* of the pregnant woman (emphasis added).

Modern abortion methods since the 1960s mean that, for most women, abortion is safer than continued pregnancy and birth. (RCOG, 2004, '2.2 Information for women', Recommendation 16, p 8; Grimes, 2006)

B. Conscientious Objection

Despite the positive outcome for access by the coincidence of safe modern treatment and the anachronistic phrasing of the 1967 Act, some women experience barriers to access, or have an unnecessarily stressful route to treatment at what is already a stressful time. A small proportion of women tell us that their GP had obstructed or delayed their referral. There is not space in this chapter to explore the issue of conscientious objection fully, but suffice to say, there is little clarity on the limits of the law. Section 4 of the 1967 Act states that (except 'to save the life or to prevent grave permanent injury to the physical or mental health of a pregnant woman'),

> no person shall be under any duty, whether by contract or by any statutory or other legal requirement, to participate in any treatment authorised by this Act to which he has a conscientious objection

The General Medical Council (GMC), the regulatory body for doctors, does not limit doctors' right to conscientious objection to carrying out abortions, providing contraceptive services or withdrawing life-prolonging treatment. The GMC's guidance states that:

> if carrying out a particular procedure or giving advice about it conflicts with your religious or moral beliefs, and this conflict might affect the treatment or advice you provide, you must explain this to the patient and tell them they have the right to see another doctor. You must be satisfied that the patient has sufficient information to enable them to exercise that right. If it is not practical for a patient to arrange to see another doctor, you must ensure that arrangements are made for another suitably qualified colleague to take over your role. (GMC, 2006, para 8)

What actually constitutes 'participating in treatment' is variably interpreted by doctors and students, with some clarification for supporting staff via *Janaway v Salford Health Authority* [1998].[2] Some objecting doctors are

---

[2] Lord Hunt of Kings Heath clarified in 2002 that to be covered by the conscientious objection clause in the Act, 'the objector had to be required to take part in administering treatment in a hospital or approved centre. Practitioners cannot claim exemption from giving advice or

known to refuse to refer patients to non-objecting doctors, to refuse to sign abortion-related paperwork, to tell women to take a few weeks to 'think about it' before they discuss abortion referral, or to ask patients to read the Bible (*Daily Mail*, 2007; *Observer*, 2007). Some medical schools permit students on relevant courses to opt out of learning about abortion treatment or the relevant ethics altogether (*Independent*, 2007), even though the Abortion Act (1967) requires doctors to be able to perform an abortion in an emergency. Conscientious objection by doctors and medical students is not registered or monitored, making it hard to know how extensive it is. Other countries such as Portugal, after introducing legal abortion up to 10 weeks in 2007, keep a statutory publicly consultable register of conscientious objectors.

In our view, conscientious objection is an important safeguard of the quality of care and is necessary to protect the professional autonomy of doctors. However, a more clearly drawn system is needed, to enable women to avoid approaching an objecting doctor and risking delay or bias, and affording objecting doctors more time to devote to patients with other needs. New guidance on personal beliefs and medical practice will be issued by the GMC in 2008 to clarify practice relating to conscientious objection within the existing law.

Medical staff in Northern Ireland are particularly vulnerable where they do work in abortion provision, as not only do they not have the protection of the Abortion Act (1967) to provide non-emergency abortions, they do not have any right to conscientious objection under the Act, adding another factor to the reluctance to provide abortion in Northern Ireland.

C. Misinformation

Autonomy is lost when misinformation is given. Some 'crisis pregnancy counselling' agencies in the UK offer poor information about abortion. Minimum qualifications are not required before offering counselling in the UK, nor is 'crisis pregnancy' work regulated. For example, 'Care Confidential' is a large organisation offering phone and online counselling and referring women to affiliated local centres across Britain. 'Care Confidential' is a function of the charity Christian Action Research and Education (CARE), whose aims are listed as 'the advancement and propagation of the Christian Gospel and in particular Christian teaching as it bears on or affects national

---

performing the preparatory steps to arrange an abortion where the request meets legal requirements. If a general practitioner has a conscientious objection to abortion, the patient should be advised and referred to another doctor if that is the patient's wish. Refusal to participate in the paperwork or administration connected with abortion procedures also lies outside the terms of the conscience clause' (*Hansard*, 2002).

and individual morality and ethics' (Charity Commission, 2008). The Care Confidential website promises 'free confidential help' but does not mention that it does not refer women for abortion (Care Confidential, 2007). LIFE is another large charity offering phone and text message counselling and referral to local centres. LIFE's website promises 'person-centred, non-directive' counselling, and says it is 'an organisational member of the British Association of Counsellors and Psychotherapists (BACP) and adheres to its Code of Ethics' (LIFE, 2008). LIFE states that 'Where appropriate, we signpost or refer to other organisations or LIFE services', but it does not mention its non-referral for abortion.

The Department of Health website offers women an understated warning:

> There are a number of organisations advertised in phone directories and on the internet offering free pregnancy testing and counselling. Some of these organisations do not refer women for termination of pregnancy. We would advise women to check this before making an appointment. (Department of Health, 2007b)

In our view this is an inadequate safeguard for autonomy. Anti-abortion groups should be able to offer women their view of abortion, but new regulation should require them to state clearly that they do not refer for abortion. Other countries are debating statutory regulation which would prohibit misleading or deceptive advertising or notification of pregnancy counselling services, such as the Pregnancy Counselling (Truth in Advertising) Bill 2006 in Australia.

In the Republic of Ireland the statutory Crisis Pregnancy Agency was established in October 2001, with functions including the promotion of state-funded crisis pregnancy counselling services to tackle the problem of '"rogue" crisis pregnancy counselling agencies' (CPA, 2006). The Irish Family Planning Association has since called for the

> statutory regulation for all pregnancy advice and counselling services, prescribing minimum codes of practice and standards, to ensure that they do not impart misleading and incorrect advice. In addition, it should be mandatory for all services to register with a recognised authority. (IFPA, 2006, p 6)

D. Choice of Methods

Autonomous decision-making in healthcare is also facilitated by providing a choice of method to patients where clinically appropriate to do so. Especially with a personal procedure such as abortion, the location, timing or other characteristics of a treatment method may mean that the treatment as a whole becomes possible, or impossible, for a woman to take up. The interpretation of the current law in respect of early medical abortion (EMA) is an example where a method is made unnecessarily burdensome for some women, limiting national capacity to provide early abortion. EMA was brought to the UK in 1992 by BPAS and is used up to 63 days' gestation. The woman swallows a mifepristone tablet (known as 'RU 486' in Europe) at a clinic, blocking the pregnancy hormones so that the pregnancy ceases to be viable. She then returns home or occupies herself for a few hours close to the clinic. Six to eight hours later, or the next day, she returns to the clinic where misoprostol tablets are swallowed or self-administered vaginally. Misoprostol causes the uterus to contract and expel the pregnancy, similarly to an early miscarriage. Women return home promptly after taking misoprostol in order to make themselves comfortable before it takes effect.

The woman's second journey to the clinic to self-administer the misoprostol is clinically redundant and can be burdensome for those with caring, or other, concerns. As the time from dosage in clinic to the onset of bleeding at home varies between individuals and can be unpredictable, the law should permit women the option of self-administering misoprostol at home. Home self-administration is common where EMA is available overseas, and is precluded in the UK only because the 1967 Act, as amended by the HFE Act (1990), specifies that an abortion (interpreted by the Department of Health to include both stages of the two-stage EMA treatment) may be carried out only in a hospital or specially approved location. In Norway, which has a law similar to the UK, mifepristone is taken in the clinic as this is regarded as the abortifacient, but misoprostol may be self-administered at home as it is viewed as a supporting medication to enable the prompt and safe expulsion of the pregnancy. An unwieldly alternative route to enable women to take misoprostol at home, by extending the legal restrictions far beyond the current list of approved locations, has been within the Secretary of State's power since the amendments of 1990 but no minister since then has permitted this. 30 per cent of women seeking an abortion in England and Wales had a medical abortion in 2006 (Department of Health, 2006), when evidence suggests that where a choice is available, the uptake would be 60%–70% of women. (RCOG, 2007a).

We see no reason to retain legal requirements resulting in sub-optimal treatment, especially as NHS treatment for non-abortion-seeking women (for example after spontaneous or 'natural' miscarriage) routinely permits home self-administration of misoprostol, allowing the pregnancy to be passed in privacy and relative comfort.

E. Identity Discourse

Contemporary rights and 'identity' discourse is being increasingly co-opted into the abortion debate in order to argue for restriction on abortion for fetal abnormality (permissible up until birth where there is risk of 'serious handicap' in the wording of section 1(1)(d) of the Abortion Act 1967), and this ground for abortion has come under particular scrutiny in recent years. Discrimination against born disabled people has been claimed in the different legal time limit for abortion for fetal abnormality.

The numbers of women involved are small: a 21- or 22-week pregnancy scan is routinely offered in antenatal care, but only 136 abortions took place in England and Wales in 2006 where gestation had exceeded its twenty-fourth week (less than 0.1% of all abortions). The interpretation of 'serious handicap' in abortion was unsuccessfully challenged in *Jepson* (2003), where lawyers for the Rev Joanna Jepson, a curate who grew up with a jaw deformity and who has a disabled brother, argued that a cleft lip and palate did not meet the Abortion Act (1967) standard of a 'serious handicap' (BBC, 2005). While some disabled individuals supported Jepson's case, many did not, and in 2003 the Disability Rights Commission stated:

> Section 1(1)(d) is not inconsistent with the Disability Discrimination Act since the latter is concerned with the rights of living persons. Moreover, the number of terminations made under the section is relatively small, and the DRC has no wish to put in question the Abortion Act as a whole.

Despite the failure of the *Jepson* case in 2003, those working with women affected by a diagnosis of fetal abnormality report an undermined confidence on the part of their doctors, with increasing referrals to hospital ethics committees before doctors will sign to certify that women meet the grounds for abortion after 24 weeks. Treatment delay for fear of litigation is an unethical basis on which to compromise women's autonomy, adding to their distress while making their treatment later and unnecessarily riskier.

F. 'Postcode Lottery'

As in most areas of NHS care, abortion provision is affected by a 'postcode lottery' resulting from inadequate resource allocation. This results in reported waiting lists of up to 13 weeks for treatment, although information about NHS waiting times is not centrally collected or monitored. Primary Care Trusts (PCTs) are also free to set their own local eligibility criteria for abortion funding (BBC, 2007a; BMA, 2007). This can result in exemplary arrangements, such as Lambeth, Southwark and Lewisham PCTs' groundbreaking 'self-referral' arrangements, which avoid administrative delays by removing the requirement for a GP's signature before abortion funding will be given.

However, local eligibility criteria also permit arbitrary restrictions, such as at Blaenau Gwent Local Health Board (LHB), where all women who have had a previous abortion must have a (clinically unnecessary) vaginal ultrasound examination, while first-time clients have the standard, external abdominal pregnancy scan. Women who have previously had an abortion must also attend a meeting with a consultant to discuss their circumstances before referral to an abortion provider is allowed. Abortion funding is not permitted by Gwent at all where the gestation is above 20 weeks, or after a woman has had three abortions. Other PCTs fund only women who have lived in the UK for a minimum of one year. Some dictate that university students cannot have treatment in their university town, but must be treated by their 'home' PCT. Until recently, some LHBs charged women for costs if they missed appointments for counselling or treatment, or required additional counselling sessions, and many PCTs and LHBs did not fund abortions before 10 weeks' gestation, before this was centrally monitored by regulators.

The practical exercise of autonomy within abortion services could be better supported by the development of a National Institute for Clinical Excellence (NICE) guideline based around the existing evidence-based Royal College of Obstetricians and Gynaecologists' (RCOG) recommendations, which the RCOG supports. NICE clinical guidance is not mandatory, but promotes evidence-based and cost-effective practice, signposting best practice for commissioners with the Department of Health actively encouraging adherence. However, NICE clinical guidance does not come with additional funding for implementation.

G. Staffing of Services

Staffing of abortion services with enough doctors and nurses can sometimes be a problem. The facilitation of autonomous choice requires appropriately skilled staffing of abortion services, and at present the law, which refers to 'registered medical professionals' is interpreted narrowly, so that only GMC-registered doctors are allowed to take full responsibility for abortion. The Royal College of Nursing argues that nurses should be able to play a fuller role in first-trimester abortions, and the RCOG has recommended that there should be investigation into the possibility of nurses and midwives carrying out early abortions, which would require a change to the 1967 Act (RCOG, 2007b).

H. Northern Ireland

The funding and access situation is far worse in Northern Ireland where, formally, abortions take place only as medical emergencies, and only in the NHS. Northern Ireland must be brought under the Abortion Act (1967) to permit equal access to funded services and remove the need for women to travel for an abortion with all the associated emotional and financial burdens. This issue has received only vague responses from government. In July 2007, Lord Alton asked the government whether they would 'resist any proposal to extend the scope of the Abortion Act 1967 to Northern Ireland' (*Hansard*, 2007). The Parliamentary Under-Secretary of State Lord Darzi replied:

> We are aware of a body of opinion in Northern Ireland that considers the current law on abortion to be either unsatisfactory or unclear, but we also recognise the strength of feeling for not changing the existing legislative provision. ... the Government believe that any change to the law should only come about at the request of a broad cross-section of the people who live there. (*Hansard*, 2007)

I. The Current Situation

Given these problems, it may seem surprising that in most areas of mainland Britain, there has never been a greater likelihood of women receiving accessible, NHS-funded abortion care. The conjunction of the *National Strategy for Sexual Health and HIV Implementation Action Plan* (Department of Health, 2002), monitoring of the percentage of PCTs' abortions taking place at under 10 weeks by the Healthcare Commission, and increased NHS investment in under-providing PCTs (Department of Health, 2007c), meant that in 2006, a record 87% of all abortions performed in England and Wales were NHS-funded. In 2006, 99.3% of the abortions were carried out in NHS premises in Scotland. In 1990, when the Abortion Act (1967) was last amended, the NHS paid for only 48% of abortions to women entitled to NHS care in England and Wales. The unprecedented high level of NHS-funded abortions at the same time as a record number of abortion treatments took place (193,700 in England and Wales, up from 186,912 in 1990) is a positive achievement for access and funded provision.

In our experience, these achievements are possible because of support from the Department of Health, parliamentarians and regulators such as the Healthcare Commission, Healthcare Inspectorate Wales and NHS Quality Improvement Scotland. However, this is contingent on the framing of abortion as a 'public health' issue, a medical solution to a medical need. Support for abortion on non-medical grounds—with respect to autonomy, or the importance that women place on planned parenthood or equality of opportunity—is not expressed, although 'patient choice' is presented as a political priority extending into quite fine details of healthcare elsewhere. The practical gains from the 'public health' approach must not be underestimated. However, if the 'public health' approach to the abortion debate is the sole direction of advocacy, this risks leaving abortion provision vulnerable and misunderstood.

One example of this is the media debate about the UK's 24-week abortion time limit for most abortions, attacked in recent years by the anti-abortion lobby using non-evidenced claims about improved survival of extremely premature babies and detailed ultrasound images of fetuses claimed to 'walk' in the womb. Restriction to late abortion is predominantly argued against using the scientific evidence about fetal viability, which in fact does not indicate that preterm survival under 24 weeks has significantly improved in the UK (Costeloe *et al*, 2000). Later abortion is rare (in 2005, 510 abortions in England and Wales took place at 23 weeks' gestation, and 136 abortions at 24 weeks' gestation and beyond), and such cases often involve women in complex circumstances, including non-recognition of pregnancy symptoms (due to continuing or irregular periods), or being delayed in the abortion referral system, suffering a catastrophic family or relationship breakdown or simply needing time to reach a decision about the pregnancy (Ingham *et al*, 2007) Policy makers rarely emphasise the point that advances in neonatal care are good news, but irrelevant to the needs of women for abortion. When no ethical case is made for late abortion, a fundamental part of women's healthcare is left vulnerable.

The House of Commons Science and Technology Committee report *Human Reproductive Technologies and the Law* recommended in 2005 that abortion law should be reviewed and separated from the law on fertility treatment and embryo research (affecting embryos outside the body). This concluded:

> We call on both Houses ... to set up a joint committee to consider the scientific, medical and social changes in relation to abortion that have taken place since 1967, with a view to presenting options for new legislation, stating that any new legislation introduced to amend the Human Fertilisation and Embryology Act should not include abortion, which should be dealt with in a separate Bill.

In 2006, Public Health Minister Caroline Flint assured colleagues that this separation would happen (*Hansard*, 2006), but in 2007, parliamentary authorities confirmed that amendments to the Abortion Act (1967) would become permissible via the Human Tissue and Embryos Bill (which became the Human Fertilisation and Embryology Bill), to be debated in 2007–08.

Parliamentarians will vote on amendments to the Abortion Act (1967) without the benefit of an inquiry including 'social changes in relation to abortion', as the Science and Technology Committee had called for. However, in October 2007 the same Committee published the results of an inquiry into the evidence on 'Scientific developments relating to the Abortion Act 1967' (Science and Technology Committee, 2007). This concluded that while preterm survival rates at 24 weeks and above had improved since 1990, survival rates had not done so below that gestational point, giving no scientific basis to reduce the abortion time limit on the grounds of viability.

The committee found no evidence for nurses and midwives to be legally prevented from carrying out early medical and early surgical abortions, and supported the removal of the requirement for two doctors' signatures for abortion certification. The committee also found no evidence to deter parliamentarians from enabling women to take the second stage of early medical abortion at home and recommended that the clinical guidelines on abortion provision should ultimately be taken over by the National Institute for Health and Clinical Excellence (NICE), also calling for more research into women presenting late for abortion, women travelling overseas for late abortions and around abortion for fetal abnormality.

The report largely echoed existing evidence-based policy within the medical and nursing professions and was strongly supported by those involved in the care of women and premature babies, and the relevant advocacy groups. The report received a reasonably sympathetic government response in a command paper a month later (Department of Health, 2007d). In the terms laid out by the public health approach to abortion, the Science and Technology Committee report provides a valuable affirmation of the safety of abortion and discussion of ways that provision can be improved. However, the scientific developments relating to the Abortion Act (1967) are only one side of the discussion that is necessary in terms of the law.

V. HOW COULD THE LAW BETTER FACILITATE AUTONOMY IN ABORTION CARE?

Our expectation is that if current conditions continue, abortion numbers will slowly rise. If more women will have better access to funded abortion services, combined with the present rate of unintended pregnancies, rise in average maternal age at first birth, trend towards smaller families and decreased social stigma associated with abortion, it seems inevitable that more women will use abortion services (possibly more than once) during their reproductive 'lifespan'. From 2005 to 2006, abortions in England and Wales rose by 3.9%, with the majority of women having a first abortion. The number of women who had had one or more previous abortions undergoing abortions in 2006 remained static at 32%, as in 2005, a small increase from 1996 when 28% of abortions were 'repeat abortions'.

Abortion more than once in a woman's lifetime is viewed with particular concern by the Department of Health, leading to a drive towards practitioners being encouraged to offer longer-acting 'fit-and-forget' contraceptive methods to women, such as contraceptive injections and intra-uterine devices (Department of Health, 2008). We work with women and men to help them prevent unintended pregnancy, but in our view, a rise in repeat abortions across the population is to be expected. This does not in itself indicate a cause for concern, whereas individuals experiencing closely spaced unintended pregnancies indicates a problem, as a suitable method of contraception has not been found. A slow rise in the rate of repeat abortions at population level may simply reflect better access to funded abortion, affording reproductive choice to more women. The view of the 'problem' of a wider uptake of abortion does not recognise the wide-ranging social and demographic changes, or positive factors to do with women's decisions to control their own fertility, employment and economic situation.

Given the expected continuation of high demand for abortion services, many calls have been made to overhaul abortion law. Since 1990, various ten-minute rule Bills have attempted reform, all with a restrictive intent in terms of autonomy. None threatened legal change, but they have succeeded in raising the temperature of the abortion debate in the media and Parliament. Meanwhile, some pro-choice groups and politicians see the introduction of first-trimester abortion 'on demand' as a central aim of reform, partly and perhaps simply because they think it is achievable. However, the long-standing demand of abortion 'on demand/request' is recognised to be legally problematic and impractical, as no other medical treatment is given 'on demand'.

While we agree that autonomy would be best served by statutory recognition of autonomous decision-making in abortion law, we question whether incorporating a new trimester distinction would be beneficial and see no need to re-enshrine the 'abortion exception'. The current approach satisfies some considerations of autonomy by having one gestational distinction at 24 weeks and broadly the same grounds at different gestations, because decision-making capacity and treatment need is not treated differently by gestation. This fits the reality of staffing an abortion service to the latest stages of legal availability, by not compartmentalising doctors into a potentially stigmatising 'late' abortion specialism.

Assuming that legally we must retain legal 'grounds' for abortion to provide an exception to the Offences Against the Person Act (1861), some have argued for a new ground 'that the pregnancy is unwanted', which could enable a more honest and respectful recording of an autonomous abortion decision. UK law is not able to recognise any 'right' to abortion, and is often compared unfavourably with other countries in Europe that acknowledge women's rights to treatment. However, where abortion is conferred notionally as a 'right', this tends to be strictly qualified and limited to the early weeks of pregnancy (BBC, 2007b). Often, in practice, Continental access is more restricted than that in Britain. For example, French and Italian law provide for abortion on request in early pregnancy, but severely limit later procedures. Women travel from European countries with codified legal 'abortion rights' to access private treatment in England and other countries at later gestations.

A MORI poll in 2006 found that 63% of a representative sample of British adults agreed that 'if a woman wants an abortion, she should not have to continue with her pregnancy', and 59% agreed that 'abortion should be made legally available for all who want it'. (MORI, 2006) To allow this would require existing abortion law to be amended in recognition of autonomy. In the ongoing debate about the abortion law, we hope that parliamentarians will support the need for autonomy, and that policy discussions on solutions to practical problems will be considered together with rights-based arguments.

BIBLIOGRAPHY

BBC (2005) 'No charges in late abortion case', 16 March, http://news.bbc.co.uk/1/hi/england/hereford/worcs/4354469.stm.
—— (2007a), 'Seven week wait for NHS abortion', 22 January, http://news.bbc.co.uk/1/hi/health/6287291.stm.
—— (2007b) 'Europe's abortion rules', 12 February, http://news.bbc.co.uk/1/hi/world/europe/6235557.stm.
BMA (2007) 'Call for end to two-signature rule in abortions', *BMA News*, 27 June 2007, http://www.bma.org.uk/ap.nsf/Content/BMAnewsarm2007weds.
Care Confidential website (2007) 'What are the health risks?', in *Your questions answered: What about abortion?*, http://www.careconfidential.com/WhatAboutAbortion.aspx (accessed 30 August 2007).
Charity Commission (2008) Extract from the Central Register of Charities maintained by the Charity Commission for England and Wales, accessed 25 March 2008, http://www.charity-commission.gov.uk/registeredcharities/showcharity.asp?remchar=&chyno=1066963.
Costeloe K, Hennessy E, Gibson AT, Marlow N, Wilkinson AR (for the EPICure Study Group) (2000) 'The EPICure Study: Outcomes infants born at the threshold of viability', *Pediatrics* 106(4), 659–71.
CPA (Crisis Pregnancy Agency) (2006), 'Introduction and Overview of 2006 by the Director', in *2006 Annual Report of the Crisis Pregnancy Agency Ireland*, http://www.crisispregnancy.ie/publications.php.
Daily Mail (2007) 'The doctor: Why I'm so passionately against abortion', 2 May, http://www.dailymail.co.uk/pages/live/femail/article.html?in_article_id=452818& _page_id=1879.
Department of Health (2001) *Good Practice in Consent Implementation Guide: Consent to Examination or Treatment*, Department of Health, London.
—— (2002) *The National Strategy for Sexual Health and HIV Implementation Action Plan*, Department of Health, London, http://www.dh.gov.uk/en/PublicationsandStatistics/Publications/PublicationsPolicyAndGuidance/DH_4006374.
—— (2005a) *Partial Regulatory Impact Assessment: Prohibition of Abortion*, Department of Health, London.
—— (2005b) *Human Reproductive Technologies and the Law: Government Response to the Report from the House of Commons Science and Technology Committee*, http://www.dh.gov.uk/en/publicationsandstatistics/publications/publicationspolicyandguidance/dh_4117875.

—— (2006), http://www.dh.gov.uk/en/publicationsandstatistics/publications/publicationsstatistics/dh_075697.

—— (2007a) *Statistical Bulletin 'Abortion Statistics, England and Wales: 2006'*, National Statistics/Department of Health, London.

—— (2007b) Register of Pregnancy Advice Bureaux, http://www.dh.gov.uk/en/Policyandguidance/Healthandsocialcaretopics/Sexualhealth/Sexualhealthgeneralinformation/DH_4063860 (last updated November 2007).

—— (2007c) *Primary Care Service Framework: Management of Sexual Health in Primary Care*, Department of Health, London.

—— (2007c) *Resource and cash limit adjustment in respect of improvements in early access to abortion services 2005/06*, London: Department of Health, http://www.dh.gov.uk/en/Policyandguidance/Healthandsocialcaretopics/Sexualhealth/Sexualhealthgeneralinformation/DH_4120276.

—— (2007d) *Government Response to the Report from the House of Commons Science and Technology Committee on the Scientific Developments Relating to the Abortion Act 1967*, Department of Health, London, http://www.dh.gov.uk/en/Publicationsandstatistics/Publications/PublicationsPolicyAndGuidance/DH_080925.

—— (2008) *Statement on Contraception and Teenage Pregnancy*, http://www.dh.gov.uk/en/Publichealth/Healthimprovement/Sexualhealth/DH_085686.

GMC (1998) *Seeking Patients' Consent: The Ethical Considerations*, http://www.gmc-uk.org/guidance/current/library/consent.asp#28 (accessed 25 March 2008).

—— (2006) *Good Medical Practice*, accessed 25 March 2008, http://www.gmc-uk.org/guidance/good_medical_practice/good_clinical_care/decisions_about_access.asp.

Grimes DA (2006) 'Estimation of pregnancy-related mortality risk by pregnancy outcome, United States, 1991 to 1999'. *American Journal of Obstetrics and Gynecology* 194, 92–4.

Hansard (2002), House of Lords, col WA 140, 7 November, http://www.publications.parliament.uk/pa/ld200102/ldhansrd/vo021107/text/21107w03.htm.

—— (2006) Select Committee on Science and Technology Minutes of Evidence, Examination of Witnesses (Questions 113 and 114), 12 July, http://www.publications.parliament.uk/pa/cm200506/cmselect/cmsctech/1308/6071207.htm.

—— (2007) House of Lords, col WA 105, 26 July, http://www.publications.parliament.uk/pa/ld200607/ldhansrd/text/70726w0001.htm#07072639000043.

House of Commons Science and Technology Committee (2005) *Human Reproductive Technologies and the Law*, http://www.publications.parliament.uk/pa/cm200405/cmselect/cmsctech/7/702.htm.

IFPA (Irish Family Planning Association) (2006) 'Legislation for RCPAs', in *Rogue Crisis Pregnancy Agencies in Ireland*, , http://www.ifpa.ie/public.html#publications

Independent (2007) 'Abortion crisis as doctors refuse to perform surgery', 16 April, http://www.independent.co.uk/life-style/health-and-wellbeing/health-news/abortion-crisis-as-doctors-refuse-to-perform-surgery-444909.html.

Ingham R, Lee E, Clements S, Stone N (2007) *Second-Trimester Abortions in England and Wales*, Centre for Sexual Health Research, University of Southampton.

ISD Scotland (2007) *Scottish Health Statistics 2006, Abortions data: 'Abortions by age and year'*, ISD Scotland/NHS National Services Scotland, Edinburgh.

Jones RK, Frohwirth LF, Moore AM (2008) '"I Would Want to Give My Child, Like, Everything in the World": How Issues of Motherhood Influence Women Who Have Abortions'. *Journal of Family Issues* 29(1), 79–99.

Lane Committee (1974) *Report of the Committee on the Working of the Abortion Act,*. HMSO, London.

LIFE (2008), http://www.lifecharity.org.uk/caring (accessed 10 February 2008).

MORI (2006) 'Ipsos Mori Survey on Attitudes to Abortion', November, http://www.ipsos-mori.com/polls/2006/bpas.shtml (accessed 3 May 2007).

Observer (2007) 'Anti-abortion GP in ethical rules storm', 11 November, http://www.guardian.co.uk/uk/2007/nov/11/health.society.

RCOG (Royal College of Obstetricians and Gynaecologists (2004) *The Care of Women Requesting Induced Abortion: Summary of Recommendations*, http://www.rcog.org.uk/resources/public/pdf/abortion_summary.pdf.

RCOG (2007a) 'Statement on the BMA Medical Ethics Committee Briefing on First Trimester Abortions', 5 June 2007, http://www.rcog.org.uk/index.asp?PageID=2009.

—— (2007b), http://www.rcog.org.uk/index.asp?PageID=1901.

Science and Technology Committee (2007) *Scientific Developments relating to the Abortion Act 1967*, http://www.publications.parliament.uk/pa/cm200607/cmselect/cmsctech/1045/1045i.pdf.

Sheldon S (1997) *Beyond Control: Medical Power and Abortion Law*, Pluto Press, London.

Legislation

Abortion (Amendment) (England) Regulations 2002, SI 2002/887

Abortion (Amendment) (Wales) Regulations 2002, SI 2002/2879 (W275)

Care Standards Act (2000)

Health and Social Care (Community Health and Standards) Act (2003)

Human Fertilisation and Embryology Act 1990

Human Fertilisation and Embryology Bill 2007

Offences Against the Person Act 1861

Pregnancy Counselling (Truth in Advertising) Bill 2006, Bill C2006B00211, http://www.comlaw.gov.au/ComLaw/Legislation/Bills1.nsf/0/8A7A8B02B EF90F2ECA25724400145410?OpenDocument (Australia)

Cases

Gillick v West Norfolk and Wisbech Area Health Authority [1985] 3 All ER 402 (HL).

Janaway v Salford Health Authority [1989] AC 537, [1988] 3 All ER 1079 (HL).

Jepson v The Chief Constable of West Mercia [2003] EWHC 3318.

R (on the application of Sue Axon) v Secretary of State for Health [2006] EWCA 372006 (Admin).

St George's Healthcare NHS Trust v S [1998] 3 WLR 936.

Index